libraries

and

cultural

change

libraries
and
cultural
change

RONALD C BENGE

CLIVE BINGLEY 𝑏 LONDON

FIRST PUBLISHED 1970 BY CLIVE BINGLEY LTD
16 PEMBRIDGE ROAD LONDON W11
SET IN 10 ON 12 POINT LINOTYPE PLANTIN
AND PRINTED IN GREAT BRITAIN BY THE CENTRAL PRESS (ABERDEEN) LTD
COPYRIGHT © RONALD C BENGE 1970
ALL RIGHTS RESERVED
85157 073 9

Dedicated to my present and former students in Aberystwyth,
Accra, Port of Spain and London

contents

acknowledgements

I wish particularly to thank Douglas Foskett and Philip Corrigan for reading through some of these chapters and making valuable comments; also Peter Wright for his considerable help with regard to the book trade; also my colleagues in the Department of Administrative Studies at the College of Librarianship, Wales—especially David Matthews—for their persistent encouragement and advice.

RONALD BENGE

introduction

This work is a contribution to the literature of librarianship and some parts of it may interest a wider audience. The chapters consist of a series of introductory explorations into several related fields. Some of these areas are usually included in curricula for library studies programmes, under a title such as 'The library and the community' or 'The social background to libraries'.

The aim of such courses is to provide a social context for the study of librarianship, and to relate library services to the wider world. It is possible to establish relationships of many kinds, and if one were sufficiently eccentric, libraries could be connected convincingly with witchcraft or the illegitimacy rate or with prehistoric man. But other associations must be sought, particularly in areas which can justly be regarded as social foundations. Some have suggested a mainly functional approach, so that the library as an institution can be related to other institutions.[1] Others would prefer to study libraries wholly in relation to an analysis of readers' needs. Such investigations usually start with libraries and attempt to show the relevance of social forces and other institutions to library practice. What I have tried, on the contrary, to do here, is to deal with some elements in the cultural background and then to note the possible implications for librarianship, so that the approach is from the outside inwards instead of the other way round.

So, for example, in the first instance, mass communication and censorship are considered without reference to libraries at all. The possible impact on libraries may then be discussed, but the connec-

7

tions between some cultural developments and libraries are not always established, either because they may not exist, or because I do not know what they are. This treatment requires some justification. I have adopted it because I consider that librarians are inevitably involved with the general cultural structure and it should therefore be included as appropriate and necessary, quite apart from professional studies in the narrow sense. This is because the librarian is part of the cultural apparatus, and, in particular, he is part of the communication world. There is a parallel here with education, which similarly requires a social context, and the area is usually called the sociology of education.

If this approach is legitimate, then we are dealing to some degree with comparative librarianship, which in library education is a relatively new development. The contribution to comparative studies resides in the emphasis on social background, without a knowledge of which all comparison of library services in different countries is meaningless.

It will be noted that as far as possible I have refrained from using the grandiose term ' sociology of librarianship '—mainly because the essays do not rest on any foundation of investigation, but also I am not a sociologist. All of the areas into which I have ventured are signposted by a vast and proliferating literature, which is in the main sociological and the scope is so wide that it may be doubted whether the approach I have attempted should be used at all. My justification is that at the present time people in general, and librarians in particular, are obliged to deal with these matters because they are confronted with them all the time. In our non traditional societies, explorations are essential, because the maps no longer relate and ' the enemy ' has taken away the signposts. Professional social scientists offer, as a rule, only limited help, since they are specialists talking to other specialists, and their investigations, in order to be exact, must relate to specific restricted topics. Moreover, they rightly do not wish to rush into the ferocious jungle where journalists, critics and television commentators trample about with impunity. (The librarians, incidentally are usually in another forest altogether.)

The separate essays are not fully integrated and the usual question about the audience must be answered. I imagine that most readers will refer only to particular parts, since some may concern students only, others may interest practising librarians and others might have a more general application.

8

With regard to the captive reader, the student of librarianship, there remains the question of level. The work is intended for any student who is expected to study the social background. In such a wide area, simplification is inevitable and more advanced studies can be undertaken only in specialised fields. In dealing with this broad range of foundation subjects, librarianship students will necessarily remain on an introductory level, even if their more specialised studies are advanced. It follows, therefore, that this contribution is not necessarily related to a particular syllabus, but to any librarianship course at any level which requires an appreciation of social factors.

RONALD BENGE

June 1969

NOTE

1 W Caldwell has always been aware of the need for a more satisfactory social framework for library studies. In his AAL conference paper published in the *Assistant librarian* (*op cit*) he suggested that the sociological theories known as ' Functionalism ' would be useful. This approach is helpful insofar as it views society as a *totality,* with the diverse parts, economy, politics, religion etc, being unified by the interconnecting functions of each. The various elements determine each other. Functionalist concepts derived from sociology (Weber) and anthropology (Radcliffe Brown, Malinowsky). For Malinowsky the functions of institutions were to serve the psychological needs of the people.

Functionalism has long been under attack, particularly from the left because it is alleged that it fails to allow for structural antagonisms. It posits a totality without contradictions; it is a conservative equilibrium theory which offers no adequate answer to the problems of social change or cultural dynamics.

In an African context this makes more sense, since African traditional life is (or was) entirely encompassed by a system of interacting forces, temporal and spiritual. The powers of the world act on one another but the driving force derives from the Supreme Being. This element in African thought systems supplies the dynamic which is missing in static interpretations of modern industrial societies.

1*

I

the nature of culture

DEFINITIONS:
Most librarians would admit that they have cultural responsibilities, but no two of them would agree what this means. They are in good company, since the word culture has two separate meanings and a wide variety of sub meanings.

The scientific approach was developed by the social anthropologists, and one of the greatest of them, Edward Tyler ('*Primitive culture*', 1871), defined culture as 'that complex whole which includes knowledge, belief, art, morals, custom and any other capabilities and habits acquired by men as a member of society'. This is how sociologists, broadly speaking, now understand the term, and used in this way it conveys a meaning which is not vastly different from the term 'society', except that society refers to animal associations as well. Human societies, on the other hand, are permanently organised in accordance with particular cultures, and human groups without culture are unknown. We know what happens if attempts are made to bring up an ape child within the human social environment: the ape remains an ape. If human children were removed from their situation and left on the proverbial desert island and yet survived, some kind of new culture might eventually develop, but it would incline to be barbaric, since cultural traits are not biologically inherited. This is what happens in William Golding's novel *Lord of the flies*—and at the end of it all the ship's officer (secure in *his* culture) says to the survivors 'I should have thought that a pack of British boys—you're all British aren't you?—would have been able

to put up a better show than that '. But they were in fact no longer
' British ', or even boys in the usual sense.

The social scientists, then, consider that all human activities are
culturally significant. But in Europe the word ' culture ' has been used
in quite another way, and one which is even now perhaps more
familiar. The *Shorter Oxford dictionary* refers to culture, *inter alia*,
as ' the *intellectual* side of civilisation '. (Incidentally, the term
' civilisation ' is now usually used to indicate a highly developed and
complex culture.) This concept of culture is, of course, the traditional view, based on the humanities as formerly studied in the
universities: it implies that there was and is an élite which trans-
mits culture from one generation to the next. For S T Coleridge and
Matthew Arnold and T S Eliot this is the fundamental thing, even
though their interpretations may otherwise be widely at variance one
from another. The particular characteristics of culture in this sense
is, first, that value judgments are introduced (Arnold: ' Sweetness
and light ', Eliot: ' That which makes life worth living '), and second,
that intellectual activity is isolated. Ortega Y Gasset refers to the
' System of ideas by which the age lives '. We still use the term
' cultured ', or alternatively ' cultivated ', to describe a certain type of
person, and the distinction usually implies a split between intellectual
or aesthetic activities and the rest of life. Because of the alleged
split, and because culture was interpreted in this narrow sense, anti-
cultural reactions have been possible. Goering's dictum is well
known: ' Whenever I hear the word culture I reach for my revolver '.
It has been suggested that the British response has been to reach
instead for their cricket bats, but if the term is used in its wider
sense, as noted above, cricket is just as much a cultural activity as
listening to Bach.[1] Possibly Malraux intended to embrace all these
things in his typically grandiose statement that ' Culture is the
heritage of the quality of the world '.

It is clear that (as so often in other fields) the scientific concept
has invaded the traditional humanistic area without fully absorbing
the older idea, so that there has been no full integration. The sociologists have recognised the difference by distinguishing between value
or belief systems (sometimes called myths) on the one hand, and
technical developments on the other—or ' ideal ' as distinct from
' material ' culture. Even so, some confusion is inevitable and it is
difficult to use the expression in any precise sense at all. For con-
venience many journalists, who wish to use the word in the Matthew

Arnold sense, refer to 'high culture', and the term is relevant to our purpose here, since we are concerned with discussing the relationship of traditional high culture with twentieth century mass culture, which can be regarded as a new phenomenon in opposition to it.[2]

It will be apparent that I am following the sociologists, since their preoccupations throw light on technological change which I wish to emphasise. The sociologists themselves use a wide variety of approaches—for example, one authority lists six major types of definition which can be used—but what is being stressed here is simply culture as a way of life—a design for living. The various parts of Tyler's 'complex whole' can be classified in many ways. One useful grouping divides culture into three, ie first: habits and customs; second: belief systems; and third: tools, machines and constructions or artefacts (technology). Such groups are useful even to the layman, since they enable us to consider cultural change with particular reference to the fact that the parts of the complex whole do not change at the same rate—and that they inter-act and influence each other all the time. Before considering the problem of change it is worth noting that the traditional function of a culture is to enable a group to survive, and this implies the conservation of the past. Such a process depends wholly on communication, since cultural characteristics have to be acquired. The role of communication is discussed in other chapters.[3]

INNOVATIONS

The scientists have carefully analysed what happens when cultures cease to be static, and certain processes obviously take place even if it is difficult to decide what is the first cause. Many would consider (and Marshall McLuhan is presumably among them) that technical innovations are the decisive factor: scientific inventions have produced new customs and modifications of beliefs, myths or ideologies. Even so, innovations, whether technical or social, are introduced by people, sometimes a group and very often by a *single individual*. Cultural patterns are modified all the time in this manner, and in every culture slight changes take place to traditional processes, procedures, fashions or manners. Skirts go up or down, household objects take on new shapes, and even traditional arts like that of the folk tale produce new variations on a theme. This is obvious enough; it is obvious also that technical inventions transform the environment out of all recognition, but perhaps less obvious, that these inventions can take place only if social conditions are appropriate. When separate cultures are generally similar, parallel inventions or theoretical discoveries inevitably occur, as for example, in the field of natural selection (Darwin and Wallace), or when the telephone was patented (Bell and Cray applied for patents on the same day). If cultures are totally different, parallel inventions are naturally improbable. It is often stated (usually as a criticism) that the Africans failed to discover the wheel, but the reasons are obscure. As a last example, it is of interest that the Eskimo's igloo is the equivalent of the dome which the Romans separately invented, but the cultures were not similar and this is quoted as an exception.

It is suggested, then, that the individual innovator plays a decisive role in many cultural transformations. The sociologists have described other types of change. For example, they refer to 'tentation', which happens in times of crisis, as when epidemics, famines, wars or economic slumps occur. At such times the cultural links with the past are broken and new remedies have to be found: those that succeed survive. Some tentation inventions are accidental, as presumably in the case of the boomerang. Finally, it is apparent, particularly in the modern world, that most of the elements in any culture are derived from somewhere else: they represent cultural borrowing or diffusion. One has only to consider eating habits to become aware how many staple items of diet have been spread all over the world. In the case of tribal societies which have been flung into the modern industrial world, the impact has come entirely from outside and traditional culture is usually entirely disrupted. This is discussed in chapter 2.

SOCIAL ACCEPTANCE

Innovations may or may not be accepted by society as a whole. If only a group of people accept a new thing, it becomes part of a sub-culture, which grows in importance, or diminishes, according to the fortunes of the struggle for survival with other sub-cultures, or with the major one. This spreading process is described as 'internal diffusion', to distinguish it from 'external' diffusion or borrowing, and in these internal clashes the degree of prestige of the innovators is important. If the innovation succeeds, cultural saturation takes place and it becomes accepted by society as a whole: it becomes a norm which can be defined simply as 'that which is done'. Often, particularly in open societies, the saturation is only partial, and various sub-cultures continue to co-exist. This, then, is how the machine seems to work; but society is not a machine and among all these complex processes somewhere lurks the dynamic of change.

CULTURAL LAGS

The concept of 'cultural lag' as originally defined by Ogburn has become generally familiar. The parts of the complex whole develop at different rates and technical advances have a relatively rapid impact upon custom, but belief and value systems are modified much later. There is a time lag so that belief systems may take one or more generations to 'catch up', particularly in conservative societies where even customs—because they are based on belief—resist change.

The cultural lag is thus the time taken for the innovations to become integrated into society, and British institutions are notoriously afflicted with these cultural hangovers. For example, the licensing laws for the selling of alcoholic liquor have produced the British 'pub', which together with 'closing time' is an institution which originally reflected the condition of the British working classes in the nineteenth century. This example is appropriate, because these customs were, and to some extent still are, rooted in political and religious beliefs. The licensing laws ensure that a number of people who have had 'one for the road', are in fact all on the road in their cars at the same time and accidents occur. The national remedy devised is not the abolition of archaic licensing laws but the introduction of a 'breathalyser' test which confirms that certain of the drivers have indeed had 'one for the road'. Other institutions of this kind abound: for instance, the British Sunday, or the trade unions, or the legal system, or the educational structure. It is in the field of statutory law in particular that time lags are inevitable, since—at least in formally democratic countries—acts of parliament must follow change in social opinion or attitudes. Near saturation must first have taken place—a process which may take a long time. Recent instances include the laws relating to homo-sexuality and divorce. It has been claimed by Michael Young (in *The rise of the meritocracy*, p 27) that a good example of cultural lag is to be found in the fact that Britain remains rural minded, even though eighty percent of the population now live in towns.

On the intellectual level, the cultural time lag is of particular interest to librarians. The mental climate changes slowly for reasons already indicated, and ideas held by an individual first permeate an élite or a group, before they are adopted by society as a whole. When this does happen, the ideas, or ideals, or philosophies, become modified or adulterated: they become embodied in institutions. This dissemination of ideas is naturally accelerated or retarded by the communication media, and this is the process which concerns librarians. The modern national state requires not only a vast network of information centres in the strict sense, but also centres of *interpretation*. This is what the communication media have to do: they are part of a cultural apparatus which includes the library.

THE DYNAMICS OF CHANGE

In the above brief description of processes, it was perhaps implied that it is technology which has totally changed our way of life. In one sense and on one level this is beyond dispute, but there is a danger that we may automatically assume that history is technologically determined. There is the widespread feeling that the machines are taking over—a feeling which overlooks the fact that machines are invented by people. Frankenstein, it should be remembered, was not the monster, but the name of the man who built him. It follows, therefore, that the discussion concerning historical motivation is as open as it ever was, and all I can do here is to note some of the possible interpretations.

The so called liberal view of history, as held by H A L Fisher and others, rests on the foundation that these various cultural and social forces react with each other and that we cannot know which is dominant or decisive, save at particular times or with regard to particular events. This view is, if only by default, reflected here, since I am not putting forward any total view of the world. The several determinist approaches, however, have been so influential that they cannot be ignored even in a work of this kind.

Technological determinism must, if it is followed through, rest on a materialist view of the world, and it is for this reason that Marshall McLuhan's gospel is specially puzzling, since he claims to be a Roman Catholic. I have noted above that one possible corrective to his and similar views is humanistic, in the sense that one can stress the role of the individual person, or of a group of people, as agents of change. Some writers (for example, Ottaway in *Culture and education*) have used this approach and regard the influence of groups to be a decisive social force. Even if we accept this, we are still left to answer the question of human motivation or incentives, and the emphasis remains on the group and not the individual. We can instead stress the role of the individual, which then carries us firmly into the sphere of the psychologist.

Some of the psychologists provide their own kind of determinism, which, like all closed systems, has its own fascination. If we seek to enquire from the psycho-analysts of the Freudian school how human motivations or drives relate to cultural patterns, we are faced with the difficulty that Freud's theories are not sociological but biologically based, so that his system postulates an essentially static and pessimistic world. He claimed that civilisation or culture *always* represses the instincts of the individual, who can only survive by a process of sublimation, which in fact maintains culture. There is no way back to the Garden of Eden, just as there is not in Christian philosophy. There is the further total stumbling block that according to Freud the human personality is fixed by the age of five. Since the master arrived at these gloomy conclusions, the system has been modified or attacked on many fronts. In some countries, for example France, Freudian psychology has had little general influence, and it is in the United States that the mental climate is pervaded by psycho-analytic influences. Anthropologists such as Margaret Mead (*Coming of age in Samoa*) and Ruth F Benedict (*Patterns of Culture*) have shown that there are cultures where Freud's analysis does not apply. However, this does not necessarily dispose of the matter, since these are relatively primitive societies and it remained for the various non-Freudians to modify (or water down) the original doctrine, by adopting a more sociological approach, which places much greater emphasis on cultural patterns and less on instinctive drives.

On a popular level, Geoffrey Gorer has followed this course in his studies of American and Russian society. The non-Freudian psycho-analysts have denied that civilisation can only be achieved by unfreedom and suffering, and they have done this by limiting, in their theory, the primary importance of the instinctive dynamics and concentrating on social and cultural factors, with the further implication that if the social reality is favourable (which it is mostly not), some kind of harmony can be obtained. This amounts to a rejection of Freud's flat statement ' There is no longer any place in present day civilized life for a simple natural love between two human beings '.

The background to all this is, of course, the natural tendency in the USA to assume that this conflict between the individual and social demands is inexorable and constant. On this side of the Atlantic it is rarely seen as inevitable or incurable, but an influential writer like

R D Laing (one of the prophets of the younger generation in Britain) has popularised the view that cultural pressures and disintegration in modern society are resulting in the collapse of the individual. His remark on education has already been widely quoted: 'a child born today in the UK stands a ten times greater chance of being admitted to a mental hospital than to a university . . . this can be taken as an indication that we are driving our children mad more effectively than we are genuinely educating them effectively.' The implication here is that the Freudian conflict between instinctive life and modern society has become so intolerable that the social structure must be broken. To be precise, the interpretation is not that there is a straightforward conflict, but that the individual has become dehumanised (*ie* alienated from himself), and, in our societies, is no longer a person, but in Laing's words, a ' shrivelled dessicated fragment '.

At this point it is impossible to ignore Herbert Marcuse, the author of *One dimensional man* and *Eros and civilisation,* and allegedly one of the theorists, if not the main one, who provides inspiration for student rebellion all over the world. This scholar (formidable in the Teutonic abstract manner) has managed to combine a revision of Freud and a revision of Marx into a new charter for revolution. In our context here he has (in *Eros and civilisation*) preserved the supreme importance of Freud's instinctive motivation as a social dynamic, but claims that in modern cultures (*ie* in the USA particularly) it need no longer clash forever with the reality, or what he calls the ' performance principle ', because it is now possible to create a different type of society based on a new reality principle. This is an up-dated version of what the Marxists used to call ' utopian socialism ', and the gospel of productivity, as preached both in the USA and the USSR, is totally rejected.

A similar message has been cheerfully proclaimed by the way-out psychologist Norman O Brown, who has an immense following in the USA, but seems little known elsewhere. He has developed doctrines which are stated in Marcuse and implied by McLuhan, who notably ignores the sexual sphere. In *Life against death,* Brown stands Freud on his head by insisting that in the new electronic world civilisation need no longer be based on sexual repression, and he envisages a return to the ' polymorphously perverse ' unfocussed sexuality of the baby. In future we shall no longer strive towards orgasmic goals, but, in the words of Marcuse, with the arrival of a new reality principle the ' spread of the libido would first manifest itself in a reactivation of all erotogenic zones . . . and in a decline of genital supremacy' (*Eros and civilisation*, p 163). The condition will be 'cool', just as it was, according to Marshall McCluhan in pre-print cultures, just as it is in the recommendations of the *Kama-sutra*. Linear time (as produced by the printing culture) will no longer operate, and the pleasures of sex will be more diffuse and constant. Brown's late work *Love's body* continues the same themes in a series of prophetic and gnomic aphorisms.

In Europe, and naturally in that part of the world which regards itself as a socialist 'camp', Marxist determinism has been more influential. The doctrine is not of course technological, but economic, since it declares that changes in the mode of production ultimately (but *only* in the last resort) cause the rest of society to change also. The other driving force is the conflict of classes. In such a system the dynamics of change are known, and all that men must do is work and fight in accordance with the laws of change—and interpret them correctly. When mistakes are made this is because the dialectically evolving situation has been misinterpreted. In the socialist society no ineradicable conflict between the individual and society can occur. In such a world every individual, including the librarian, has a duty which is, to use a favourite phrase, crystal clear. By giving this perfunctory account I have implied that this doctrine is foreign to the approach used in this work. It should, however, be added that there is a great deal in Marxist analysis which has, by any standards, cultural relevance, and this is mentioned elsewhere in this chapter.

Finally, we should not omit the traditional Christian view, which regards the system of beliefs, and particularly religious belief, as the decisive element which causes cultures to change: when religion declines (*any* religion), culture declines. The civilisations of the past collapsed because of the decline in belief. Perhaps even more than the other total answers mentioned here, this analysis cannot be proved or disproved, and evidence can be found for or against. It may well be that each culture has a soul or pervading spirit which moves in its own mysterious way. If this is so at the present time, one can only urge the librarian to watch and pray.

The above discussion may seem to some to be an interpolation, but in any discussion of cultural matters the importance of the social dynamic is really fundamental. It is of course a typical problem of the hen (culture) and egg (childhood or instinctual situation) variety, and, as was stated at the beginning of this section, no total solutions are offered.

So much has been written on the alleged split between the world of the arts and the world of science that a summary of the arguments is scarcely necessary. Many have claimed that there is no inherent reason for this divergence to exist, and if it is now there, or appears to be there, then this is the result of historical circumstances and of the development of education systems. Certainly the gap is less noticeable in the Soviet Union or in the USA, and more evident in Britain where the humanistic (in the academic sense) tradition is deeply rooted. In the case of the controversy between Leavis and Snow, the argument became a slanging match between antagonists who had, in fact, already taken up positions on either side of a fence which others like them had erected in the past. As Lionel Trilling has pointed out in *Beyond culture*, the dispute is really a revival of the famous controversy between Matthew Arnold and T H Huxley in the late nineteenth century. Arnold was concerned to defend the traditional primacy of the humanities in education, and Huxley was insisting that the development of science had created a new world and that scientific values were essential for modern education.

What is new in the present dialogue is that Snow has stressed *social* responsibilities and the relevance of science to modern political life, and has pointed out that many of the great literary figures of our time, for example, W B Yeats, Ezra Pound, Wyndham Lewis, T S Eliot, D H Lawrence, have taken up social attitudes which can be regarded as contemptible and reactionary. In fact Snow indicts modern literature on social and moral grounds—and Leavis (following Arnold's dictum that literature should be a 'criticism of life') takes up a moral position also. Trilling claims that in fact the most significant modern literature has questioned life itself, and must go beyond the somewhat narrow moral preoccupations which both antagonists share. 'A lively young person of advanced tastes would surely say that if ever two men were committed to England, Home and Duty they are Leavis and Snow—he would say that in this they are as alike as two squares ' (p 153).

To leave the matter at this point would, however, be an evasion—since if we ignore the manner in which this controversy was conducted, it remains true that Leavis was deeply concerned that Snow's main analysis was wrong because it was based on wholly false foundations. He alleges that Snow was *inventing* two cultures by assuming that it is simply a question of two different areas of *knowledge*, whereas they are in reality two different modes of experience. He pointed out, quite rightly, that you cannot compare Shakespeare's King Lear with the second law of thermodynamics in any meaningful way. Furthermore, an understanding of science does not rest on the acquisition of knowledge, but on a training in scientific habits of thought and method.[4] It follows, therefore, that although some scientists may appreciate the arts, a useful scientific education for non scientists is not possible except in a most general and limited sense. There can be no total two way communication, and it is this which Snow is demanding. Somebody has referred to the two types of experience as ' That which makes life possible ' (science), as distinct from ' That which makes life bearable ' (the arts). If one accepts this one must accept also that the question of communication between the two areas is largely irrelevant. This does not, of course, dispose of the matter, but it suggests that the problem is really another one. Behind all this sound and fury remain many unanswered questions. It is evident, for example, that there are not in fact two but many cultures.

A full consideration of the matter would involve a comparative study of education systems and of psychological theory, in order to establish whether individuals are inherently likely to lean towards the sciences or the arts. It is well known that many talented people cannot understand mathematics, but this may happen because of the way they have been taught, or for some psychological reason. There can be no doubt that in both spheres students have been alienated by inadequate teaching methods, which have ' killed ' particular subjects for them. Many people cannot learn in areas where they cannot see the point or purpose. It certainly appears that an intelligent person should be able to acquire a *general* understanding of both science and the humanities, and that early specialisation makes this impossible. It has also been noted, particularly with regard to intelligence testing, that many people fail to develop or maintain a spirit of enquiry, and the element of ' creativity ' has been isolated and stressed. Two American investigators, Getzels and Jackson (*Creativity and intelligence*, 1962) claimed that there are two distinct styles of thinking— ' convergent ' and ' divergent '—and it is only those with the former who regularly excel in intelligence tests. Further research has suggested that this difference can be used to explain the science or arts bias in the individual. ' Divergent ' people tend to show greater creative ability, and it is they who often prefer arts to science subjects. But once again this may simply reflect the way that science has been presented.[5]

Another traditional element involved is that, at least in Britain, the divergence has represented class differences. The cultivated man was a gentleman who knew the classics and appreciated the arts but science and technology were beneath him. Similarly, even in the scientific sphere, pure science was considered superior to applied. These traditions die hard and what was previously regarded as a general education was, in fact, often mainly humanistic in the narrower and élitist sense. As W K Richmond states (in *Culture and general education*, p 135), 'No excuse need be made, therefore, for placing the two cultures in the class warfare context where it belongs'.

Finally, it is worth noting that with many people prejudice against science represents what might be called a cultural lag. They are often thinking of nineteenth century mechanistic science, or of the abuses of the Industrial Revolution, or of the misuse of machines, 'Science' in the past has often appeared to be wholly anti-biological, mechanical and inorganic.

All this is naturally of fundamental importance for librarians, since much of the discussion about documentation rests on the assumption that a key difference between the traditional librarian and the 'information scientist' is the kind and degree of subject knowledge. If the above criticism of Snow's dichotomy is sound, this analysis is inadequate. It may well be that this emphasis on 'knowledge' has obscured the nature of the problem, and that the essential activity of the librarian both in science and the arts is something else. This is discussed in chapter 14 where I have noted the importance of relationships.

THE NEW CULTURE
Elsewhere we have recognised the common distinction between 'high' and 'pop' or mass culture—a distinction which now obscures the older stratification of highbrow, middlebrow and lowbrow. Many have claimed that it is no longer possible at all to isolate cultural levels in the old manner, and that the key factor now is the relationship between minority culture and that of the masses. It has been claimed by several schools of criticism that high culture has lost its way or reached the end of the road.[6] This was a common theme with Marxists in the thirties, and it was assumed that it was capitalist culture that was dying and that a new healthy proletarian culture based on the doctrines of social realism would arise. It is difficult to make such assumptions

now, and I wish to examine more recent manifestations in high culture which are significant, not only because they indicate that the old road still continues (whether it is regarded as capitalist or not) but because they are relevant to the theme of this book.

THE RELEVANCE OF ANTI-ART

The radical tendencies which we are discussing here can be observed in all the arts. The modern movement cannot appropriately be called ' *avant garde* ', since the term implies continuation, whereas it can be claimed that the new art represents a decisive break with the past and is based on wholly new attitudes. These trends have been designated ' neo-modernist ' by Frank Kermode, to distinguish them from other twentieth century innovations which are now seen to be part of the main tradition. The first noticeable characteristic is a total rejection of the concept of formal order. Art as it was formerly understood is to be abolished, since it is considered not only impossible but undesirable to impose any form, or imaginative order, on the confusion of the world. It is the chaos which is important. (One of the texts of the movement is Morse Peckham's *Man's rage for chaos*.

Linked with the rejection of orm, pattern, or order, is a denial that art should concern itself with purposes, goals or ends—hence the label ' anti-teleological '. There is no question of trying to get anywhere because there is nowhere to go. The work of art does not *mean* anything; it simply exists like life itself, and there is the further implication that life is inherently superior to art. But life itself has no meaning, so that it is pointless to attempt to ' understand ' either life or art, and rational choice is an illusion. It follows that art *ceases to be communication* and becomes re-absorbed in life; it cannot be judged but only experienced. The arts and the new media of communication are not means of interpreting the world, they *are* the world, the only difference being that they deal with *images*. Art must therefore necessarily be impermanent, random, unpredictable and often farcical just as life is: there is an emphasis on the element of *play*.

In traditional terms, such attitudes would have been regarded as nihilistic and defeatist, but the general outlook of the anti-artists is cheerful—even optimistic; art is regarded as an affirmation of life. This happy note is perhaps typically American, and it is from the USA that much of the inspiration for the movement has come. The new men are no longer alienated, they are simply cheerfully dis-

23

connected from society, and work and rationality have become obsolete. Given such an approach with its concentration on the moment, on spontaneity, on the primitive, the traditional preoccupation with 'maturity' is no longer relevant: it is neither possible nor desirable.

The 'happenings' which have taken place as part of the movement are now no longer notorious or even remarkable. They include John Cage's musical composition 4' 33", where a performer sits at a closed piano and the audience listens to whatever noises drift into the hall. (Silence, incidentally, is an important part of the non-communication process and this is the title of one of Cage's books. Perhaps his most famous utterance is 'I have nothing to say . . . and I am saying it'.)

In music, a key contemporary figure is Stockhausen, who produces works which can be performed in any sequence, just as the novelist Burroughs' later work, with its fold-in technique, can be read in any order. One musical performer attacked a piano with a chisel, rubber hammer and a bicycle chain, and on another occasion with a saw. Another burnt a violin stuffed with concert programmes. In painting, the happenings include Rauschenberg's famous 'Bed', which is simply a bed, and the tins of Campbell's soup signed by Andy Warhol (fifty years earlier Marcel Duchamp had produced his 'ready mades', which were objects picked up and signed by the artist). Happenings include various 'assemblages' or 'combines' which incorporate objects from the real world into the work of art. In sculpture, there are a number of mobile creations, of which the best known are probably the fascinating constructions of Jean Tinguely, such as the famous machine 'Homage to New York', which actually destroyed itself.

Pop art represents an important link with mass culture, ambiguous though the relationship is, for most pop artists are far from unsophisticated. Marshall McLuhan explains their work by noting that the artists use objects in our daily life, in an 'anti-environmental' fashion, so that new perceptions are possible. The total difference from older art forms is particularly noticeable when the productions of these artists can be seen amongst traditional painting or sculpture, as for example, a real wash basin that was exhibited in the Tate Gallery. (The first one-man pop art exhibition to be held in the Tate Gallery was of work by the American, Roy Lichtenstein. Characteristically, he explained his paintings by stating that he takes a wholly assimilated cliché, like a bad strip cartoon, and intensifies the cliché quality to

24

make us look at it again. For this exercise the subject matter must be banal and vulgar.)

As has been noted above, many of these manifestations originated in America, but similar signs and symptoms can be found all over the developed world: if they are present in the Soviet Union they are part of the underground movement which is known to exist. The same tendencies precisely have long been prevalent in the French school of anti-novelists, such as Alain Robbé-Grillet, and in the plays of Samuel Becket and the theatre of the absurd, generally. The movement in drama is particularly significant because of the element of violence, and the considerable influence on the French student movement of Artaud and the theatre of cruelty. In fact, some of the neo-modernist trends, as described here, have probably had more political influence than specifically political prophets like Marcuse.

Enough has been said to indicate the characteristic features of anti-artistic activity. These trends can be regarded as a symptom of total cultural collapse, or as an amusing joke, or as the activities of a lunatic fringe minority which is always with us. If the last explanation is adopted then there is no break with the past, and the cultural traditions which have prevailed since the Renaissance will continue. Many critics have taken this view, but it seems to me that these manifestations cannot be so easily dismissed and that many of them are not fringe but central in recent cultural developments. The ideological influence has extended far beyond the realms of what used to be high culture, and what I wish to stress is that the key elements *are also present in mass culture*. The alleged total gap is not there at all, at least not at present.

I am suggesting that the break is in fact between the present and the past, although this is by no means generally agreed. It is a question of whether we live at a time which is revolutionary, in an exact sense, or not.

IMPLICATIONS FOR LIBRARIANS

I stated at the beginning of this chapter that it is possible to interpret the librarian's cultural responsibilities in many different ways. My main intention here is not to define what they should be, but to insist on their importance. For example, if one takes the view that the old high culture is menaced by a new barbarism, presumably this view would be reflected in library policies. Alternatively, if one considers that the librarian must come to terms with mass culture—then policies will be modified accordingly, particularly in public libraries.

The first attitude is more in accord with the traditional role of the librarian. The new barbarism (if that is what it is) rejects the past: it is irrationalist to an extreme degree, and the implication is that libraries should be destroyed because they are symbols of a dead past. (The Italian ' futurist' movement of forty years ago included the abolition of libraries as part of their programme. Their manifesto said ' Come! Set fire to the libraries '.) On the other hand, one can take the view, which I have in the main adopted here, that a totally changed world requires new roles. That is why I have attempted, in a superficial manner, to discuss the nature of culture in the broad sociological sense, and also certain features of the cultural climate at the present time.

NOTES

1 In *Notes on a definition of culture,* T S Eliot stated that ' It [culture] includes all the characteristic activities and interests of a people: Derby Day, Henley Regatta, Cowes, the 12th of August, a cup final, the dog races, the pin table, the dart board, Wensleydale cheese, boiled cabbage cut into sections, beetroot in vinegar, 19th century Gothic churches and the music of Elgar. The reader can make his own list.' The curious thing is that readers have *not* made their own list and Eliot's catalogue of activities has 'been repeatedly quoted as if it had some peculiar merit, whereas it is largely restricted to *recreational* interests: it is a consumers' list and remarkable for its omissions. It suggests, in fact, a different definition from the one I have quoted. Behind these notes on a definition lurks Mr Eliot, the fastidious poet, who recoils from the world of Sweeney and the weeping multitudes who droop in a hundred ABC's.

2 In recent years cultural studies in France have been dominated by ' structuralist ' doctrines, and particularly by the work of Claude Levi-Strauss. He used a method which had been developed in the growth of structural linguistics to analyse kinship systems, a basic problem in anthropology. He claims that the same method can be used for all cultural studies. It involves an abstract analysis of systems of communication (used in its widest possible sense). In his own words, ' a structural method in the study of social facts is characterised by its examination not of the terms of a system but of the relationships between the terms '. Certain patterns are discovered, analogous to the rules of games which are based on structures which can be mathematically or formally treated.

This fashionable movement in France is influenced not only 'by Levi-Strauss and structural linguistics, but also by studies in *Semiology* (the science of signs). All three approaches have 'been used in the study of mass media of communication. At present the doctrines seem too abstract to have become generally familiar in the United Kingdom, and I am not alone in failing wholly to understand them.

3 It has often been suggested that the extraordinary vitality of African traditional art can be explained not only by the fact that this art was an

26

essential and integral part of life, and in this sense functional, but also because one of these functions was communication. In non literate societies the only cultural links between the generations are forged by oral tradition and by art forms. (Certain techniques of divination resemble writing but these are secondary.)

4 Samuel Goudsmit, an American physicist (' Consequences of the knowledge explosion ' in *The knowledge explosion, op cit* p 79) declares that the gap exists particularly for non scientists because science can only be understood and appreciated by active participation. There are other activities which can be enjoyed and judged by outsiders, but with science this is not possible at all. He concludes that the gap cannot be closed at least for this generation.

5 In 1966 Liam Hudson, in *Contrary imaginations,* published the results of his research amongst English schoolboys using the converger-diverger distinction; his conclusions lend support not to a simple equation that scientists are always convergers, or that divergers are necessarily always more creative, but to the thesis that the distinction is a useful one. Most of the evidence suggests that creative people ' seem to differ not in their intellectual equipment but in the use that they see fit to make of it '. This is so whether they are scientists or arts specialists. He also notes that experiments indicate that most scientists are surprisingly like their popular stereotype, *eg* (p 146) they tend to avoid peronal relations. ' Evidence here is drawn from many sources, and indicates that the scientist's unsociability usually sets in as early as the age of ten.'

6 In *The struggle of the moderns* Stephen Spender contrasts the ' moderns ' with the ' contemporaries ' in twentieth century literature. The moderns (for example Joyce, Eliot, Lawrence, Pound, Yeats) set out to invent a new literature because they feel that our age is unprecedented and outside the convention of past literature and art. The contemporaries, on the other hand (Shaw, Wells, Bennett, Snow), support the cause of progress and wish to modify an older tradition to provide for the results of scientific technology.

2

the clash of cultures

I have chosen this aspect of culture to consider partly for reasons
of personal experience, and partly because in a world that is supposed
to have become a ' global village ' the clashes make a persistent noise.
The subject is so large that I have simply selected one or two themes
of personal interest.

THE IMPACT IN REVERSE: THE GARDEN OF EDEN
Much has been written on the destruction of tribal societies through
the impact of ' advanced ' or technological cultures. This is the
history of imperialism and is beyond our scope. Alan Moorehead, for
instance, has produced his account of how Europeans destroyed the
culture of the South Sea Islands. The trader, the missionary and the
soldier have succeeded in doing this all over the world. It was
required by Progress. Moorehead called his story *Fatal impact,* but
much less has been written about the process in reverse, *ie* the
influence of ' primitive ' cultures on Europe and America. This
exposure led to many innovations in the field of the arts, for example
the negro element in jazz music. It resulted also in a vast literature
of travel and exploration. Here I am concerned only with one concept,
the notion of the Garden of Eden.

The impact of tribal culture on those who destroy it is, of course,
not fatal at all, but its effect may be more far reaching than is
generally appreciated. Complex industrial societies generate a reaction
against themselves which is nowhere more apparent than in creative

literature. Nobody idealises Rousseau's noble savage now, but the concept behind the literary fashion was and is valid. The feeling persists that the civilised product of a technological culture is cut off from elemental truths and satisfactions which he imagines must exist in more simple societies. This is of course an illusion, or rather it is an illusion to imagine that the simplicities of a tribal past can be recaptured. The attempt to do this has resulted in various ' back to the land ' or simple life movements. The anthropologists and psychologists have their own explanations—usually involving a parallel between the individual childhood and the childhood of the race.

The Christian doctrine of the Fall is also relevant, since in a rather imprecise fashion the arrival of urban, or industrial, or technological, or capitalist society—to many people—came to represent the Fall. Freud's atheistic doctrine of sublimation ironically reinforced these attitudes, by presenting civilisation as a process crippling to individual development.

THE IMPACT OF THE ARTIST

This cultural motif could in the first instance find expression in the idealisation of bucolic bliss—the joys of Arcadia. It is significant that this word dates from about 1590 when the Elizabethans wrote pretty nonsense in the classical tradition about shepherdesses and their swains. But as more and more people came to live in towns, the myth became charged with a greater intensity, and the *peasant* was allotted his role of child of nature; and from the outside his culture seemed so valid that he became a dominant theme in European literature. One has only to mention Hardy, Zola, Tolstoy, Dostoevski, Jean Giono, Knut Hamson, Sigrid Undset to see what is meant. (The nineteenth century Russian writers are significant here because they were living in a state of cultural clash, confusion and even shock, and hence the supreme importance of their literature.) These internal conflicts were produced by the onset of the industrial society. In twentieth century Britain the peasant had almost ceased to exist, but the tradition was strong enough to provoke Stella Gibbons's parody *Cold Comfort Farm*. It is not without interest that many of these writers, like Britain's Henry Williamson, were attracted by the anti-industrial blood-and-soil attitudes of the German nazis.

If within a fragmenting society the indigenous peasant—all unaware —was bearing this symbolic burden, the tribes of distant lands came to exercise the same appeal to the romantic imagination with an even

29

greater force. They enjoyed the additional advantage of a tropical or sub-tropical setting. (As a rule the Eskimos were not involved in all this: it is significant that the word ' exotic ' originally meant simply foreign or alien.) The vast literature of travel became imbued with Garden of Eden mythology. This literature is at the present time losing its traditional significance—not because there is nowhere left to explore, but because there are few communities left which are willing to become, as it were, pegs or props for other people's fantasies. This world is no longer large enough, and interest is passing to other worlds and to the realm of science fiction which satisfies our need to be frightened.

The idealisation of the primitive dates from the time of the eighteenth century, when polite society had become artificial and excessively rational. The discovery of the South Seas engendered enthusiasm for the paradise islands, and Rousseau's back-to-nature and the innocence-of-the-child themes contributed to the general Romantic reaction against the drawing room world. In its early form the myth dwelt on how the guiltless and harmonious culture of the islands was destroyed by the barbarians from the West. Captain Cook arrived in Tahiti in 1769 but Admiral Bougainville preceded him by twelve months or so.

In his *Supplement au voyage de Bougainville* Diderot wrote, ' One day they (the Christians) will come with crucifix in one hand and the dagger in the other to cut your throats or to force you to accept their customs and opinions; one day under their rule you will be almost as unhappy as they are.' At that time the population of Tahiti was about forty thousand: seventy years later it was down to nine thousand and Diderot's prophecy had come to pass. Since then there have been other developments, but the old culture was destroyed and this is what is relevant here. Herman Melville in his semi-autobiographical works *Typee* and *Omoo* carried the same message.

When, in the next century, Africa was opened up and the missionaries intensified their holy wars, the tradition became more complicated and it was the ' savagery ' of simple cultures which was stressed. This further enriched the myth, and the brew came to contain *all* the primitive instincts; violence and cannibalism as well as lotus eating and sex in the sun. By this time the more sophisticated writers became conscious that it was their own predicament they were dealing with (the impact in reverse). Incidentally, some of these writers and artists never left their own countries, but the difference is irrelevant.

The archetypical figures are French: Rimbaud, Gauguin and Baudelaire explored the theme in depth. As Moorehead points out, it is significant that the title of one of Gauguin's best known paintings is 'Nevermore', and the maiden in it can be taken to symbolise a culture destroyed. Gauguin was a banker; it was a customs officer, the 'primitive' painter Rousseau, whose work creates the symbolic tropics in a unique manner. The typical individual who took part in this exploration (which was really an inner or subjective search) is described in a single poem of Baudelaire 'Le voyage'. The story begins with the child 'amoureux de cartes et d'éstampes', continues with 'les vrais voyageurs . . . qui partent pour partir', and concludes with 'le vieux vagabond pietinant dans la boue'. Such might have been the origin of the celebrated 'nostalgie de la boue' motif. The British contribution was less profound. Somerset Maugham is really outside this tradition, except on a superficial level; Robert Louis Stevenson chose to *live* the myth, but his best work lies elsewhere. Conrad understood the matter, but he was an expatriate in more than one sense, and his story *The heart of darkness* betrays the tensions that were inherent in his cultural conflict, leaving one with a feeling of unease because the theme is not really Africa at all. The Africans are symbolic.

We could continue with a catalogue of the motif in various disguises as it is displayed in Laurence Durrell, whom somebody has unkindly suggested is Rider Haggard brought up to date. (For now, alas, 'the Rudyards cease from Kipling and the Haggards ride no more'.) And so at the end of the survey we should come to Graham Greene, whose typical anti-hero is a burnt out case, who neither finds nor expects to find anything on his travels. Or we should encounter Anthony Burgess, whose schoolmaster non hero, having ludicrously survived for three whole novels in the Far East, then comes to a pathetic and largely meaningless end.

EROS AND CIVILISATION
Central to all this literature and to the experience itself was the theme of sex: this was always part of the search. Bougainville called Tahiti the 'new Cythera', and Baudelaire's poem of disillusionment is called 'Voyage à Cythère', which recognises the symbolic nature of the quest.

'Dans ton île O Venus, je n'ai trouvé debout,
   Qu'un gibet symbolique où pendait mon image.'

Here we encounter the clash of cultures in its most extreme form, since the tortured eroticism of the European puritan (and in this context all Europeans are puritans) is not to be found in the pre-erotic culture of peasant peoples. Sex for them (apart from normal external frustrations) is pleasant and necessary, but, except in extreme youth, it cannot be isolated from the rest of life. This fact has led many writers to regard romantic love as a European disease based on the poetical conventions of the troubadours of twelfth century Provence. Denis de Rougement, in *Passion and society*, considers that passionate love, together with the down-grading of marriage, developed at this period (the time of Heloise and Abelard) partly because of Christianity itself, partly as a result of the underground Celtic pagan resistance to Christian monogamy, and partly because of the influence of Manichaean doctrines which originally came from Persia. (The Manichees, like the Celts, believed in the eternal war between good and evil as symbolised by Night and Day, and, as far as this world is concerned, it is the Devil who is in control.) The same authority claims that the Cathars must also share responsibility for the cult. They were the formidable twelfth century Christian heretics whose mysticism took the form of a Manichaean exaltation of romantic love and a virtual annulment of marriage. They were liquidated with appropriate ferocity in the Albigensian crusade, and their culture, including their literature, perished with them.

Whatever the precise origin of romantic love (which of course is still with us in the debased Hollywood form), there can be no doubt that it represents an amalgam or cultural diffusion which includes Christianity, Christian heresy and Arab mysticism, together with Celtic and Germanic paganism as expressed in the myth of Tristan and Iscult. It is all still there in Wagner, including the Manichaean element and the preoccupation with death as the grand solution.

I have dwelt on this element in our culture because it is not or *was* not present in other parts of the world, for example, in the civilisations of the Far East.

THE ARABISTS

In relation to this idealisation of the stark and simple virtues, it is impossible not to mention the curious British cult *vis-à-vis* the Arabs. Doughty, Richard Burton, Lady Hester Stanhope, T E Lawrence and others added to the legend. The way of life of the desert Arab has consistently appealed to the imagination of the British, and has often distorted their politics. This experience also is coming to an end and the Arabs are abandoning the role. Soon they will be like everybody else and those theatrical robes will be no longer available for eccentric Englishmen to wear. Even in Aden the educated sophisticates of the National Liberation Front have taken over, and it was left for Wilfred Thesiges to seek out the last strongholds of the myth in the arid wastes of the Empty Quarter, and among the swamp Arabs elsewhere.

THE POLITICAL MYTH

It may well be that these same ingredients are to be found in the realm of politics. But political myths have their own kind of reality, and it remains true that the people of the underdeveloped countries and/or the non white races have taken the place of the urban masses who were destined to inherit the earth. The proletariat is dead: long live the peasants of the world. It is possible that the Chinese and Frantz Fanon and Fidel Castro will yet prove correct in their analysis, and that the peasants of Africa, India and Latin America will revolt against their present rulers, who have merely taken over the privileges and attitudes of the foreign imperialists.[1] And the ghost of Che Guevera will be knocking on the door. But to explore this would take us beyond the sphere of culture.

SURVIVALS

The impact of industrial countries on underdeveloped regions raises so many complex issues, which have already produced a vast literature, that I can here only refer briefly to one or two aspects. The problem is now so familiar that the question is not whether the more ' primitive ' culture will survive, but whether any part of it will remain. How can the best things in the old way of life be preserved? In a library context I have—in a superficial fashion—referred to this elsewhere.

The leaders of the new countries of Africa have been very conscious of this need to preserve what seems to be most valuable in the traditional way of life while adopting the new technology to raise their standard of living. At African cultural congresses much time has been spent in discussing such concepts as ' negritude ' and the 'African personality '. The significance of negritude is, of course, that it was developed by Africans and West Indians from French ex-colonial

33

territories, where people were brought up as black Frenchmen, and for them the search for identity has a desperate meaning. It must be admitted that many of these theories are not very convincing. The cynic could claim that for the developing areas the cultural clash results in the adoption of the more malignant habits and values of Western society, and the preservation of all the worst elements in their own. I can only suggest that this would be a superficial judgment. It is at least apparent that a scientific culture is directly opposed to the *mores* of the folk and is likely to splinter them totally. Two examples should suffice. It was hoped that in Africa ' superstitions ' could be eradicated and art forms would survive. Traditional African carving, as is well known, made a profound impression on European artists, but in spite of the efforts of cultural centres such as those in the universities, it has ceased to have much meaning for educated Africans because for them the utilitarian and the symbolic meanings are lost or no longer relevant. Much has been made of the very real social advantages of African communal life. But the emerging ' middle class ' or the professional elements do not want to live in this way any more. They are often condemned for aping the burgeoisie of the West, but anyone who was brought up in a village where there was no adequate housing, or sanitation, or transport, or electric light can be excused for wanting above all things a bungalow and a car. In consequence, it is only nationalist fanatics, or antiquarians, or sentimentalists, or *foreigners* who are concerned very much about the indigenous past.

If this trend is apparent everywhere, it does not follow that the old ways become extinct altogether. There are, of course, numerous important and persistent *survivals* from the past. Cultural change is slow. Inevitably, contradictory elements co-exist in all cultures and in the minds of the same individuals. It is a commonplace that many educated Africans still believe in ' juju ' and witchcraft, but less often appreciated that Europeans or Americans exhibit the same characteristics. For example, in Europe institutional Christianity has never wholly absorbed many deeply rooted pagan traditions which survive after a thousand years. Confusion is absent only in death.

The current political resurgence of Scottish and Welsh nationalism is a variation on this theme. The Welsh, for example, naturally wish to preserve their own distinct culture which is embodied in their language: this genuine living folk tradition. At the same time they demand the material benefits of industry and tourism, which have nothing to do with the folk and will in large measure destroy them. The conflict is inherent in the situation. There can be either the biblical (subsidised) sheep upon the hillside, or alternatively the coastal caravans of alien tribes, but in the long run they are probably not compatible. The caravans may breed in a disgusting (commercial) manner, but they do not have to eat the grass. Factories are something else, but their cultural significance is not local or regional, or even national at all.

A striking indication of the power of cultural survival is to be found in the West Indies, where every attempt was made to destroy the culture of the African slaves. Many African customs and words have nevertheless survived; not only this, but these vital residues have combined with other elements to set up new cultural forms. The world famous Carnival of Trinidad is the obvious example. As one writer has said: ' The rich folk life of a small isolated society inevitably dies or suffers radical changes upon contact with " modern western " culture. This same modern western culture, for all its myriads of forms, has not shown any viable creative expression among its folk. But from what would seem to be the least likely place, a small and culturally fragmented island, there has emerged a folk life and a number of art forms without precedent. Taking as material and subject the tritest products of commercialism, movies, popular songs, pulp magazines (and old steel oil drums), new forms of expression have been created and other forms extended and revitalised. Trinidad . . . has shown what can be done.'

It is open to doubt whether Trinidad has done anything of the kind. It is improbable that similar circumstances exist or are likely to exist elsewhere.

It remains to add that the social anthropologists deal with the impact of ' advanced ' upon simple cultures by distinguishing between ' nuclear ' and ' peripheral ' areas of cultural organisation. The nuclear, or central, area is resistant to change, and if this is destroyed then the culture collapses, while in peripheral regions all kinds of modifications can be made. In any particular context what is nuclear and what is peripheral seems to elude easy definition. Head hunting in Borneo is the nuclear custom usually cited, but this is not a particularly common pastime in the modern world.

A well known contribution to this debate has been made by Ruth Benedict. In *New lives for old: cultural transformation—Manus 1928-1953* she describes how after twenty five years she revisited the Manus people of the Admiralties Islands (New Guinea) to find that the people there had passed during that interval entirely from a stone age culture into the modern world. Admitting that the conditions in these small islands were ' very special and quite unrepeatable ', she suggests that this experience (and evidence from elsewhere) may indicate that ' rapid change is not only possible but may actually be desirable ' (p 372). Each human culture is a whole, and it may therefore be easier to change totally from one pattern to another than slowly to introduce isolated changes which by themselves are too little and too late. Such a thesis, obviously applicable in some places, carries the implication that the careful building of bridges between the old and the new may be a mistaken policy: the grafting of new habits on an older structure may result simply in collapse. So ' this study of the Manus suggests the great importance of whole patterns, that it is easier to shift from being a South Sea Islander to being a New Yorker—as I have seen Samoans do—than to shift from being a perfectly adjusted to a partly civilized, partly acculturated South Sea Islander . . .' (p 376). It is a cogent argument and the last chapter, ' Implications for the world ', is a valuable summary of the various attitudes adopted by administrators and anthropologists.

THE LAST REPATRIATES

I conclude this chapter with a comment on the role of expatriates in ex-colonial countries. They are caught up in the cultural clashes which they no longer control. This often causes them to become incongruous figures in the landscape, but affords some of them at least unique opportunities for understanding. It is a journalist's commonplace that anyone who takes up a post in an ex-colonial country will need different interests, attitudes and qualities from those members of that now almost extinct species, the colonialists, who spent their lives abroad in the past. This is so obvious that we can ignore it. The new role, however, carries with it the possibilities of at least vulgar errors, or in some instances total disaster.

One set of unsuitable attitudes derives from the wish to *identify* with the new environment. Members of the American Peace Corps, for example, before they go forth on their pioneering activities are briefed in the thorough American manner, and in consequence disaster in the field is only averted because of the good sense of idealistic young people. Some Americans concentrate so intensely and consciously on ' adjustment ' and ' adaptation ' that they forget who they are and lose the naivety and spontaneity which is otherwise one of their most attractive failings. The ironies of this situation are best illustrated by a scene in which an American dressed in African ceremonial robes might sit down to consume indigenous food (using his fingers) together with an African friend in evening clothes who eats his steak and two veg with knife and fork. No more need be said.

A second more dangerous fallacy is a subtle new version of the white man's burden theme. It arises from a feeling that these people who are being 'helped' should be grateful, or if not, that they should accept without question the guidance of the expert from another culture. It is easy enough to declare that we should forget our own cultural norms when dealing with other societies, but much less easy to do this in practice, because the norms are often unconscious—almost instinctive.

In the sphere of librarianship, Lester Asheim mentions the use of the linear alphabet in the countries of Asia, which results in totally different catalogues. A person from an English speaking culture may well come to think of his cataloguing rules as a law of nature. If he does not he will almost certainly feel that his attitudes to work or efficiency, or time, or money, or sex are in some sense absolutes.

A peculiar variation of this cultural confusion can be observed in the behaviour of a number of white radicals who have been to Africa, sometimes in an academic capacity and sometimes specifically as advisers. Disillusioned by the political gods that failed in Europe or elsewhere, they saw (quite rightly) in the underdeveloped areas of the world new possibilities of social reconstruction or revolution. In particular they looked to the 'socialist' countries of Africa to build up communities where human solidarity would be paramount. Many of them were to be found in Nkrumah's Ghana: they are not there now. Where then have they gone? Tanzania? Cuba? socialist Britain? None of these countries will do. The answer, of course, is that they are mostly to be found in the USA, where their inexhaustible fervour can swell the chorus of protest. They are mentioned here in order to indicate that their socialism was not really relevant. They were the products of another culture who belonged to it because they rebelled.

NOTE
1 Franz Fanon's message in *The wretched of the earth* (*op cit*) was that cultural renewal is impossible for the countries of the Third World until they become truly independent and create a national consciousness. The new culture cannot be built on the folk ways of the pre-colonial past, nor

on imitation of Europe, but will emerge as a result of the struggle for independence and social justice. These developments in most of Africa still lie in the future and formal political independence is only the beginning of this revolutionary struggle. Since he wrote, this movement has received many setbacks and much of black Africa remains in a neo-colonialist condition

3

communications

RELEVANCE: There is now a daunting amount of communication about communication—a literature which relates *inter alia* to cybernetics, neurology, linguistics, psychology, social anthropology, physics, group dynamics, semantics and the sociology of culture. We must also add library studies and documentation. The librarian is indirectly concerned with communication because his collections of material need to be organised for use, and until they are so organised an important agency in the communication process breaks down. The information role of the librarian involves him in the world of communications, and that is why students should study methods and types of communication. What follows is an outline of some communication problems, but I have been particularly concerned to make clear that the sphere of information is a limited one, whereas communication is basic to our culture in a different and more fundamental sense.

ANIMAL CONTACTS
The ability to communicate is a key element in culture, and most living things have developed rudimentary methods of communication which include sound as well as visual display. The communications of animals include cries, gestures and thumps which express simple responses to stimuli such as the mating call, or the alarm signal, or the warning display. The porpoise has apparently gone beyond this stage of development and uses a language which linguists are trying to decipher. Claims are even made for the domestic fowl, which,

according to one authority, possesses an international 'language' made up of thirty basic sentences. The social insects such as the ants have communications systems, and the bees do their ' dance ' to indicate the location of a new source of nectar.

But non-human creatures have not evolved a formal language in the true sense, and it is this which in this context distinguishes them from humanity. In the beginning was the word. Apes possess several characteristics which are necessary for culture, such as the ability to walk and to use thumbs and vocal cords. In addition, their children mature slowly and they share with man the dubious blessing of a continuous sex urge. Indeed, sexual activity may well be the most basic of all forms of communication. The vast literature of sex probably owes its origins to the fact that sex relations represent an attempt at total communication, and an escape from isolation. Furthermore, sexual union exhibits one important characteristic of true communication insofar as it is, or should be, a two way process: to use the current jargon, feed-back occurs.

Hence the only valid objection to solitary masturbation as a practice is presumably that it excludes communication with others. McLuhan's otherwise dubious dictum that the medium is the massage is perhaps most applicable in this sphere. But to return to the animals, they cannot be said to possess true culture because they cannot symbolise, and the essence of human culture is accumulation—the retention and passing on of cultural manifestations from one generation to another. The extraordinary cries of birds, for example, can be recorded and even preserved in libraries, but this, of course, is for our benefit, not theirs.

LANGUAGE

It is established, then, that when *homo sapiens* uttered his first words human culture really began, just as the child enters the cultural heritage when it begins to speak. But the original cause of spoken language is not known. Conflicting theories have been advanced and they are commonly and seriously known by fanciful names. The ' bow-wow ' theory claims that men learnt speech by imitating animal cries. The ' pooh-pooh ' adherents believe that language developed as a result of involuntary noises provoked by violent stimuli, in contrast to the ' ding dong ' people who propose that men must have imitated all kinds of noises in an onomatopoeic fashion. The ' yo-ho-ho ' explanation is that men acquired speech to assist in co-operative labour, just as songs are used in the same manner today. Finally, other linguists have suggested that the first words were used to accompany gestures which must have long preceded speech.

Whatever the origins, we know that the languages of the world can be classified into families which were produced by the wandering of tribes and peoples. The resultant babble of tongues is one of the most obvious barriers to communication. When our earliest fore-fathers built the city and the tower of Babel, the people had one language and were therefore building a true community wherein ' nothing will be restrained from them which they have imagined to do '. But in developing their isolated city culture they were neglecting their global responsibilities as laid down, which required that they should be scattered abroad upon the face of all the earth. Accordingly, the Lord said ' " Go to, let us go down and there confound their lan-guage that they may not understand one another's speech ". So the Lord scattered them abroad . . .'

That was long ago, yet we are still confounded and are likely to remain so. The proposals for an international language (such as Esperanto) ignore cultural realities, particularly the fact that languages are not artificial creations but reflections of a way of life in time and place. The foreign language barrier is, of course, a great obstacle to all forms of international communication, and is felt so particularly in the field of scientific research where speed of communication is important. There is in consequence a bibliographical problem with which we are not concerned here. What is more relevant to our theme is the fact that obvious foreign language barriers may be less dangerous than the other divisive elements in culture mentioned elsewhere. In most countries people officially speak or write the same language as each other, but the *use* of language may vary so much that communi-cation fails. Groups in one country often have more in common with groups in another country than with their own compatriots, in spite of the language complications.

PICTURES

After the invention of language the next step was the development of the ability to produce pictures to correspond with a thing described in words. Those symbols which literally represented things pictorially are called pictograms, whereas what is called ideogrammatic writing used symbols which indicate by association. The ancient Egyptian hieroglyphic contained both forms, and the Chinese language to this

41

day is based on the dual principle. Such methods of writing have the advantage that they are 'international', in the sense that algebra or chemical formulae or musical scores are, but the corresponding disdvantage is that there is no link with words. It is an entirely visual medium—and those who used it had to learn two 'languages' which were not at all related. Modern scholars can decipher early pictorial languages, but they do not know what they sounded like when 'read' aloud. If visual communication had remained pictorial, written languages would have remained separate from spoken languages and the latter would have succumbed to a proliferation of dialect and jargon. That is what happened in China.

THE ALPHABET

The Egyptians' hieroglyphics included some signs which represented sounds, but they did not develop a phonetic linear alphabet. This was the achievement of the Phoenicians, who produced a practical alphabet, the main limitation of which was that it contained no vowels. Modern semitic languages such as Hebrew also have this characteristic. The final development—that of providing vowels—was carried out by the Greeks, and the alphabet had by that time become substantially what it is now. Usage in the Western world was fixed by the Romans, who wrote horizontally from left to right in descending lines and used the letters which we still use.

PRINTING

The fourth stage in the evolution of media was the invention in the fifteenth century of printing from movable type. It has remained the main medium of visual communication for the last 500 years. Its significance is too well known to warrant description. It is because of printing that the repository role of the library became so important, since libraries were able thus to accumulate culture. The role of the librarian is to make communication possible. In our time the mass media of communication are to some extent modifying the role of print, and this is discussed in the next chapter.

MYTHS, SYMBOLS AND IMAGES

So far we have been discussing what is mainly *rational* communication involving the conscious levels of the mind. There remain those regions where people communicate by means which involve other faculties and other types of perception. Some of these are still a matter for conjecture and dispute, so that I shall omit telepathic communication or psychic phenomena such as messages from beyond the grave or from supernatural beings. In any event, these are not normally considered to be part of a librarian's responsibility. It is however impossible to ignore the fact that, even though language or print may be used, messages are sometimes conveyed by indirect means, often in order to try to express the inexpressible. Thus the literary artist will use words to reflect a multiplicity of human experiences which has many levels and many meanings. This incorporates both the aesthetic sphere and the technique of suggestion used by the advertiser and the propagandist.

ORAL SOCIETIES

Pre-literate communications were oral, and when human memory is the cultural connecting link we invariably find it impossible to distinguish between history and legend. Indeed history without written records *is* myth (unless it can be substantiated by precise archaelogical research); who knows whether King Arthur ever did ride to Camelot? Having noted this it should be added that many myths have been explained in other ways without reference to history; they have been variously described as parables, allegories and early scientific theories. Freud, basing his theory on the remarkable similarity of content in the myths and folk tales of the world, and on his analysis of individuals, claimed that myths are thinly disguised representations of unconscious fantasies common to all mankind. Jung carried this theory further with his concept of the collective or racial unconscious, which lies below the personal unconscious, and beyond this yet again the deepest levels common to all humanity. For him the collective unconscious is the deposit of ancestral experience for millions of years, and he calls certain themes which recur in dreams and in mythology ' archetypes '. The postulation of a collective unconscious seems to suggest that certain ' ideas ' may be inherited, and it is not one which scientists will normally accept, but Jung's work has been influential and much of his terminology has passed into our culture.

The Preacher, then, apparently overstated his case when he asserted that ' There is no remembrance of the former generations, neither shall there be any remembrance of the latter generations that are to come, among those that shall come after '. But his words serve to remind us that those who invented the alphabet also invented Time, which eventually became fully mechanised with the arrival of printing and with the invention of the clock. When this happened the old organic cycle of generation, birth, development and death lost its full meaning. Non-literate cultures do not have this impatient sense of time as duration.

LANGUAGE AND MEANING

As soon as we consider language as a medium of communication it becomes apparent that language and reality are not the same thing. Language is not a mirror of experience, not even a distorting mirror, because it exists in its own right, and interacts with other social realities. A word is in fact a *thing*—in addition to being a symbol of some other thing. As Jesse Shera says (in *Documentation*, p 66) ' We do not know the effect of the symbolic structure that is language upon the behaviour patterns of society '.

We do know, however, that language can be used consciously or unconsciously to conceal objective truth. This is obvious enough in the case of detectable untruths, and psycho-analysis has made us all familiar with the processes of rationalisation by which individuals deceive others and, more particularly, themselves. If people are unable to communicate with one another, it emerges at once that language (or the thinking based upon it) serves many other purposes than external communication, and many of these purposes are either evil or superstitions. The word itself, as Ogden and Richards emphasised in *The meaning of meaning*, may gather round itself occult powers and the aura of taboos. There have been many deities whose names are held to be unmentionable, and so on. As a *thing* the word is inevitably a conservative force, and produces the kind of cultural lags discussed in chapter 1, because it reflects (insofar as it reflects at all) a reality which no longer exists. In a time of rapid change, such as the present, this is one reason why the middle aged (*ie* any one over thirty) cannot understand the young—and why the young try to invent a new language.

It follows, therefore, that words are not labels but social tools, whose use and meaning depend on conventions which differ according to the class and group affiliations of individuals. If this relates to education at all it only does so insofar as the education structure may reflect (or modify) diverse social backgrounds. In fragmented societies there are various partially separate groups or subcultures who use language in a way which may not be comprehensible to other groups. For complete understanding, a community of experience and thought is required, and when this is absent we state literally that people ' are not speaking the same language ', even though their vocabularies may be identical. It is the *understanding* which is lacking, and this is nothing to do with language as such. This is commonly appreciated with regard to conversation: many people, particularly those past middle age, either do not talk at all, or else rarely finish their sentences, because they have lost faith in language as a means of communication. The other groups have gone beyond the pale—and one group, or one individual (the ' outsider ') or one class becomes culturally alienated. This overworked term (alienated) expresses a variety of meanings, but the common factor in all of them is a psychological condition produced by social isolation. Where no real community exists there can be (by definition) no communication, and alienation is therefore very relevant to communication problems.

The concept of cultural alienation as originally used by Marx, and before him by Hegel, Schiller and other German philosophical idealists, is worth a further note, since it is a part of Marxism which has become relevant at the present time—and one which has brought about an attempt by some European Christian thinkers to continue a ' dialogue ' with Marxism. According to Marx, man has become self-estranged, or dehumanised, or alienated, because what he produces becomes objectified—turned into a ' thing ' or ' reified ' as something separate from him which he can no longer control. Marx, at least in his early work, blamed Christianity for this process, because of its ' otherworldly ' nature and because of the emphasis on the individual which meant that collective social life was ignored. But ultimately and more particularly in his later work he regarded alienation as fundamentally economic in nature, so that it could only be healed by political revolution. These ideas have been developed and modified in Sartre's influential *Critique of Dialectical Reason*, 1960, and, like many American writers also, Sartre automatically supports the ' anti-social ' alienated individual (such as Genet), which the English tradition, as exemplified in Leavis, does not. Raymond Williams, for example, has always stressed social values and his belief that alienation need not occur even now, and will be overcome in a return to a true socialist community.

It will be seen that the term ' alienation ' as commonly used at present means something much less precise than this, and may simply refer to cultural or social fragmentation which results in separate

45

sub-cultures, such as those of the teenagers, or the black Americans, or the very poor—or, in another sense, that of the intellectuals.

The use of language, then, rests on assumptions which are shared: these are present in all of the members of a particular group. Since everybody belongs to some types of in-group, how can the influence of closed groups be modified or destroyed? Aranguren, in *Human communication*, p 140, suggests that this is the special social function of the intellectual: 'An intellectual is someone who is capable either of emerging from the social group to which he belongs or else of criticising it from within'. This is why intellectuals are usually only partially integrated in society. At a further extreme, this is why, in Aldous Huxley's words in *Literature and science*, p 13, ' The elements of experience which are unique, aberrant, other than average remain outside the pale of common language '.

It remains to note that in ' open ', or pluralistic, societies these groups are partly an abstraction, since individuals *may* belong to several different ones. But the result in cultural terms is the same, and from the point of view of the individual, conflicts between groups will naturally be reflected in his mind—which is not necessarily a bad thing, since it helps to ensure social progress.

SCIENTIFIC INFORMATION

Meredith, in *Instruments of communication*, stresses the social elements in scientific information work: ' Social communication among scientists is an essential condition of their work '. He claims further that because of the limitations of the printed word, it is more important in science to talk to people than to read books. Noting the traditional classical concept of oratorical argument where, because uncertainty prevails, emotive techniques can be used, he points out that there are not only depths of emotion which traditional rhetoric recognised, but also depths of understanding which it failed to distinguish. It follows that communication problems are rooted in social and technical changes which go far beyond the realm of language studies. From the more narrow point of view of librarianship, the implications have been recognised by many of those engaged in the retrieval of scientific information. A number of investigations have indicated that scientists use information retrieval systems and library information services far less than might be expected, and that social factors are largely responsible.

46

There are, therefore, or there should be, as many types of spoken and written language as there are types of readers, and bad writing is simply that which is inappropriate for its purpose, and which fails in the full sharing of understanding. When one considers that the most effective means of communication in modern physics, for example, is often the use of mathematical symbols alone, but that the results of its researches must also be presented to the understanding of the layman, the extent of the problem becomes apparent. Kapp, in *The presentation of technical information* has indicated the main difference between functional and other kinds of writing, by noting that a good functional style maintains receptivity in the reader: it should not be ' creative ', since receptivity cannot be stored. But as far as scientific research or discovery is concerned, there is obviously a ' creative ' element, which means that scientific activity is by no means as wholly objective as sometimes alleged. The creative aspect in science includes subjective insights, and in consequence there are often accidental features in research and discovery. The information scientists have also had to recognise this element, hence the increasing attention which has been paid to ' serendipity ', or random selection.

Apart from these factors, language in itself often fails as an instrument of communication because of the rapidity of change. There is in fact a language crisis now, because the old association between words and the things they represent becomes impossible. The older use of language was much more rhetorical, in the sense of the word used above: this rhetoric may now hinder contact with ' reality ', which, at least as far as the material world is concerned, is increasingly scientific.

STRUCTURE OF LANGUAGE

Within the field of linguistics itself, a number of authorities have studied the fact that our *thinking* is determined by the structure of particular languages. This work has been particularly associated with the theories of B L Whorf, who, in *Language, thought and reality,* claims that language actually *organises* reality. According to Whorf, the world is presented in a kaleidoscopic flux of impressions which has to be mentally organised—and this is done not by classification systems, but largely by the linguistic structures in our minds. The pattern of our language imposes an obligatory codification.

THE GROWTH OF NON-COMMUNICATION
Increasing concern has been expressed in many quarters that an outstanding defect in modern cultures is a failure in communication.[1] The proliferating literature on communication studies exhibits the same use of specialists' jargon, incomprehensible to the layman, which characterises other specialist topics: the communicators are talking to themselves. Seligman's *Encyclopedia of the social sciences* defines communication as a ' network of partial or complete understandings '; one might equally well substitute the word ' misunderstandings '. What follows is a discussion of some of the possible reasons for this relative failure.

THE INFORMATION EXPLOSION
The increase in the quantity of information (and the speed with which it appears) is the factor which most librarians think of when considering how to control the flood of publications by bibliographical and library means. The first problem is to ensure that relevant information gets to users at the right time. As is indicated in my book *Bibliography and the provision of books*, these matters are fundamental to library and bibliographic organisation. The same figures are constantly repeated for the quantity of publications, with particular reference to science and its exponential rate of growth. One authority (Professor Price of Yale University) has pointed out there if the present rate continues, there will soon be more scientists than people; another has calculated that there are more scientists *alive* today than in the sum total of the past.

The answers to the explosion lie in the field of social and bibliographic organisation. Yet even if solutions on this level were to be found, there is no evidence that real communication would be achieved. The fact that information is emitted or disseminated, and even received, is no guarantee that communication occurs. The transmission in itself has no meaning, and the information has to be *deciphered and interpreted,* and as a result it is frequently not understood.

There are, in fact, more fundamental barriers to communication, some of which we have already noted in relation to language.

INDUSTRIAL COMPLEXITY
Within the field of information flow as a social process it is evident that a modern society requires a far-ranging network of communica-

48

tions in order to function at all. It is only to be expected, therefore, that information often fails to circulate. The apparatus of the welfare state, for example, is so complex that many citizens (particularly those who need the services most) are not aware what actual benefits they might receive. State agencies, and all organisations within the state, organise information services, and this is an essential element in management technique. As a social process the free flow of information is wholly dependent on the existence of free democratic (ie politically unrestricted) institutions at all levels, and on the absence of censorship or authoritarian suppressions. As is noted in the last chapter, it is possible to have a free flow of some types of information within particular organisations and still not have a free society, because there is some overall control. The growth in size of modern organisations, particularly those engaged in scientific research, may also produce, and indeed is producing, a situation where individuals work on a specialised job without knowing for what purpose their particular operation is intended, or what the complete venture is. This is a further example of the dehumanisation which can occur. It follows that a man may be working, *could be* working, on some totally anti-human form of research without even being aware of the fact.

One response to this and similar problems is the current demand for ' participation ' in all forms of social, political and economic life. This amounts to a claim that information itself, is not enough and a consideration of it would take us beyond information as such, and into politics.

THE FAILURE OF RATIONAL EXPLANATION

It was suggested above that the use of language is often inadequate because it no longer describes reality. This seems to be part of a trend which has many facets. In chapter 1 is discussed the growth of irrationalism in the arts. In Kafka's nightmares, the main protagonists never discover what is happening or why. The ' theatre of the absurd ' is truly absurd on one level at least, because nobody can communicate at all, and Becket's clowns and tramps are primarily studies in the manners of non communication. The key factor in modern developed society, as Herbert Marcuse constantly proclaims, is that social structures *seem to be* wholly rational but rebellious individuals instinctively feel that this rationality does not satisfy human needs. As Daniel Bell states in *Technology and social change*, edited by Eli Ginzberg, p 59, ' The whole breakdown of the rational cosmology is imminent and will ultimately create the most serious problems for society because of an alienation of the modes of perception about the world '. Society is unable to find cultural terms for expressing what is happening—and twentieth century thought lacks confidence in the rational solution of social and cultural problems.

The implication can only be that the ' rational solutions ' are inadequate. Many radical critics would dispose of the matter in the traditional Marxist manner by pointing out that capitalist ideology inevitably obscures the real nature of society. (It should not be forgotten that the word ' ideology ' means, or originally meant, a system of beliefs which does not explain, but explains *away* reality, just as rationalisation obscures reality for the individual.) If this is the case, as it certainly is in the USA, it is probably true in the USSR also, where the official ideology corresponds even less with life as it is experienced—and furthermore any attempts to radically modify this discrepancy cannot appear above ground.

There is therefore a blockage in the communication of *ideas*. Traditional political or religious faiths provided an analysis of social reality which *inter alia* explained how society (and the universe) was believed to work. At one time the Christians, and the Marxists, explained everything to the satisfaction of millions of adherents. Up to the end of the century even the scientists provided answers whose implications could be understood by everybody. The gods have failed now because their analysis is irrelevant, and in consequence their panaceas do not help. As McLuhan has claimed, the overworked concept that God is dead really refers to the Newtonian universe that has passed away, and the ground rule upon which so much of the Western world is built is dissolved. Because of this we cannot control events, and *nobody knows what is happening*. (Harrington deals with this at length and that is why he calls his book on our times *The accidental century*.) In many spheres where ideas are important, few people have anything valid to say, and for this and other reasons we stop listening to the message and there is a widespread growth of disbelief, scepticism and negative criticism. Our leaders seem to be more in the dark than anybody else, illustrating in a new guise Acton's dictum that power corrupts. As Bob Dylan has it, ' Something is happening but you don't know what it is—do you Mr Jones?'.

It is most noticeable in the case of the revolting young that they tend to use terminology—for example anti-capitalist slogans—which does not really express what they are trying to say. They are groping towards a new language—a true communication—but, meanwhile, inadequate slogans from the past must serve. The millions of young people who stick a poster of Che Guevera on their wall do not share either his beliefs or his language. Most of them are aware of this circumstance: they are also very conscious that there is this need for true communication, and the leaders of the pop world like the Beatles have frequently said so. This is why the trends in clothes and long hair are to them so important: they are fundamentally methods of communication. There is a Beatles song called 'All you need is love', which on the face of it is a banal and puerile statement, but they are not simply referring to the usual commercial concept at all. Sex as a basic form of communication was discussed above. On another level it is beyond doubt that without love, in the sense used by most of the great religious leaders, true human communication is impossible. If society as it exists does not allow for this act of communication, either because the structure is wrong or because of social injustice or because there is no freedom to express opinions, then the social consequences will be revolutionary.

The trumpet calls for human solidarity are based on a recognition of this, but what usually happens in practice is that the kind of solidarity which is based on human love only occurs temporarily within small groups (opposed to other groups), or where societies are at war or in times of revolution and crisis. Or else these human needs are perverted and rendered evil by false prophets like Hitler, who must base their movements on error. This brings us back to those radical opposition movements which fundamentally reject modern societies, since what they are fighting is hypocrisy in all its forms: where untruth prevails, communication breaks down. That is why this chapter is not about technical processes such as ' positive and negative feedback loops '. All the loops in the world cannot obliterate fabrication.

NOTE
1 Thus Simenon the novelist: ' The fact that we are I don't know how many millions of people, yet communication, complete communication, is completely impossible between two of these people, is to me one of the biggest tragic themes in the world. When I was a young boy I was afraid of it. I would almost scream because of it. It gave me such a sensation of solitude, of loneliness. This is a theme I have taken I don't know how many times. But I know it will come again. Certainly it will come again ' (in *Writers at work,* edited by M Cowley, Secker & Warburg, 1958).

4

mass communications

WHAT ARE MASS MEDIA? Communication as a 'mass' activity (*ie* directed to a mass of recipients) is not new, but in the past the audience was smaller than today, as in the case of the medieval churches which communicated entirely with isolated rural communities. When we are discussing mass culture it is important to keep this in mind. It is generally agreed that the mass media include the cinema, the radio, the press (together with large circulation periodicals), and above all television: many authorities also include paperback books, which have a mass circulation.[1] The terminology is not precise, and some publications have used a statistical yardstick to indicate when the audience or readership becomes 'mass'; for example, UNESCO in one publication uses the figure of one million. (It is of interest that about one million people regularly listen to the third programme of the BBC.) The concept, however, is clear enough: it implies a vast number of people at the receiving end of the communication process, usually receiving *at about the same time*. In the case of radio and television, the messages stream into our own homes and there is no immediate group psychological reaction, such as obtains in large public gatherings, or even (to a much lesser degree) in the cinema. With all the media it happens that cultural minorities can be catered for and alternative programmes can be provided: these minorities, being smaller, are less of a mass than the larger one which forms the basis for popular culture. Best-selling publishing has always shared most of the characteristics of the mass media generally. Some writers have apparently assumed that *libraries* in general are agents of mass communication, but they are not so considered here, if only because their role is intermediate and more passive. A well organised information service is of course, a communications agency which also *interprets* the literature, but this is done for a relatively small number of people.

SAVAGE TORPOR

Because modern mass culture has been largely created by modern technology and the communication methods which it has engendered, there exists a very considerable literature on the subject. Much of the discussion does not lead anywhere in particular, and in view of the fact that the full impact of television has been felt only within the last fifteen or so years, this is not surprising. The literature inevitably includes representations by those who lament the passing away of the folk, or the threat to traditional high culture. Because of the academic humanistic attitude to culture already noted, there are constant laments over the evils of vulgarisation and popularisation. These prophecies of doom began more than a hundred years ago when the mass society was set in motion by the effects of the Industrial Revolution. At that time, the poet Wordsworth complained that ' a multitude of causes unknown to former times are now acting with a combined force to blunt the discriminating powers of the mind and unfitting it for all voluntary exertion to reduce it to a state of almost savage torpor '.

It was at this time also that the alleged evils of commercialism became apparent, since, at least in the sphere of journalism, writers had become dependent on the public for financial support and the long dialogue began between those who believed in giving the public what ' it ' wanted, and those who wished to educate it, and thirdly, those who tried to do both. There were always respectable or leading figures who not only accepted the new trends but welcomed or took advantage of them. Sir Walter Scott was one of the first; Wesley, the evangelist, was another who used the new possibilities in his preaching campaigns, in his publishing programme and in the organisation of his church, which took advantage of group psychology. Whatever the reaction, the point being made here is that by the middle of the last century, the so called mass society was already in existence. During the early nineteenth century, book clubs and circulating libraries were flourishing, and in 1832, Charles Knight's *Penny magazine* was selling 200,000 copies a week. In the second half of the century, the process accelerated, and the popular press extended its influence to the lower middle and working classes. In this development, Charles Mudie and W H Smith, the pioneers who appreciated the commercial significance of railway transport, are key figures. By 1870, the periodical *Titbits* had a huge circulation: in 1896, Lord Northcliffe founded the *Daily mail*, and as far as the publishing world is concerned, the mass communication process was complete.

THE CRITICS
The critics who deplored the trend were rooted in the culture of the past; today Malcolm Muggeridge is the living embodiment of the frustrations which such a stance produces. He uses the communication channels of mass entertainment in order to attack it (which no doubt accounts for his waxworks presence in Madame Tussaud's). The critics mentioned so far are largely writers and journalists who have committed themselves to one side or the other, but there has been, inevitably, an academic industry which has tried to treat these matters scientifically. Since the United States is the country which represents mass culture in its most advanced form, much of the academic analysis has come from there. It has frequently been noted that the sociologists, so far, have not yet supplied any *conclusive* evidence one way or another. This point is made forcibly by J D Halloran in *The effects of mass communication,* published in 1968. He goes on to show that although this is the case, *some* conclusions are possible and these will be noted later in this section. There is, for example, evidence obtained by the Television Research Unit at Leeds University that, with regard to politics, television did not affect attitudes or voting behaviour at any particular time, but that we do not know what the long term impact might be and the short term questions are much less important. But even if the social scientists, following further research, were to supply much more information, we should still find that many of the answers would lie beyond the disciplines of the social scientist. There are, to be sure, scientific values mainly concerned with the search for Truth, but the moral judgments ultimately involved in any assessment of the wider aspects of mass culture must come from elsewhere.

THE OBJECTIONS
It is revealing that most of the critics have concentrated on the debit side. The Pilkington Committee on Broadcasting stressed that, as far as its evidence went, the tendency to deplore television was almost

54

universal: ' Though it was generally said to us of sound radio, this is admirable, none was willing to say it of television '. Or, again, another comment is relevant: ' What is most striking about much of the research work is its failure to take into account what good the mass media may do, and the obvious fact that teaching people to become more selective is at least as important as any question of changing or censoring the content of the media '. Another confusion which runs through the literature, is a tendency not to be able clearly to distinguish the media from their use. It is not easy to establish what is *inherent* in television, for instance, when many of the objections of the critics really refer to abuses, or to the way that the medium has been used to far.

POWER AND CONTROL

It is commonly alleged that the mass media enable a few people to manipulate opinion or to create needs where none exist. People everywhere are exposed either to political pressures or to direct or indirect influences from financial interests. Modern psychological techniques are used to substitute persuasion for debate or brainwashing for persuasion. We are at the mercy of those who are trying to sell commodities (USA), or to perpetuate their own political control (USSR). With regard to both types of exploitation, it is obvious that the situation in Britain is not so disturbing to the liberal mind, since there are built-in safeguards which to some degree protect the individual. In broadcasting and television the device of the public corporation preserves the media from government control, at least to some degree, and the financial interests do not directly determine programmes as in the United States. But in all ' free ' societies the powers of the advertisers have increased and are increasing.[2] This is partly because of the use of more sophisticated psychological techniques. As Raymond Williams has warned, modern advertising ' has passed the frontier of the selling of goods and services and has become involved with the teaching of social and personal values '. The audience is regarded as a passive mass which has to be converted into a *market*. This is done by ' subliminal ' or indirect means, and the message is concealed. It is significant also that the techniques are visual and there has been a shift from language to image. The language that is used is of a special kind similar to that found in popular literature. ' The line between the language of advertising, the language of popular literature and the images of the commercial cinema is fast disappearing '. These are the power and control aspects which Raymond Williams has stressed, and it follows that it is not necessarily the media themselves which are a social menace, but the use to which they are put. The task of a liberal society is, therefore, to organise a communication structure where these abuses or misuses cannot become too serious. That was the intention behind the setting up of the Pilkington Committee on Broadcasting.

The above refers mainly to ownership and financial pressures which affect the media as institutions. There has also been discussion about the influence of the media as propaganda agencies. As indicated in chapter 5, the usual conclusion is that the media reinforce attitudes which are already present in their audiences, but otherwise do not radically affect people's beliefs. This can be accepted, since the attitudes of most individuals are largely determined by their ' peer groups ' and by their immediate environment. We shall return to this point below. Beyond fundamental attitudes, it remains true that in many areas people have ' floating ' opinions or none at all. As a Head of the BBC Audience Research has stated: ' You cannot reinforce something that is not there '. At times of crisis or shock these patterns, of course, break down and anything can happen, but it should be clear enough that the media do not *cause* the crises, which are rooted in long term social, economic and political realities. As with pornographic influence, a particular radio or television programme, a specific issue of a newspaper or journal, may act as a trigger mechanism, but that is another matter.

To conclude, it is probable that television does not realise its full potential beyond the strictly recreational sphere, and that the educational possibilities will be much more fully explored when the Open University is set up. Much of this failure, particularly in the United States, can be attributed to the nature of ownership and control. These are political issues.

PASSIVITY

Quite apart from the attitudes of those who provide radio or television programmes, or the daily fare of popular journalism, it is alleged that people are, in fact, passive consumers. They do not participate; there is no active response or feedback, such as should happen in true communication. (In this context, what would these critics say about the religious sermon, which was a major communication medium for centuries? It would appear that the psychological situation was the same.) There is the further allegation that television in particular fosters apathy and indifference to the outside world as it is reflected on the screen. This cannot be proven and it may well be that this indifference is something which, in the majority of people, was always present. The objection seems to be mainly an objection to the medium as such: the term ' hypnopathy ' has been used to describe the effect of television on viewers, and this type of reaction seems to be particularly apparent in relation to news programmes.

But there is another kind of passivity which takes the form of fantasy on vicarious living, and in this case the viewer *is* involved, but not with reality. Millions of people relate themselves to Mrs Dale or the Archers (radio), or to Dr Findlay (television) or to the characters in some trivial soap opera, but they do not know, or want to know, their next door neighbour. It is possible to believe that this situation is undesirable, but the phenomenon is neither new nor created by radio or television: certain types of literature have always played this role. Much to the chagrin of Conan Doyle, and subsequently to some members of his family, Sherlock Holmes became more ' real ' throughout the world than Conan Doyle or any living person could ever be. The same critics have rarely condemned the immortality of characters such as those of Dickens or Shakespeare because they are part of high culture as well as low. What should we say of James Bond, who apparently has no intention of following into the grave the writer who created him? One can think of numerous other archetypal figures who exist for the same reasons, *ie* because of basic human needs.

In any event, these fulminations about passivity should not be accepted too uncritically, because the critics, in fact, do not really know what happens in the mind of television viewers who apparently do not respond. As we shall see, Marshall McLuhan takes an opposite view and in this respect he has not been alone. For example, in many activities there can be a total *absorption,* which is not the same thing as deep concentration, and afterwards nothing is remembered, but this does not prove that nothing has happened. The critics may accept this analysis but dismiss this type of reaction, on the grounds that it is simply a drugged condition. There is an assumption that all drugs are undesirable: there is a further assumption that all fantasy is deplorable. Neither of these assumptions can be accepted without question; they are based on an attitude which automatically condemns certain kinds of pleasure as ' escapism ', with the further implication that it is wrong. The commonsense conclusion would seem to be that escapist material is not necessarily harmful *per se*, although it may be for some people in particular circumstances. The human requirements which are met by fantasy are various, and while some of them may be socially undesirable, others are not.

THE PSEUDO WORLD

It is alleged that the media create their own world which is not the ' real ' world. Journalists have always had to face the accusation that what is newsworthy is not *typical* and that in consequence a gross distortion occurs. To an even greater extent, the daily fare of television news portrays a world where violence, disaster, chaos, disorder, crisis and calamity go on all the time, whereas, in fact, the world is not like this at all. The implication seems to be that anything which is typical has some peculiar significance : this is only true in peasant or static cultures. Modern man is aware that he is condemned to live among extreme situations. The same insistence on the typical appears in the aesthetic theories of ' socialist realism ', which have inevitably produced anti-literature. The same emphasis was placed by conservative economic historians, who dismissed the social misery of the Industrial Revolution in Britain on the grounds that it was not representative.

What these people are really saying is that if a man bites a dog this is disgraceful and should be ignored. They also obscurely feel that the news of the dog-biting man may provoke a general outbreak of dog-biting. In general, such reactions derive from a deep seated conviction that exposure to alien patterns of behaviour, or disturbing events in other parts of the world, beyond whatever pale or fringe they live within, will disrupt a settled and limited way of life. This is indeed possible and the instinct is sound but increasingly irrelevant, since it is now dishonest to pretend that what happens elsewhere need not concern us. The machines have abolished time and space, as it was formerly understood, and television brings the dog-biting man into our homes and nothing will send him away. But television has not invented the man and cannot be held responsible for him. Who or what then is responsible? The answer to such a futile question will depend on individual attitudes and on what level we choose to answer it. The apostles of social commitment would claim that in the last resort we are all responsible, even if the social and political solutions are not yet available.

In 1962, Daniel Boorstin, in *The image*, analysed at length the creation of pseudo-events and, by concentrating on personal 'images', the construction of fake personalities or celebrities. He noted that in the USA there is a public *need* for this process and this is the key factor. Americans, he claims, insist on living in a world of illusions because their expectations are extravagant. 'We want and we believe these illusions because we suffer from extravagant expectations . . . we expect too much of the world . . . we expect anything and everything'.

This particular element is less apparent in Europe, for Europeans can no longer afford this type of illusion. (It may well be that the American dream itself has been shattered by the Vietnam war and the realities of racial civil conflict.) Even so, the same tendencies are noticeable everywhere. The ' image ' of people and events has become important because in television what we experience *is* an image and the image is part of the world. Leaders in mass societies become symbols, but this is not a new phenomenon. Abuses and cults of personality occur, but when the myths are insufficiently rooted in permanent psychological reality, having served their purpose, they wither away.

The same process lies behind the creation of film stars or pop singers. Ordinary people—because of the cinema or television—achieve the status of myth. Some observers claim that this is simply the result of the activities of commercial operators—the agents—the middle men of the entertainment world. In the world of fashion they claim the same thing. This simple theory overlooks several factors. One is that there is always a particular kind of talent present, which happens at any given time to meet some indefinable social need—a need which is already there and is not *created* by communication media, or commercial operators, or by anything so tangible. This situation places an almost intolerable strain on those who are chosen or doomed for a star role. They want to be real people. The classic example is, of course, Marilyn Monroe. The gods and goddesses of the old religions enjoyed the advantage that they did not exist in the flesh, or if they did, the mythologising took place only after their death. The Virgin Mary did not have to bear this burden in her own life time. At present —because of the mass media, and for other reasons, the dreams and fantasies of millions are festooned around people who were to begin with ' real ' in an everyday sense.

TRIVIALISATION

The mass media and television in particular, the critics claim, reduce everything to the commonplace. This happens everywhere, but in the United States the process is more noticeable and pervasive because communication and salesmanship are inextricably mixed. There is a cult of mediocrity, and the common man is flattered because he is the market for both consumer goods and for the mass media themselves. To the masses, great men must be shown to be just like everybody else. It is suggested that our sensibilities are inevitably blunted when a series of unrelated images, some tragic, some significant, some ridiculous, are all given equal weight and importance, and are all brought into our homes where some kind of domestic life may be in conflict with them. The terrible image of the war in Vietnam must be followed by top of the pops, and both may be diminished by the tantrums of Aunt Mabel when bitten by the baby. The Pilkington report noted that ' triviality resides in the way the subject matter is approached and the manner in which it is presented '. More significantly it adds ' triviality is a natural vice of television ', and this surely can be accepted only if we add ' in our experience to date and under the circumstances in which television has so far developed '. If we ignore economic considerations, or if we think of the possible use of the Open University, it is at once apparent that this quality is not inherent in television at all.

THE ABOLITION OF THE PAST

We have already noted that industrialisation and technology destroy the culture of the folk and shatter the old ways of life. The mass media, as cultural agencies have made their own contribution. It is also claimed that high, or minority, culture is threatened with extinction. All that need be said here is that high culture was rooted in a social reality which has now changed, and because of this the past is no longer what it was, and we no longer believe in automatic progress towards the future. T S Eliot and James Joyce ransacked the past because it had become a lumber room.

Another element in this discussion arises from the concept of ' roots '. It is noteworthy that many British contributors, particularly Raymond Williams, are concerned that what is worthwhile in regional or local culture should not be dispersed by the metropolitan, cosmopolitan, rootless influences which emanate from centralised broadcasting and television networks, or from national newspapers. Although McLuhan claims the opposite, it is generally agreed that this tendency is present, and many would regard the resurgence of national and regional feeling in the UK simply as a reaction against the encroaching power and influence of the centre. This view is probably too simple, and it is a fact that many of the important cultural influences of the past twenty years have had their origin in the provinces and not in the capital. Instances abound in the novel and in drama and in pop music. It is no longer fashionable, or socially advisable, to possess a ' BBC accent ', if such a thing still exists. Insofar as centralised networks may be diminishing local culture, one remedy naturally lies in the development of local and regional broadcasting and television—a process which is continuing. The local newspapers still survive.

THE CORRUPTION OF HUMAN RESPONSES
The most damaging attacks on the popular press, on popular films and on a great many television programmes, come from those who insist that they ' exploit ' our worst instincts and desires. It is not surprising that many of the individuals and pressure group organisations who submitted evidence to the Pilkington committee, particularly stressed this aspect. The report summed up these objections by noting that, in general, it is claimed that television is likely to worsen the moral climate of the country. When one has discounted the fact that religious and political bodies have always protested about moral situations, of which they know very little, it remains true that children *may* be adversely affected, particularly by violence on television. To quote the Pilkington committee again: ' Dr Hilde Himmelweit told us that all the evidence so far provided by detailed researches suggested that values were acquired, that a view of life was picked up, by children watching television '. It is probably true also that the average child may suffer from occasional nightmares as a result of exposure to ' Dr Who ' or worse. Finally, it can be accepted that the values implicit in many American comics are so alarming that the young should be protected from them. Wertham points out that these comics wallow in sadism and every known form of sexual perversion. The villains are always ' foreign born, Jews, Orientals, Slavs, Italian and dark skinned races '. But these publications are exceptional, at least in Britain, just as maladjusted children are exceptional. In the case of television, one answer, which is perhaps too facile, is that parents are after all still responsible for their children and should control their viewing according to their own view of their responsibilities. The fact remains that many parents are not particularly concerned. In one

sample survey it was found that in the case of secondary modern school children, two thirds of their families, and in the case of grammar school children, one third, never switched the television set off at all.

It must therefore be accepted that violence on television will probably adversely affect the minority of ' deprived ' children who have violent tendencies. It must also be accepted that the safety valve theory of vicarious satisfaction, whether it is valid or not, does not operate with potentially delinquent children. What practical conclusions should be drawn from this is a matter for dispute, since, as with pornography, it seems wrong that the interests of average or ' normal ' people should be governed by the impact of the media on those who are highly maladjusted.

THE PRESUMPTIONS OF THE YOUNG

The current war between the generations, about which so much ink is spilt, is mentioned here because in the field of mass entertainment the young have taken over media with which the mandarins of high culture cannot easily come to terms. In former times, growing up was called ' adolescence ', or ' puberty ', and the process eventually resulted in an integration into adult society—an absorption into the main cultural stream. At present it is likely that this advance to ' maturity ' will not take place, since there is nothing to be integrated *with*. Traditional cultural or moral values are still *there*, it is true, but they are often untenable for people generally, although the older generation still profess to cling to them. The mature have given up and sold the pass to an enemy they cannot identify, and they have, in a sense, betrayed the values they imagined they upheld, particularly in the acceptance of too many deceptions, too many lies. The Vietnam war (in the American context) was an extreme example of this betrayal: the crushing of the Hungarian and the Czech revolutions was another: hypocrisy about racism and sex is another. Young people, therefore, incline to ignore the values of the past, not because they disagree with them, but because they have become irrelevant or ' square '. This reaction against the attitudes of the ' Others ' takes many forms, and in the USA beatniks are followed by hippies, or yippies, or flower people, but the foundation is always the same—a mixture of revolt and opting or dropping out. The same trends are presently apparent all over the world, and student revolutions indicate the crisis as it confronts the universities. Meanwhile, for reasons suggested above, adult society shows signs of a failure of nerve—an ominous vacuum is beginning to expand—and how this void will be filled is not yet clear. What is clear is that student unrest will intensify, and that the young will probably remain part of a permanent and aggressive sub-culture, constantly increasing in size.

We are concerned here only with the communication media where the impact is sufficiently obvious. Pop culture is founded on the assumptions of the young, who have grown up with the electronic media. As is noted in another chapter, the leaders of mass culture have always been aware that they are concerned with communication in the extended sense in which McLuhan has used the term—and it is now relevant to consider his contribution.

MARSHALL McLUHAN: THE ELECTRONIC APOSTLE

I have chosen to discuss McLuhanism separately because his work is not so much a new theory or collection of theories, as a close system which defies conventional academic analysis. Many critics have regarded him as a charlatan or worse, and have refused to take his doctrine seriously, yet his approach has already produced marked changes in the climate of opinion on this subject. His four books repeat the same simple message, and the essence of it can be found in *Understanding media,* or, with reference to the past, in *The Gutenberg galaxy.* Part of the hostility which he has provoked is caused by his deliberate habit of flat assertion, as if his truths were self evident and normally obscured by fools or vested interests. These critics are regarded as idiots, ' Semi-literate book-orientated individuals who have no competence in the grammars of newspaper, or radio, or of film, but who look askew and askance at all non book media . . . Their current assumption that content or programming is the factor that influences outlook and action is directed from the book medium with its *sharp cleavage between form and content* ' (my italics). This prophetic manner has alienated ' experts ' (a word which for him is a term of abuse), but has awakened a response in many, particularly among the young, who find the usual analysis inadequate. The manner is deliberate, because he regards his statements not as coherent structures, but as ' *probes* ' or explorations. He objects to classification. ' There is an alternative to classification and that is exploration. This doesn't easily register with nineteenth century minds . . . they have never acquired the verbal means of grappling with a pictorial world ' (*McLuhan: hot and cool,* edited by G E Stearn, p 320).

The element of *shock*—again deliberate—is present throughout his work because it is based on a fundamental thesis which runs counter to most normal assumptions. This thesis is simply that the media of communication, and particularly the electronic media, have created a revolution in our time. This has happened not because the masses have been exposed to new knowledge, but because the nature of the media themselves has totally changed our outlook on the world, irrespective of the content which they communicate. By use of this single concept, or device, or trick (whatever one chooses to call it), he arrives at the startling conclusion that the media both now and in the past have been responsible for historical change on a vast scale. The concept is based on a theory that the environment as an overall pattern eludes perception, so that when a new technology creates a new environment (as for example clothing, or speech, or script, or the wheel), we can only understand what is happening if there exists an anti-environment or counter-situation. So as an environment television is not perceptible except in terms of content. We fail to notice that it has profoundly altered our sensibilities, our sensory ratios, so that we have become merged with a mass environment in the same manner as pre-literate tribal societies. The ' disassociated sensibility ' (T S Eliot's phrase, not McLuhan's) which characterised mechanised print-orientated society is on the way out. There is a return to the organic world of the African tribesman, and hence his use of the term ' global village '. Traditionally, the arts and the sciences have acted in the role of the anti-environment, and this is the function of the liberal arts which train perception. Art should not be a retrieval system of past culture, but an exploration, and that is how Blake regarded it. The artist (and for that matter McLuhan himself) represents a ' Distant Early Warning System ', commonly referred to in his work as a ' Dew-line ' system. (There is now a monthly publication called the *Marshall McLuhan dew-line newsletter*.)

The type of ' insights ' arrived at in this manner are best illustrated by quotation (part of his technique is to use slogans or catch phrases after the manner of commercial advertising. So, for example, with regard to the telegraph : ' In the same year, 1844 . . . that men were playing chess on the first American telegraph, Soren Kierkegaard published the Concept of Dread. Thus the telegraph (one of the first of the new media) " ushers in " the Age of Anxiety and the philosophy of Existentialism '. With regard to the telephone : ' No more unexpected social result of the telephone has been observed than its elimination of the red light district and the creation of the call girl '. It is typical that he claims that the telephone *causes* this development, whereas most observers would merely note that the telephone made it possible. (Similarly the poetry of E E Cummings was ' caused ' by the typewriter.) Or again, the resurgence of regionalism and nationalism in the UK is produced by the radio. ' Ireland, Scotland and Wales have undergone resurgence of their ancient tongues since the coming of radio . . . Radio is not only a mighty awakener of archaic memories but a decentralising pluralistic force . . .' The impact of radio is therefore quite different from television. Radio is the medium for frenzy: this is why Adolph Hitler would have been impossible in the TV age. But it is television for which he makes the highest claims. It has produced electronic man, who is now totally and deeply involved in the human condition. After the mechanisation of life which happened in the nineteenth century, and which so many great writers deplored, it is now possible to return to the organic society.

Central to his analysis is the much discussed distinction between ' cool ' and ' hot ' media, and this is where he parts company with those critics of television who emphasise the passive state of ' hypnopathy '. Television, according to McLuhan, is a cool medium because it ' involves us in moving depth but . . . does not excite, agitate or arouse '. This is an ingenious explanation of the effects of television, which is no more implausible than any other. The hot media, on the other hand, such as radio, print, the cinema or the photograph, are low in participation because they do not have to be completed by the audience: they produce ' high definition ' because they are well filled with data. The hot media of the past, particularly printing, produced the cultural fragmentation of the mechanical age and from this atomisation we shall be saved by television. ' The hotting-up of the medium of writing to repeatable print intensity led to nationalism and the religious wars of the 16th century '. Mechanised techniques extend the human body: electrical techniques extend the central nervous system. ' In television there occurs an extension of the sense of active, exploratory touch which involves all the senses simultaneously rather than that of sight alone. You have to be " with it ". But in all electric phenomena, the visual is only one component in a complex interplay '.

McLuhan also associates the pre-electronic type of man with rationalism. Western culture in the past has been rational because it was *visual*. This sequential rationality was largely caused by the bead-

3

like linear construct of the alphabet. ' Western history was shaped for some three thousand years by the introduction of the phonetic alphabet '. He also uses his basic theory to explain most of the key social and cultural problems of our time. If the young lack ambition this is because fame, which was once an incentive, is now dependent on television which creates celebrities. So ' getting ahead in the world ' no longer means anything. ' There is no " ahead " in a world that is an echo chamber of instantaneous celebrity.'

The reference to the instant leads us to McLuhan's emphasis on different kinds of time. The invention of clocks produced the sense of duration characteristic of the mechanical era, and time became separate from the rhythm of human experience. The clock dragged the individual out of the grip of nature and out of the clutch of the tribe. But in the electric age we are in an instantaneous space time world, and we find clock time frustrating: new multiple rhythms become necessary.

This brief outline of McLuhanism should be sufficient to indicate his contribution. It is not difficult to see the reason for both his notoriety and his influence. Where others have no explanation he provides one. His analysis seems to confirm both the attitudes of pop culture and those of the existentialists (total involvement). With regard to the latter, it may be added that the existentialist *attitude* is prevalent, even if the developed philosophy is not. With regard to pop culture, there is an obvious appeal in the fact that here, for once, is a kind of panacea which involves no prolonged effort on the part of the individual. The appeal of certain kinds of Eastern meditation techniques is of the same kind. The complete doctrine has the fascination which all total answers, and all philosophies of first causes, possess. As with Marxism, the key, once it is found, unlocks all the doors. If his methods are unacademic and his procedures unscholarly, so much the worse for scholarship. Whether one accepts the basic doctrine or not, many of his insights do provide a new illumination and a much needed new approach to the subject. As Frank Kermode has said, ' He offers a fresh and coherent account of the state of the modern mind in terms of a congenial myth ' (*McLuhan: hot and cool,* p 209). To which McLuhan has replied, in another context, ' When man is overwhelmed by information he resorts to myth '.

Meanwhile, orthodox opinion will continue to hold that ideas are more important than the means of transmission, and that form and content can still be differentiated in any medium.

66

CONCLUSIONS
The various authorities I have quoted differ profoundly concerning the possible effect of the media. Without following McLuhan all the way, it is a matter of common sense that in any society these communication agencies *must* have considerable consequences, even if we do not always know what they are. The *psychological* difference between literate and illiterate people is very striking, as anyone who has lived in an illiterate community will witness. If this is the case, there must clearly be similar differences between those who have been exposed to particular types of media and those who have not. This must be considered against a background where whole populations are involved. In the UK it has been reliably stated that the average figure for television viewing is over two hours per person per day, and that the average teenager watches television for seventeen hours a week. At any one time a programme may be watched by twenty million people. This is a typical situation in an advanced society. In the underdeveloped regions of the world, the transistor radio is the most important agent in breaking down tribal isolation forever. The effect of the media on illiterate communities as compared with literate is, of course, different altogether. It is now well established that people in illiterate communities react in an unexpected fashion to the film or other visual media. So much so is this the case, that they do not see what those who make or provide the films expect them to see, nor do they react to educational films along expected lines. Their perception of the world is different (in some countries illiterate voters cannot relate a photograph to the candidate, even when he is present). The same people may, however (as McLuhan claims), respond more easily to television. The point I am making here is simply that there is obviously a considerable impact. There can be no doubt that the portrayal of the good life, as lived in different societies, by television and films has provoked demands for social justice among the underprivileged and dispossessed everywhere. In the USA this has happened with particular intensity among the Afro-Americans, because officially they are supposed to be included in the American dream.

At times of national crisis television may obviously have a decisive influence and the 'masses' temporarily become a community. It is generally accepted that the Czechoslovaks' peaceful revolution of 1968 was only possible because of television. This remains true whatever the eventual outcome may be. When President Kennedy was assassinated, this temporary ' unification ' of the people happened not only in the USA

67

but all over the world. For the time being the gulf between the private and the public realm was annihilated. The incident has a unique significance, firstly because Kennedy had achieved symbolic status involving the hopes of millions, and secondly because the assassination actually took place on the screen. And everywhere people wept in the streets.

THE LIMITATIONS OF THEORY

It can be said without fear of contradiction that none of the theorists have provided an adequate analysis. At first, following nineteenth century attitudes, most commentators, even up to the twenties and thirties, postulated that ' the masses ' could be *manipulated* by the mass media. During the first world war it appeared that quite simple propaganda techniques had, in fact, worked. It is well known that the infamous Dr Goebbels, Hitler's propaganda minister, believed and practised the ' big lie ' theory of mass indoctrination. Yet it eventually became apparent that this approach was altogether too simple, and an appreciation grew that, *at least in relatively normal times,* ' the masses ' do not exist. (Nazi Germany and Britain in wartime were, of course, not in a normal situation.) At this stage it was generally agreed that modern society is not, in fact, wholly atomised, and that the decisive units remain the individual, the group and society in general. These distinctions survive, and American advertisers have recognised them by appealing to group affiliations. Arising from the emphasis on groups, some recent research has concentrated on the idea that well informed persons pass on information, supplied by the media, to groups and other individuals. These people are ' interpreters ' or opinion leaders, and it may well be that the library is an agency of this kind.

Other writers have attempted to shift the emphasis in the study of the media away from the media themselves and their message, to an examination of the social needs which they cater for. The work by Hall and Whannel already cited provides a more balanced view for the general reader. We should, therefore, be concentrating not on the human *responses,* but on what people in the first instance *need.* A common element in a number of modern cultural interpretations is an attempt to understand or stress the *play* element in culture, partly on the grounds that the nineteenth century puritan emphasis on the gospel of work is no longer relevant. This approach can be used, and has been used, to stress the importance of the recreational function of the mass media—there being the further implication that there can be no real distinction between recreation and education.

To sum up, I have suggested that some of the common attitudes concerning the mass media should not be too lightly accepted, since they fail to analyse the social *value* which is either present now or potentially there. Clearly there are certain qualities and advantages which each of the media uniquely possess.

Those who persist in regarding all television programmes as a menace to the imagination should ponder the phenomenon of the television serialisation of *The Forsyte saga*. However the experience is defined, the fact is that millions of people have now been involved with this boring family, and have publicly debated the great issues underlying the conflict between Soames and Irene Forsyte. It is difficult to discuss this without irony, particularly when one considers that this same serial has made a tremendous impact on the people of Marxist Yugoslavia; yet what is relevant here is that these millions would never have encountered the original novel, or have responded to it if they had. The experience is of a different order to the reading of literature, and involves, it may be, a majority of the people. That is what ' mass ' culture is about, and it is not the same thing as the ' low ' culture of the past.

This is only one example: there are so many others which can illustrate the same point. What, for instance, are we to make of 'Alf Garnett', who was so horrible that everybody loved him: this has nothing to do with literature and cannot be regarded as an inferior substitute. Finally, let us consider the quality of the television programme ' The magic roundabout ', which, although apparently intended for children, is watched nightly by four million adults. It is, in fact, a brilliant commentary on contemporary human responses, and what is significant in the context of television, is that nobody need be aware that it is anything but nonsense for the children. In earlier times there was *Alice in Wonderland,* but she really belongs in a book and not to the small screen—even though she has sometimes appeared there.

Having noted the special possibilities of television, it must be accepted that the media can be and have been misused, and it is probable that they could have done much more than they have so far to improve the quality of our lives. Even so, the general level of popular culture (insofar as it can be compared at all) is probably higher than in the past. The ' admass ' tendencies are admittedly there, but they

69

were in the first instance created by modern technology and not by mass communications.

THE WIDER CONTEXT

In the above discussion I inevitably returned to the point that we cannot reach any conclusions concerning methods of communication without reference back to the nature of modern technological society. I therefore have to conclude by noting that the machines are producing a new situation with regard to the use of leisure. Machines are taking over tasks, both skilled and unskilled, which were formerly done by human beings. They produce the goods, and so it follows that society needs to employ people in another fashion, for example, in the public or social services. The kind of specialisation which once involved millions of people and consisted of tending machines, can now be done by the machines themselves. For the first time in history the individual *must* work less and consume more. If this is valid it means that the nineteenth century doctrine of the importance of work is no longer relevant. One of the most fundamental assumptions of Western life will disappear. As Keynes, the economist, noted, ' We shall be able to rid ourselves of many of the pseudo-moral problems which have hag-ridden us for 200 years, by which we have exalted some of the most distasteful human qualities into the position of the highest virtue '.

If the religion of work is to be abandoned, what is to take its place? Whatever answer is made will involve the problem of the use of leisure —the type of education which should be provided. The latter will have to allow for the fact that there will be a new type of work, and people will switch from one job to another in a way which was not possible when people rather than machines were performing specialist tasks. It seems probable that it will no longer be necessary to train a young person in one skill to last a lifetime, and that it will become more important to provide a liberal education which will enable him to change his skill. Another consequence of affluence, which may happen, is that it will become a social duty not to save but to consume, and if this does take place many social attitudes, which were formerly (rightly) condemned as ' decadent ', may become generally accepted.

In chapter 1 I suggested that the old distinction between high and low culture is no longer the most important one: as Susan Sontag, in *Against interpretation,* has argued, Matthew Arnold's idea of culture is no longer tenable, and art cannot now be regarded as a kind of moral journalism. She claims that it is still possible to maintain standards while accepting the 'pluralistic' view—and it is this view which I have adopted. From such a standpoint the world of work and personal responsibility is not, and should not be, the only one. It is one kind of reality and there are other realities which are apprehended by the artist or the mystic. On another level there are the necessary realms of dreams, myths, fantasies, games, gossip, chatter and nonsense. In any culture, all these elements, and possibly others, should have their place, since we are born with unequal potentials and some people will inhabit one of these worlds and others two or three simultaneously. Whatever the type or the quality of these experiences may be, they will rest on the communication process.

NOTES
1 In Alice Payne Hackett's *70 years of best sellers 1895-1965* eleven books sold over six million copies in America, ten had sold over five million, fifteen over four million and forty four over three million. The minimum figures bestseller status chosen are one million (paperback and hardback), 750,000 hardback only.
2 In a special number of *The listener* (31st July 1969) devoted to advertising, Lord Hill, Raymond Williams, Enoch Powell and others discuss the impact of advertising on the mass media. Their attitudes are predictable and at variance with each other, but there is general agreement that *control* of the mass media by advertisers as in the USA is socially wholly undesirable.

5

censorship

HISTORICAL BACKGROUND: The expression of ideas has always been subject to social control and all that has changed through the ages is the various means by which this control has been exercised. A full account of the persecutions of the past is beyond the scope of this chapter and I have restricted the discussion mainly to the present situation in the UK.[1] In former times the main emphasis was on the crimes of religious heresy or political sedition, and the modern preoccupation with obscenity and pornography is mainly a result of the extension of literacy and the development of the mass media of communication.

Before the invention of printing the most common method of dealing with those who expressed dangerous ideas was imprisonment or torture or death at the stake. This inevitably happened because heresy was a crime against the state. It was naturally only after the invention of printing in the fifteenth century that it became necessary to control the publication of materials. The Christian church met the challenge by instituting the censorship of manuscripts *before* publication, and later, in 1559, the first Roman index of prohibited books attempted to control literature *after* publication. In various forms this *Index librorum prohibitorum* continued until it was abolished in 1967, by which time more than 1,000 titles were on the list. (It is significant that it was not until 1897 that obscene books as such were broadly prohibited.) The index, of course, was not an instrument of total censorship, even for the faithful, and complete control has only been exercised in those countries where the Roman Catholic Church and the state power have been identical. For example, the situation in Eire is that for the Irish Board of Censors the index was dangerously libertarian in its omissions, and the board's list of banned books was at one time almost a national bibliography of Irish writers, quite apart from the literature of the rest of the world. The list grew so long that in 1967 as a result of a new censorship Act several thousand titles were struck off.

There was also an *Index librorum expurgatorum,* which was never published: this listed works which could be read after expurgation. Finally, it should be noted that the church has always controlled the publications of those in Holy Orders by requiring them to obtain permission before publishing books in such subjects as law, ethics or theology. It was for this reason that Teilhard de Chardin was unable to obtain publication of *Phenomenon of man* and other works. For literature which is approved by the Holy See as doctrinally sound, the church provides the blessing contained in the *Imprimatur* or *Nihil obstat.*

To return to the sixteenth century, when the Reformation came in Britain and elsewhere new forms of heresy became possible. Henry the Eighth persecuted both papists and reformers (Moore, Fisher, Tyndale). For his successor Edward the Sixth, the papists were the heretics but this was reversed in Mary's brief reign. Elizabeth was faced with Puritans as well as Papists, and so the religious struggle continued until some degree of toleration began to emerge at the end of the seventeenth century. Henry the Eighth used the Court of the Star Chamber for censorship purposes—a procedure which continued until the court was abolished under the Commonwealth. Queen Elizabeth introduced other controls and in particular used the Stationers' Company, which was given a monopoly of printing on condition that it prevented the publication of undesirable literature. This was, in fact, a *licensing* procedure which persisted in various forms until 1692. The Stuarts intensified these censorship laws and also passed laws to control the importation of books. Since the end of the seventeenth century in Britain, books and journals have never been censored by law before publication.

It was during this period that some of the classic statements were first made repudiating the persecution of the expression of ideas, including Milton's *Areopagitica* (1644) and Locke's *Letter concerning toleration* (1689). These works are quoted so often that it is as well to remind ourselves that neither Milton nor Locke advocated complete freedom of expression in practice. *Areopagitica* called for the suppression not only of ' popery and open superstition ' but also ' that which is impious or evil ' and that ' which is blasphemous, atheistical or libellous '. Milton also made the claim, often repeated, that given open expression, truth will emerge triumphant. We are less confident now and perhaps Coventry Patmore's lines supply the corrective :

' For want of me the world's course will not fail
When all its work is done the lie shall rot
The truth is great and shall prevail
When none cares whether it prevail or not.'

John Locke's importance in this context resides in his attempt to formulate a private sphere beyond the reach of the state. He was prepared to tolerate pagans and non-conformists but not catholics or atheists.

Christianity is not of course the only religion which has been fanatically exclusive. The Muslims have a similar authoritarian record and it is appropriate to conclude this section with a reference to Omar, who in the year 642 destroyed the library at Alexandria. Being economically minded he used the books as fuel for the public baths: 700,000 volumes were sufficient for 400 baths for six months. His reasons remain as a classic statement on behalf of suppression : ' The contents of these books are either in accordance with the teaching of the Koran or they are opposed to it. If in accord, then they are useless since the Koran itself is sufficient, and if in opposition they are pernicious and must be destroyed '. Given the premise the argument is irrefutable.

SINCE 1800 : OBSCENITY AND THE LAW
After the political and religious convulsions of the seventeenth century, the age of reason was relatively free from censorship. There were very few publications to disturb the stability of the state and bawdy literature was relatively safe, bearing in mind that there was no ' mass ' reading public. There were some convictions, usually as common law decisions, for example, against the bookseller Edmund Curll in 1727, who published *Venus in the cloister or the nun in her smock,* and against the radical John Wilkes (who escaped to the continent), but on the whole writers and publishers were left to themselves.

All this was changed with the turn of the century, and after the inevitable cultural lag, the activities of the anti-vice societies (dis-

74

cussed below) and the rise of puritan middle class morality was reflected in legal activity. There were prosecutions in common law or under such statutes as the Vagrancy Act of 1824 (obscene prints) or the Metropolitan Police Act of 1839. Even so, beneath a facade of respectability, pornography flourished and the law failed to check it.

The change came with the Obscene Publications Act of 1857 which enabled magistrates to order the seizure and destruction of books. This Act, it was claimed by the Lord Chief Justice, did not alter common law, but in 1868 Lord Chief Justice Cockburn provided his famous definition of obscenity in the Hicklin case, which involved an attack on the Catholic Church in a pamphlet called *The confessional unmasked*. Cockburn's interpretation of the Act remained valid for nearly a hundred years (and in the United States similar statutes were in force). His definition was that ' The test of obscenity is this, whether the tendency of the matter charged as obscenity is to deprave and corrupt those whose minds are open to such immoral influences and into whose hands a publication of this sort may fall '. The implication of this judgment was that society's literary needs were to be determined by standards of the feeble minded or by those of children, and publishers were exposed to possible legal action on wider grounds than formerly. Prosecutions did take place and, as C H Rolph has stated (*The author*, Autumn 1968), ' Since the turn of the century, the end of a long spell in which the only prosecution for obscenity had been that of the bookseller Vizetelly in 1886 for publishing Zola's *La Terre*, official anxiety about what we read has taken on the character, roughly speaking, of a seven year itch '.

Throughout this ninety year period the Cockburn interpretation was attacked not only by publishers, authors and critics but by judges both in the UK and in America. For example, in the *Ulysses* case of 1933 in the USA, the judge declared that the book ' must be tested by the court's opinion as to its effect on a person with average sex instincts . . . it is only with the normal person that the law is concerned '. The same judge insisted that the work should be judged ' in its entirety ' and not by select passages. This particular prosecution concerned importation and the ban was lifted.

Similar warnings were made by judges in the UK—and for a long time it was generally felt that a new statute was needed. The urgency became greater after various prosecutions on moral grounds in the fifties. There was a ' purity ' campaign which happened when Sir David Maxwell-Fyfe—later Lord Kilmuir—was Home Secretary,

75

1951-54, and after 1954, Lord Chancellor. This crusade was directed against homosexuals, prostitutes and pornographers. (It was traditionally understood that all three groups are necessary in a well organised society provided that they can be prosecuted from time to time.) In 1953, 197 prosecutions were made against obscenity, and in 1954, five relatively serious novels became subject to legal scrutiny—with varying results. In consequence, sections of the British public became alarmed at the threat to legitimate publishing interests and wrote letters to *The times* and questions were asked in the House of Commons. In 1954 the Society of Authors set up a committee to consider the matter, with Sir Alan Herbert as Chairman, and its recommendations were embodied in a Private Member's Bill which, under the ' ten minute rule ', was presented to the House by Roy Jenkins and then got no further. A similar Bill was introduced by Hugh Fraser later in the same year but this was ' talked out '. A third attempt at reform by Lord Lambton in 1957 secured a second reading in the House and the Bill was then referred to a select committee under the chairmanship of Sir Patrick Spens, which reported in March 1958. The Herbert committee was then in a position to draft a new Bill based on the select committee's proposals. This was introduced by Roy Jenkins as a Private Member's Bill and eventually became law in 1959 as the Obscene Publications Act. (Meanwhile the Children and Young Persons (Harmful Publications) Act 1955 made it possible to ban imported American ' horror comics '.) The Attorney General is responsible for prosecutions under this Act.

Changes in the 1959 Act: During the passage of the Bill through the House, its sponsors found that in order to get it accepted at all a number of modifications and compromises had to be made. In consequence the final version was a ' watered down ' one and the new test of obscenity was not all that different from the old one. The definition is that ' an article shall be deemed to be obscene if its effect . . . if taken as a whole, is such as to tend to deprave persons who are likely, having regard to all relevant circumstances, to read, see or hear the matter contained or embodied in it '. It should be noted that the word ' article ' in the Act refers not only to reading matter but also to sound records, ' and any film or other record of a picture or pictures '. In spite of all the compromise there were certain advances; for example, the use of the words ' taken as a whole ', which prevents the isolation of particular passages and the reference to ' all relevant circumstances '. The Act also allows for expert evidence concerning literary and artistic merit, and confers the right to choose jury trial if preferred. Moreover, for the first time Parliament had accepted that, in the words of the Act, 'A person shall not be convicted of publishing an obscene article . . . if it is proved that publication of the article in question is justified as being for the public good on the ground that it is in the interests of science, literature, art or learning or of other objects of general concern '.

These were the new provisions which were tested in the *Lady Chatterley's lover* case the following year, and in the *Last exit from Brooklyn* case in 1967. In the former it must be supposed that the 35 expert witnesses who gave evidence that the work was ' for the public good ' made a suitable impact on the jury. In the second case the jury was not convinced and it was only at the Court of Appeal that *Last exit* was cleared, the publisher, John Calder, having claimed that the jury had been misdirected by the trial judge.

Since 1959 there have been two further modifications of the law. In 1964 another Obscene Publications Act was passed, the main provision being that there is a new offence which consists of ' *having* an obscene article for publication for gain ', which makes it possible for the police to prosecute a publisher for having stocks of books or magazines considered by the police to be obscene. The second amendment came with a clause in the Criminal Justice Act of 1967 which made it impossible for private persons to bring ' destruction orders ' against books of which they disapproved—all such actions being limited to the police or the Director of Public Prosecutions. Various anomalies in the law remain, consisting chiefly of unrepealed sections of earlier acts such as the Vagrancy Act of 1824 which made it an offence to show obscene or indecent pictures or exhibitions in a public place. Also there still survive some rules of common law which may be invoked. Apart from these, there exist various other controls, legal and non legal, which are discussed below.

The conclusion can only be that in Britain, although the law is slightly more liberal than it used to be, censorship remains a reality, and publishers cannot tell when or how the censor will strike again. Quite apart from the main provisions of the 1959 Act omissions remain: for example, neither HM Customs and Excise nor the GPO was mentioned, so that seizure of material at the ports or in the mail may continue. Also the printers are still liable to prosecution as well as the publishers. Finally, a confusion exists with regard to ' nudist ' magazines. It is doubtless for some of these reasons that there is a Private Member's Bill before Parliament once more in 1969.

In view of the reference to the United States above, it is of considerable significance that in America within the last decade the old legal tests of obscenity have been virtually scrapped. This change has been largely brought about by Charles Rembar, a lawyer, who has succeeded in obtaining judicial decisions from the Supreme Court that censorship violates the First Amendment to the Constitution which guarantees freedom of expression. Under a Supreme Court ruling made in 1966, no work can be declared obscene which can be shown to possess a minimum of literary merit. It would appear, therefore, that in the United States the courts have managed to isolate traditional hard core pornography at last. Rembar has described this very important change in his work *The end of obscenity*. Such a remedy is, of course, not available in Britain as there is no written constitution.

The customs and the post office: It is a curious fact that customs officers have powers in their discretion to seize ' obscene ' material at the ports, and even more curious that the Customs Commissioners compile to aid this purpose a blacklist of their own which may include books which have never been the subject of legal action in the UK. *Ulysses* remained on this list until 1953, and the works of Genet even longer, as was discovered by the Birmingham Libraries Committee, which did not challenge a seizure. These powers derive from the unrepealed sections of the Customs Consolidation Act of 1876 and the Customs and Excise Act of 1952. Under this last act the seizure may be contested in the courts, where the commissioners are required to prove the obscenity of the book concerned. In 1957 it was reported that only two travellers had troubled to contest seizure in the past twenty years, but this is scarcely a justification for the power. It is, of course, a method of control much used elsewhere, as, for example, in Australia and in South Africa. It may be rightly assumed that customs officers (like policemen—as was successfully pleaded in a case in 1963) are immune from corruption by pornographic influences, but if this is the case it is difficult to imagine how they can detect these corrupting influences in the first place.

Under the Post Office Act of 1953 it is an offence to send indecent matter through the post, even though under cover. The post office employees may open suspect packages, but the ' consignee ' must be informed so that if he wishes he can attend the ceremony: there is also legal provision for packages to be opened by warrant of a secretary of state. It is not altogether clear how the officials detect the obscenities inside the packages.

Printers: The 1959 Obscene Publications Act made no reference to printers and the British Federation of Master Printers had previously stated that it did not wish to be protected, a surprising attitude which Craig (*The banned books of England*, 1962) suggested was due to commercial vanity. Certainly it does happen from time to time that printers are cautious about the risk of prosecution. It was not until 1954 that Zola's *La terre* was republished in Britain and this was partly because at least a dozen printers had refused to print it. In some cases outstanding works have had to be printed abroad.

OTHER TYPES OF LEGAL CONTROL

There are basically four kinds of ' libel ' (which means a writing— from *libellus*, little book). The Obscene Publications Act of 1959 removed the term 'libel' from the former phrase 'obscene libel', since it caused confusion, especially for juries. Apart from obscenity, censorship may operate against blasphemy, defamation, sedition, and ' official secrets '. Blasphemy is now an anachronism, but, legally, blasphemous utterances or publications are punishable if they endanger the peace or the security of the state. Defamation, the publication of a false, unjustified and defamatory statement, is governed by the Defamation Act 1952 and the judicial decisions stemming from it. It may take the form either of a libel or slander, and the former is a criminal offence as well as a civil tort, though criminal proceedings for libel are rare in the extreme. The 1952 Act gave some protection in the case of innocent ' publication of a defamatory statement, since the innocent defamer is now allowed to defend himself by making an adequate correction and apology. Formerly this was not accepted in mitigation. It is a benefit of particular importance to newspapers and magazines.

Control of the other media: The writer for the Press is restricted in many ways quite apart from the law, and the same applies to those who work in television, radio and films. All these mass media reach instant audiences of millions and are therefore circumscribed by the pressures of majority opinion. TV and cinema programmes are the product of teamwork and an internal and commonsense censorship based on a knowledge of current audience responses is inevitably brought to bear. At the BBC there is no formal censorship machinery, but the ITV companies are watched over by the Independent Television

Authority which, under the Television Act of 1964, must ensure that nothing is included in the programmes which offends against good taste or decency or is likely to encourage or incite to crime or to lead to disorder or to be offensive to public feeling. With this wide range of possible causes of offence, the television companies inevitably 'edit' their programmes carefully, and some degree of timidity must result. Mrs Mary Whitehouse's 'Clean-up TV' campaign has particularly concentrated on the BBC, and on the fact that Sir Hugh Greene (the former Director-General) did not believe in written rules on censorship, having written 'In my view there is nothing to be achieved by coercion or censorship, whether from inside the corporation or from outside—nothing, that is, except the frustration of creative people who can achieve far more by positive stimulation of their ideas in an atmosphere of freedom'.

In the cinema the British Board of Film Censors, an independent body set up by the industry itself, keeps watch over films as they are made. The board operates within the Cinematograph Act of 1954 and has followed a fairly liberal policy, apart from occasional vetoes and cuts which are not always easily explicable. Beyond this the local government authorities have the final say in passing or rejecting films for local consumption. The secretary of the Board of Film Censors may also advise producers at work who seek guidance, sometimes even before the films are made. In the theatre, control by the Lord Chamberlain was abolished in 1968, and dramatists are no longer constricted as they have been by this source of censorship for at least 200 years.

NON STATUTORY LIMITATIONS

Pressure groups: As was noted above, by the time the eighteenth century was over the anti-vice societies were already on the march. They knew what vice was and they were against it. A methodist body, the Society for the Suppression of Vice, founded in 1802, was energetic in prosecuting printed pornography. At their instigation, for example, the bookseller Edward Truelove was fined and imprisoned for publishing Robert Owen's tract *The individual family and national poverty*. America followed suit and various moralist societies were founded in the USA, until almost every state had obscene laws forced onto the statute books. One of the most important in effect was the New York Society for the Suppression of Vice, founded by Anthony Comstock, Congressman and self appointed 'Roundsman of the Lord', who persuaded Congress to pass the first federal law on obscenity in 1872.

'Comstockery' flourished and its originator claimed at one time to have destroyed fifty tons of vile books, 28,425 pounds of stereotype plates, 3,984,063 obscene pictures and 16,900 negatives—a splendid achievement.

At the present time there still exists in the USA private organisations such as the Watch and Ward Society of Boston, and the National Organisation for Decent Literature. In the UK we have the Public Morality Council, founded in 1899, which was particularly active in the nineteen thirties, and in 1938 conducted a campaign against the book *To beg I am ashamed,* by Sheila Cousins. As a result the publishers withdrew the work from circulation. Winnington Ingram, Bishop of London, was prominent in the activities of the council for many years and he it was, according to Craig, who said of contraceptives that he 'would like to make a bonfire of them and dance about it' —a not very practical proposal. There was also the National Vigilance Association, a Protestant Society, founded in 1888, which conducted many prosecutions for the cause, including in 1888 the case (mentioned above) against the bookseller Vizetelly who had published bowdlerised versions of Zola's novels.

Enough has been said to show that these societies, usually representing a vocal minority, were remarkably successful in their repressive endeavours, at least for a while. To the outsider it is clear that the pursuit of other people's vices can become an obsessional vice itself, but Pharisees have never been deterred by criticism or mockery.

There are other pressure groups besides these crusading bodies, and to some extent active minorities may operate informally in every community. It is groups of this kind, or even individuals, who may bring influence to bear on book provision in public libraries, on standards in broadcasting and in the press. It is mainly television which the moralists attack, under the invariable claim that they represent ordinary decent people seeking to protect themselves against television programmes which typify the attitudes of only a very small proportion of the British population.

Booksellers: After a book has been published it may come up against restrictions imposed by the distributive trade. W H Smith & Son Ltd, for example, from time to time decline to stock books and magazines because of their contents. *Private eye* and *International times* are perhaps the best known examples. Since this chain of bookstores is the largest in the country, and in many smaller towns its shop is the only bookshop, it is clear that this form of censorship—if such it can be called—can considerably affect both sales and the availabilty of material to sections of the public. How it can be countered is another matter.

Expurgation: The varieties of expurgation of original works could fill a chapter by themselves. The devices range from simple omission (declared or undeclared) through the use of classical or foreign tongues and dots and asterisks, to actual rewriting as was done by the notorious, egregious and eponymous Dr Bowdler. In his defence it should be emphasised that his purifications were perpetrated to accommodate the excellent Victorian habit of family reading. Even now, school editions of literary classics are commonly expurgated, and series for adults such as ' Everyman ' do not have accurate texts in many cases. Some publishers also have the tiresome habit of producing two editions, one more expensive which is de luxe and complete and the other for the common reader. This practice is a relic of the undemocratic past when erotic literature was reserved for the wealthy—censorship by means of the purse. It may well be that there are good reasons for expurgating children's versions of the classics, although these are not the ones usually offered. The idea that children need to be *protected* from sex or simple violence is probably an illusion. They are already protected precisely because they do not share adult emotions, and their enjoyment of certain types of horror or violence is often natural and healthy. (I am not here referring to the kind of values which are implicit in some of the horror comics.) Those reformers who would eliminate the terror from fairy tales or nursery rhymes are misguided. Would any child grow up with a bent or twisted imagination because the blackbird came down and pecked off the maid's nose? The sex issue is more complicated, because it can make adults appear ridiculous to the child, which might be considered a subversion, but popular songs about ' love ' produce this reaction in any case. On balance the expurgators almost certainly do more harm than good, except insofar as, like all puritans, they contribute to the drama of existence.

Control of the Press: For journalists, apart from the law of defamation, there exist other controls and limitations. For example, there are para-legal devices, such as the ' gentleman's code of honour ' which must be observed by newspapers who are ' advised ' by the government, or in some cases by an agreement amongst newspaper owners. The trouble over ' D notices ', a form of gentleman's agreement over the publication of classified official material, in the sixties indicates the difficulties which may arise in interpreting the code.

82

Many would claim that the press is not 'free' at all, because both at national and provincial level it is controlled by a few newspaper magnates who are responsible to no-one except their shareholders, and whose political attitudes are conditioned by the need not to offend the advertisers who supply most of their revenue. These commercial influences undoubtedly operate in many ways which are more subtle than the direct distortion or total suppression of news. This danger, always inherent in the capitalist control of the press, is now intensified by the monopolist trends in the newspaper industry. The pressures here are, of course, mainly political and political censorship is noted below.

Private control: Some writers have destroyed their own work before publication or directed that it should be published only after their deaths. Nothing can be done about this. There remains the possibility of private control by others, particularly by the relatives of 'controversial' writers. There is no law to prevent an inheriting widow from destroying her late husband's literary remains, and diaries by their nature are particularly vulnerable. Byron's and Richard Burton's were consigned to the flames in this way. Pepy's diary has never been published in full, and Boswell's journal had to wait two hundred years for publication. Roger Casement's diary was (officially) not allowed to see the light of day for half a century, ostensibly because of Anglo-Saxon obsessions about homosexuality.

Control by libraries: All libraries have to select materials, and items are rejected according to criteria which may include moral or political considerations. This is, of course, not censorship in any exact sense because, at least in Britain, the exclusion operates for one library system only and the effect is local not national. However, the case against national censorship is also applicable to libraries, and it can be argued that librarians and library committees have no more right to attempt to control what people should read than have national governments. Indeed, in free societies they have less right and their legal responsibility is entirely governed by legislation. It might appear, therefore, that so long as libraries do not supply material which is proscribed by the government they should not concern themselves with the matter at all—and no more need be said.

Unforutnately, much remains to be said, and librarians in Britain and in the United States have regularly excluded material of which they disapproved on political or religious or ethical grounds. This censorship ' in various forms has operated in all types of libraries even, for example, in the British Museum, where certain holdings are not included in the public catalogues. The ' problem ' is, however, much more urgent in public libraries and there has been perennial controversy, much of it on a low level, as was evident from a debate in the *Library Association record* from December 1968 to March 1969. The argument for this type of control rests mainly on three grounds : first that it is a professional duty to select material according to policies which exclude what is regarded as ' bad ': second that the public librarian and his committee are wholly responsible to a local community which might object to certain types of literature : third that the library may need to protect the young and the unstable from evil or from disturbing influences which they might not otherwise encounter. These arguments should not be too lightly dismissed—ridiculous though they may seem to some outsiders—since they spring from the practical experience of public librarians.

However, if one leaves aside practical expedients which *may* be necessary in dealing with certain types of community (for example, the reserve or ' blue ' shelf) the only one of these reasons or excuses for library ' censorship ' which should be taken at all seriously is the first one listed above. If a library has to select material, it follows that some items must be rejected on various grounds. These grounds are frequently not ' literary ' in the narrow sense, nor are they entirely determined by the nature of public demand. They are inevitably influenced by values which are to some extent personal, since in an open society there are no fixed standards outside the law.

A public library is, or should be, a liberal institution, and liberal minded librarians naturally object to the exclusion of material that some people consider is obscene. Suppose, however, that in the foreseeable future racial tension develops in certain areas of Britain, and there is at the same time an increase in racist literature which to the liberal mind is wholly obnoxious. What should be the attitude of a librarian then? One has only to ask the question to realise that liberal institutions cannot easily survive in an illiberal community, and to note that there is a case for the exclusion of such material. If this is once admitted it becomes less easy to claim that under no circumstances should a book be rejected because it is objectionable. This is the classic liberal dilemma in the face of totalitarian doctrines. This challenge does not face British librarians at the moment, and if there are librarians at work who are totally opposed to the so-called permissive society and wish to crusade against what they regard as corrupting and

84

evil influences, then they should resign their posts immediately—and devote their paternalist energies to some other cause. The public library movement, both in Britain and America, is firmly committed to a positive struggle against the local book-banners, and the library associations of both countries have issued documents towards this end. In the last chapter of this work it is argued that a devotion to the ideals of intellectual freedom should be an essential part of the professional ethic.

In British public libraries the main danger has not been the open withdrawal of books following objections from pressure groups, but a hidden policy of censorship before the selection process starts. Such policies are difficult to detect, and it can always be claimed that books are rejected on other grounds. In 1955 E T Bryant ('Book selection and censorship', *Librarian*, April 1955, p 65) quoted the results of a questionnaire which showed that out of seventy one libraries in the North West region, only fifteen possessed more than ten out of a list of twelve important works which might be regarded as 'controversial'. This test, in fact, proved nothing, but it does suggest that 'censorship' of this passive kind was operating, and this may happen all the time. (As a student has suggested, it would be interesting to find out how many public libraries do not provide the thoughts of Chairman Mao.) It is, moreover, reasonable to suppose that some public librarians both in Britain and America share the prejudices which are typical of the lower middle class from which they are often recruited: others belong to religious organisations which provide guidance on reading matters and whose activities are likely to extend beyond their flock.

Fortunately there are many librarians who take a different view of their responsibilities, and in the United States some of them fought courageously and consistently against the terrible political pressures which were directed against them during the McCarthy era. It is a test which British librarians have not been required to face, and this is why the present chapter has not attempted to deal with political censorship, which is the major type of control in most countries of the world. A survey of this problem in Czechoslovakia, for example, would raise issues which makes the controversy about obscenity seem trivial and irrelevant. In Britain at least the discussion is a luxury which we can still afford.

To return to practical considerations the proposals put forward by James Carter ('Censorship and the librarian', in *Libraries and the book trade*, edited by Raymond Astbury, 1968) seem to me eminently sensible. They include the point that every library authority should define its book selection policy and if necessary incorporate extracts from statements by the British and American library associations; also if the reserve shelf is used to restrict the issue of certain books, then the reasons for this policy should be declared and the contents of the reserve stock should be listed and publicly displayed. Similarly, if particular books are deliberately not purchased and the cause for rejection might be ' controversial ', a record of the decision and the reasons for it should be made. The same writer notes, quite rightly, that the arguments for some kind of control often seem reasonable but that once it is admitted that any kind of control is necessary, the pass is sold and the censors have won.

The arguments: Even the most cursory examination of the literature on this subject reveals that much of the argument is conducted on a level which ranges from the superficial to the idiotic. One of the reasons is probably that this is an issue where most men feel obliged to take up attitudes which are most appropriate for the battlefield. One is either for or against censorship and the middle ground is occupied by the hollow men. The compromisers are regarded, as in the Revelation of St John: ' So then because thou art lukewarm, and neither cold nor hot, I will spew thee out of my mouth '. Another more fundamental reason is that this battle is really part of a much bigger war which goes on all the time everywhere. The struggle is both religious and political in the most profound sense, and the attempt to *isolate* the issue of freedom of expression results in arguments based on unexplored assumptions about the nature of society or the meaning of existence. Much writing of this kind figures in an American Library Association compilation called *The first freedom*, which is an anthology of writings in favour of intellectual freedom. The intention is admirable, but quite apart from the question of repetition, which is perhaps inevitable in an anthology, we are left with the feeling that fundamental issues are ignored. In other words, one can say that intellectual freedom was and is an essential element in the development of liberal capitalist democracy, and must be defended by those who believe that such societies represent the good life in its most developed form. But in areas of the world where different traditions exist, if we object to control of expression, we cannot be content with the same arguments or the same analysis. It is to be doubted whether intellectual freedom should be an absolute in all circumstances. It must be admitted that this idea is a dangerous one which can be used to justify every kind of tyranny, but this chapter is really based on the assumption that all ideas are dangerous and that all important literature is ' subversive '. In any case, it is a matter which should be carefully examined—since the issues, both moral and political, are desperately important.

WHAT IS OBSCENITY?
Much of the anti anti-vice literature makes great play with the fact that obscenity cannot be satisfactorily defined. In this field the lexicographers' habit of circular definition is very noticeable, and the six famous adjectives: lewd, obscene, lascivious, filthy, indecent, disgusting, are used to refer to each other. (Roget's *Thesaurus* inevitably gives a splendid range of near synonyms which includes the word ' free '.) Beyond the sphere of the dictionaries we can accept that, in fact, no satisfactory logical description can be provided for a subjective interpretation. This leaves us with the notion that as a matter of common sense everybody knows what obscenity is, and it is usually stated that anything which arouses ' lustful thoughts ' is obscene. One American source uses the happy phrase that anything in literature might be regarded as obscene if it arouses ' genital commotion '. If we agree with this we can eliminate a large part of the literature which was under attack in the past—as a result of Victorian attitudes. We can safely assume that few sane people would now object to scientific or medical literature about sex. The battle for free distribution of information on sex techniques or birth control has been won, or in countries where it has not been won, the objections are not based on the issue of obscenity. The possibility of effective birth control renders traditional attitudes obsolete over a large area. Virginity is dethroned. For this we have to thank not only scientific advances, but the promotional efforts of pioneers such as Havelock Ellis and Marie Stopes.

The issue thus becomes limited to the realm of imaginative literature which has the power to stimulate sexual response. Here we encounter a confusion rooted in the realities of class differences and intellectual snobbery—and (to be fair) legitimate aesthetic and moral attitudes. Traditionally there has been an attempt to distinguish between ' hard core ' pornography, which has no other purpose than sexual stimulation, and literature which must deal with the whole of life. This difference is common understood, and the American writers E & P Kronhausen (*Pornography and the law*, 1959) have expressed it by distinguishing between what they call ' erotic realism ' and pornography proper. As they rightly point out, the great artist illuminates the mystery of evil. Cardinal Newman noted that ' We cannot have a sinless literature about sinful men and nothing is barred *per se* '. The pornographer, on the other hand, wallows in ' evil ' illuminating nothing.

With regard to literary criticism this analysis is sound, but it does not dispose of the matter, since it leaves out the readers' response which is by definition *subjective*. If legal sanctions against pornography are being considered, it is at this point that the argument breaks down. The evidence is overwhelming that these distinctions cannot be maintained in a court of law, even if as a general literary principle they might be otherwise valid. The provision of the 1959 Act for trial by jury was welcomed because it was thought that the judgment of a group of people was preferable to that of one individual judge. Yet in the case of *Last exit from Brooklyn* the jury condemned a book which, in the opinion of most critics, would have come under the heading of ' erotic realism ' as noted above. This could obviously happen again—and this case reinforces Alec Craig's point, mentioned earlier—that if there have to be laws against obscenity, then it is well nigh inevitable that serious literature will be affected, not least by the publishers' fear of prosecution. Other remedies have now been suggested. For example, John Calder considered that there should be, firstly, a provision ensuring that jurors in an obscenity case have certain minimum literary qualifications, and secondly, that prosecution witnesses should be called first, as in any other kind of trial. It is doubtful whether these reforms would make any difference. Perhaps it was always naïve for the liberals to suppose that twelve good men and true chosen at random would be impressed by the motley arguments of two dozen assorted eggheads. David Sheppard, parson and MCC cricketer, who was the last witness for the prosecution, almost certainly made a greater impact than all of them.

The argument then must be carried further by accepting that all kinds of literature, from the standards of literary value, good or bad, may stimulate lust. (One student in an American survey mentioned Motley's *Rise of the Dutch Republic*, but perhaps she was joking.) The other myth to be cleared out of the way is that educated people find pornography boring. This is regularly repeated, for example, by N St John Stevas (*Obscenity and the law*, 1956): ' On the whole, perverts excepted, educated people do not read pornography, since their taste for reading is fully formed and they find it dull and uninteresting '. For ' educated people ' some works may be boring for other reasons, but to suggest that they are immune from sexual stimulation is plainly against all experience. The class element in all this is clear enough. Pornography was no problem in a pre-industrialised society where it was available only for the educated élite. The distinction has been preserved by censorship by price, so that certain material is available only to the wealthy scholars with library facilities. The system is practical but the moral argument is dubious, since the implications are that whereas a minority may be exposed to corrupting influences, those who are neither wealthy nor *bona fide* scholars may not. The further implication is that this large excluded section of society is potentially delinquent. This appeal to literary standards should be abandoned except as a practical expedient; it is now increasingly accepted that the real moral issue is whether sexual stimulation is wrong. The Victorians thought it was: at the present time we tend to think it is not. The feeling is that if people want to indulge themselves in this way, that is their own affair and why shouldn't they? Indeed the trend is so well established that most young people fail to see what all the fuss is about.

The Victorians adopted this attitude partly because they had a pathological horror of masturbation. This is no longer with us, although it should be noted that D H Lawrence objected violently to pornography for this reason. His opinion merits further examination. What made him so angry and hysterical was, of course, the isolation of sex as a thing in itself from the rest of life. This he regarded as a major disease in modern industrial society, and travelled in Mexico, the Mediterranean and Australia, in search of a country where the ' dark gods ' were in their proper place and people were not obscene. These journeys represent the failure of the kind of quest which is discussed in chapter 2. It must be conceded that ' sex in the head ', to use his phrase, is a characteristic of advanced societies, but it would be futile to suppose that the censorship of literature would make any difference.

There remains one other fallacy to add to this pathetic catalogue. The pioneers of sexual freedom claimed that legal restraints *produced* the demand for pornography. As Havelock Ellis said, ' It is law *alone* which makes pornography both attractive and profitable '. During the twenties and thirties the ' prog ' people firmly believed that *secrecy* was the cause of all the trouble. As Ernst and Seagle claimed (in *To the pure*, 1928) the real obscenity lies in taboo. Edward Carpenter, somewhat earlier, took King Lear's bitter ejaculation straight, and advocated universal public copulation. Such attitudes are less common now and would seem to be based on the kind of rationalism which evades the nature of cultural reality—a reality which must include human frustrations.

THE SOCIAL PROBLEM

Most of the attitudes discussed above revolved around the traditional idea that anything which provokes lust must be evil as far as the individual is concerned, and the counter claim that sex under modern conditions is a private affair and freedom from interference is one of the rights of man and woman. We accept this latter claim, but serious social implications and complications remain.

Pornography, violence and crime: What has to be answered is the accusations that the free circulation of 'obscene' literature and of publications which glorify violence provoke or increase crime. The answer is not easy because the evidence is not conclusive. It has been established that some horrible crimes have been committed by people who have been influenced by the reading of pornographic and sadistic literature. Pamela Hansford Johnson's book *On iniquity*, an attack on the permissive society, was written because she was appalled by the 'Moors murders' of 1966 and by evidence that the young murderers had read De Sade and other apostles of sexual violence. They had become monsters and the literature contributed. It included *The history of torture through the ages, Orgies of torture and brutality, Sex crimes and sex criminals, Kiss of the whip, Pleasures of the torture chamber, Cradle of Erotica, The life and ideas of the Marquis de Sade*, and about forty similar titles, including works on fascism and nazism. Miss Johnson goes on to admit ' No one can prove a causal connection between what these two people read and what they did'. But she stresses that there remains the possibility that there is a causal connection. There is plenty of evidence that many criminals do read this kind of literature, but we cannot prove that they would *not* have committed crimes if they had not read it. All that we can say is that the literature—to use the usual expression—' triggered off ' an explosive force which was already there. It is possible, although again not proven, that there would have been some other equally decisive influence to provoke them.

On the other hand there are sociologists and others who hold that the literature of sex and crime enables people to act out their criminal propensities in fantasy and that so far from being a menace, such literature is a safety valve. Secondly they claim that part of the attraction exercised by this kind of reading matter is that it is forbidden. Such arguments no doubt influenced the Danish government in 1967 to remove all controls over literature. It is claimed that after the lifting of censorship there was a heavy demand at first but this has now subsided. On the other hand, there are authorities who insist that *some* people are bound to try to carry over their fantasies into anti-social actions. Those who have attacked horror comics both in this country and in America have been influenced by this view. It is reasonable to suppose that, whatever the answer, the issues with regard to violence are exactly the same as those raised by sex in literature. Wertham in the USA has carried on a prolonged campaign against horror comics and similar literature on the grounds that there *is* sufficient evidence to show the connection with crime, particularly with regard to young people. This evidence is marshalled in *Seduction of the innocent,* 1954.

One has also to remember that much of this literature is pictorial rather than verbal, and the visual influences are obviously greater. In the USA there is a vast adult reading public for ' horror comics ' and to a lesser extent in the UK also. As far as children are concerned, the British government passed the Children and Young Persons (Harmful Publications) Act in 1955.

At this point we should dispose of another argument which has been often stressed, namely, that literature really influences people very little. This is a view which no librarian could hold. One is forced to the conclusion that in this field it is *impossible* to collect evidence which in a free society could lead to irrefutable conclusions, if only because the obscenity issue is part of a much larger predicament. Many would regard it simply as a symptom of a more general social disorder. This is probably the case and only a fanatic would claim that reading or looking at pornographic photographs is a *cause* of crime. It is claimed, for example, with regard to prostitution—in the words of Donald Soper—' The main and most frequent reason is *excitement* . . . in the promotion of this sense of excitement pornography plays a most decisive part '. Neither Dr Soper nor anybody else would claim that if pornography could be eliminated the need for excitement would disappear: that is the crux of the matter.

One aspect remains to be noted. In free societies commercial interests batten on the appeal of pornography—and the apostles of censorship have concentrated on this 'victimisation' of human weakness by money-makers. Most of these critics do not object to commercial interests in other fields, and their position is dubious since commercial interests inevitably exploit all human failings, particularly in their advertising role: that is what businessmen are for. One could make out an even more telling case against the sale of alcoholic liquor, yet the history of prohibition shows that it succeeded neither in suppressing drink nor crime: on the contrary. On the other side of the curtain it was once believed and is still the official doctrine, that when the just society is established and the exploitation of man by man abolished, then all these problems, including that of crime, would disappear. St Augustine—who might be considered, psychologically speaking, as the first modern man—was much concerned with this concept of an ideal organisation (the church), but his last line of defence was that the City of God exists elsewhere. We can only hope that it does.

CONCLUSION

In the above survey I have maintained that much of the discussion on this subject proceeds on a superficial level. Many have called for more *evidence* about the possible effects of allegedly pornographic literature. Even if such were forthcoming it is doubtful whether the confusions would be any less. Authoritarian and puritanic societies produce a climate of opinion in which many human responses, both emotional and intellectual, are considered anti-social and taboo. They can therefore only be expressed, if at all, within restricted or underground groups. In more open societies the burden of censorship (in Freudian terms) is borne by the individual, and in consequence a variety of attitudes co-exist within society. Some people (perhaps correctly) are afraid of their buried selves, and it is often these who want to control the pleasures of others. These others may be content to live in their private world if society will let them, and if they want to behave in a kinky fashion then 'that is their thing'. Behind much of the argument the real issue revolves round the nature of evil. God may indeed be dead but what of the Devil?: is it possible that he is still lurking somewhere in St John's Wood or sleeps in Potters Bar? It is safer to call up the police.

To be more explicit, I believe that all censorship is futile, ridiculous and wrong; but like all absolutes, this must be related to existing societies, and once one has made the qualification, the issue is befogged again.[2] For example, it would be absurd to remove all kinds of censorship if a majority of the people in society were *actively* in favour of it, or if sudden exposure to unfamiliar modes of thought and feeling should provoke solid citizens to rush out like lemmings from their customary bounds. In simple or primitive societies the people need protection from influences beyond the tribe. It may be doubted whether Britain is a society of this kind, and if there are minorities, like children or delinquents, who do need protection and control, then some way of doing this should be found which does not penalise the rest of the community. It follows that Britain would do well to take the example of Denmark and the United States and remove the existing controls.

Beyond this, however, when one considers the thousands of people who rot in prisons all over the world just for attempting to bear witness to what they regard as the truth, the problem fades into insignificance; to those who are incarcerated in the political gaols of totalitarian countries, our preoccupations must appear at worst a kind of frivolity—at best a harmless indulgence.

NOTES

1 It is of interest that Anatoly Kuznetsov, the Russian writer who sought political asylum in Britain in 1969, stated that the Nazis burnt half his library during the war, the Soviet authorities burnt the other half in 1937 and his own books in 1969. He claimed (*The listener* 21st August 1969) that all books which are regarded as hostile to the Soviet regime must be burned, because ' if they are just sent along for pulping the workers might take them for themselves '.

2 This chapter has been overtaken by events. In July 1969 a working party set up by the Arts Council issued its recommendations which called for a total repeal of the obscenity laws for a five year trial period. (The report is reprinted *in toto* in the *New Statesman* 8th August 1969, and discussed in *The bookseller* 19th July 1969.) In the present climate of opinion the report is probably too radical for its proposals to be implemented by statutory legislation in the near future. It is significant however that the membership of the committee included representatives of all the main bodies concerned with the production and distribution of literature, *eg* the Publishers Association, the National Book League, the Society of Authors and the Library Association. Evidence was obtained from as wide a field as possible. The committee urged not only the abolition of the 1959 and 1964 Obscenity Acts, but that certain other relevant Acts should be amended or repealed. The main reason advanced for these sweeping proposals was the existing legislation represents a ' total nonsense '. The arrangements for films, television and sound broadcasting are not affected, and the report would leave intact the Children and Young Persons (Harmful Publications) Act, 1955.

The reader is referred to the twelve points in the report which sum up the reasons for the recommendations. The case for abolition has never before been put so succinctly and with such cogency.

6

reading and the use of leisure

Other parts of this book deal directly or by implication with the fact that technology is creating not only more leisure but the means by which that leisure time is filled. This chapter relates mainly to the use and possible value of reading, and other aspects are ignored. There is also a section on the literacy problem, but this refers to the more straightforward topic of reading as a practical necessity in the modern world and whether it can be made universal. In such a context leisure pursuits are secondary to urgent everyday needs.

One of the difficulties is that it is almost impossible to discuss reading as an activity or leisure time pursuit without reference to the type of literature that is read, and any attempt to do so may be misleading if not dangerous. There are too many imponderables.

There are three elements in this equation or communication process: first the writer, second the piece of literature and third the reader. The literature can be evaluated by a professional critic according to values which may or may not be generally accepted, but the process, although often fundamentally influenced by these values, is affected by psychological factors both in the writer and the reader. In other words, communication is never total or subject to rational analysis. One might say that *all* communication processes are partial failures, but the nature of the failure varies according to the medium and to particular circumstances. One element in all this is the presence or absence of what the communication scientists call 'feedback', a jargon word which has come into significantly general use. If a message can be checked or clarified or interpreted, by whatever means, then the communication procedure becomes more total, in the sense that what the originator wrote is more accurately transmitted. On one level and with regard to factual information, we can assume that this ideal of total communication is wholly desirable, but on a less rational level this may not be so—particularly with any type of writing which may be called 'creative'. These matters are also discussed in chapter 3, but what is relevant here is the element of *necessary* failure. Readers read in their own way and for their own peculiar purposes, which may have little bearing on what the writer intended to convey or thought he was writing about. (To avoid misunderstanding I should make it clear that in the strictly information realm the attempts to improve reading efficiency are no doubt valuable within their necessary limits.)

The above considerations arise particularly if we think of *individual* reactions to reading matter, and these are important if we are not to fall into the simple fallacy of defining certain types of reading matter as 'recreational', or whatever, without reference to the reader who uses it. The *social* functions of reading are vague and difficult to define, partly for the reasons mentioned, but provided we bear in mind that these are abstract social generalisations, the categories mentioned by Landheer in *The social function of libraries*, are useful. He distinguishes four types of reading: achievement reading, devotional reading, culture reading and compensatory reading. These terms do in fact relate to distinctions which are commonly made and should need little explanation, except possibly the last, which refers to what we usually call recreational reading. He uses 'culture' in the narrow sense of intellectual activity, and it is here that confusions inevitably arise, because the pursuit of knowledge for its own sake is always mixed up with other motives such as social status and class conventions. The discussion which follows mainly relates to the way that culture reading changes with each generation.

SALVATION WITHOUT WORK

The peasant of old, tired after his dawn to dusk labours, was content with simple pleasures or simply to sit still. Neither he nor anybody else minded how he spent his spare time, and he did not want holidays, nor did he get them, except as seasonal interruptions to his work. As soon as men and women were crowded into towns, what they should do with their leisure time (little though it was) became a 'problem', and nineteenth century moralists were worried, not without good

95

reason, about the numerous evil pursuits which might disturb the existence of the more comfortable elements in society.

Since then the working classes have become respectable, and have been admitted to (or have won for themselves) some of the benefits of affluence, so that now the moralists are worried by the possibility that leisure may be used in a negative, mindless or an uncreative fashion. Journalists are filled with alarm at the thought that automation will create more and more leisure for other people.

This is of course part of the challenge that the cybernetic age will bring to the advanced regions of the world. We have no evidence that these new opportunities will not be taken up, and there are already signs that they are being well used. For example, the 'do-it-yourself' movement has become general, and is likely to spread if only as those manufactured goods which are produced by traditional methods become more expensive. There is abundant evidence that all kinds of 'worthwhile' pastimes like bird-watching have vastly increased. It is probable that many more people than formerly cultivate their gardens or play golf or go fishing. How we regard these various leisure time activities depends on our scale of values. For example, in the past the puritan ethic tended to regard most forms of enjoyment, recreation or pleasure as automatically suspect. This attitude is receding and the current tendency is to consider that recreation is a necessary part of community life. Some authorities, for example Huizinga in *Homo Laudens*, have gone further, and claim a more important and positive role for the play element in cultural life. This is too large a subject to pursue here, but it is sufficiently clear that the *quality* of our lives is very much in question. Even if we are not puritans, and in consequence not our brothers' keepers, there is to most observers something peculiarly depressing about the spectacle of thousands of people in cars crawling head to tail from our cities to sit side by side along the coast, and then crawl home again, having done little but eat sandwiches and look at the sea when they are there? Gertrude Stein's comment is appropriate for this and so many other similar leisure activities: ' There is no " there " there when you get there '.

The relevance of this to reading is, firstly, that the more positive or active or individual activities do tend to increase the demand for the relevant literature, as public librarians will bear witness. Secondly, the discussion concerning the right use of leisure also concerns reading in the sense that some types of leisure reading may be (and usually are) considered more valuable than others. Furthermore, this culture reading plays a different role in different types of society. The salvation without work dilemma was much in evidence in nineteenth century Britain. The social reformers (as was indicated in the debates on the first Public Libraries Act) were not in the first instance thinking of the culture value of reading, but were mainly concerned with 'getting people off the streets'. (The same negative motives are noticeable today in developing countries, and it is an effective argument to use in persuading local worthies to set up community libraries.) This was no more than a debased modern equivalent for the procedures in the monasteries, where the monks were required to read because ' Idleness is an enemy of the soul '. It is really a fifth type of reading to those identified by Landheer, which might be called moral or ethical—or reformatory—or therapeutic. The difficulty, of course, was that the literature involved might lead the readers back to the wickedness outside, and in consequence various kinds of censorship were also essential. (There are still librarians among us whose daily tasks used to include blacking out the horse-race betting news in the daily newspapers displayed in the reading rooms!)

READING AS AN EVIL

Since literacy began there have been many dire warnings about the harmful consequences of reading and two of them, one ancient and one modern (quoted from Hall and Whannell, *Popular arts*, chapter 14, p 387) should serve our purpose: Socrates (as reported by Plato) said ' For the discovery will create forgetfulness in the learners' souls, because they will not use their memories; they will trust to the external written characters and do not remember of themselves . . . They will appear to be omniscient and will generally know nothing; they will be tiresome company having the show of wisdom without the reality.' This is a typical reaction from a society where oral tradition was the rule—it is well enough known that people from such communities, particularly the bards and story tellers, possessed phenomenal memories and used to recite long sagas by heart.

The modern reference raises objections which are not dissimilar: ' Reading is one of the insidious enemies of the kind of leisure required for creative thinking. Reading is insidious because it is a praiseworthy intellectual activity '. The first statement says (quite rightly) that reading in itself cannot make men wise: the second appears to warn against the reading of *any* kind of literature as an enemy of creative

97

4

thinking. It is quite true that 'creativity' whether in science or art, is not a conscious process in its origins and not immediately subject to will. It is also true that too much reading may obscure whatever vision an individual may have; this is a well known occupational disease of academics, who become incapable of making a statement unless it is supported by somebody else's statement and so on *ad infinitum*. However, it is clear that reading does not *always* cause people to evade problems and projects, so that once again we are back with the variety of individual experience. Just as a drug like LSD will affect two persons (and the same person at different times) in totally different ways, so the impact of reading must vary. The actual content or quality of the literature read may be irrelevant, since, as we noticed in relation to pornography, it may simply act as a trigger mechanism. No doubt one man's compensations are another's culture, just as some people read the *Bible* for cultural or aesthetic reasons and not as a devotional exercise. Possibly some of the most important literature is that which can carry out all or several of the functions mentioned above, and the *Bible* may be one example.

Before leaving this point it is necessary to mention again the problem of compensatory or recreational reading. The arguments about 'escapist' literature, like all discussions concerning fantasy, cannot be pursued without becoming embroiled in fundamentally religious or philosophical problems. One can proceed from a standpoint that it is wrong to try to evade or escape from reality, but this immediately brings up the questions of what 'reality' is, and whether the reality that some people have to endure is worth remaining with. Throughout this book I have taken the view that most people need some kind of drug some of the time, and in this context the reading of compensatory literature, whether it is 'good reading' or rubbish, is a relatively harmless sedative.

The contrary argument is often made that the human need should be met not by useless fantasies but by genuine myths or beliefs which illumine or reconcile us to the human condition. For example, an English literary critic objected to the Tolkien Society of America on the grounds that its members were ignoring the true nature of Tolkien's work: 'Myth has always been an attempt to come to terms with the world—not to avoid it'. There are 'Sherlock Holmes' societies all over the world, and presumably they can also be condemned as even less 'serious'. But a plea must be made that light reading may have a place in the scheme of things and this is nothing to do with the value of great literature. Whether public libraries should deal in compensations of this kind is another matter. All that I have tried to establish is that the same piece of literature may have many uses and some of them may be more evil than others. The use of reading matter in hospitals and prisons provides other examples. If they read novels dealing with their diseases some people may be helped; others may get worse. Prisoners who read about the pleasures and pains of crime may become more criminal or less so: it appears to depend on who they are.

THE USE OF SURVEYS

If it is difficult to make any helpful generalisations about why people read, it should at least be possible to ascertain *what* people in general or particular social groups read. Sociologists have conducted social surveys which have included reading habits, and librarians have produced reading surveys which have their value, but this is often limited by the poor quality of the surveys or by the inability of the surveyors to come to any useful conclusions. There is a survey of surveys available and I need not pursue them here except to note that, with regard to use of libraries, one of the most interesting was Groombridge's survey of public library use in London (1964). It was valuable because the investigator knew what he was looking for, and this surely is important. Many sociological investigations fail, particularly it seems in the USA, because vast quantities of facts are collected and then the surveyors do not know what to do with them or how they can be interpreted.

CULTURE READING

As distinct from ' achievement ' or utilitarian reading, which is concerned with immediate practical ends such as passing an examination or learning skills, ' culture ' reading can be regarded as useless in any direct sense, but always very important in any society. It involves the disinterested pursuit of knowledge, truth, beauty or goodness. even though it is always mixed up with other motivations such as the search for social importance (knowledge is power), or for status and acceptance, or for the comforts of a dream world, or for the individual self realisation which involves the establishment of a personal identity. The young reader reads to discover who he is and what his role should be. In order to indicate how the nature of this role changes I have

99

selected two themes, or perhaps they are two aspects of the same theme.

The literature read by the young in the process of coming to terms with the world is always of special cultural significance for obvious reasons. Most people's basic attitudes are fixed by the age of 25 and, subject to some modifications, these attitudes remain for the rest of their lives. In a healthy or integrated society some kind of balance is kept, so that if the young rebel or revolt, as is normal, they will eventually become nevertheless part of the ' acceptance world ', which has meanwhile changed. So, if we consider the closing years of the nineteenth century, several elements can be noted. For a long time culture reading had been individualistic in the sense that Disraeli was expressing when he referred to the world as his hero's ' oyster '. The young were entering into a cultural heritage which had been preserved and developed in a century which had experienced not only the earlier liberation of the romantic movement, but also the vast energies released by the industrial revolution, the extension of political demo-cracy and the expansion of Empire.

But the great Victorian society had paid the inevitable price, and the revolt and dissent was expressed in their best literature, just as it has been in twentieth century America. So it was that for the young reading became a liberating experience which released them from Victorian attitudes. This revolt took several forms, one of which was the aesthetic movement of the nineties. Undergraduates went about the streets chanting the more dithyrambic bits of Swinburne ' Thou hast conquered O pale Galilean—the world has grown grey from thy breath '. Late Victorian clergymen pottered along muttering to them-selves the quatrains of Fitzgerald's Omar Khayam, and Walter Pater was so distressed by the subversive influence exercised by the last chapter of his work *The Renaissance,* that he omitted it from the second edition: ' I conceived it might possibly mislead some of those young men into whose hands it might fall '.

The other stream in this tide was more directly social and political, with Shaw and Wells pointing towards the new Fabian Jerusalem, at the same time as novelists, like Samuel Butler in *The way of all flesh,* were reflecting the revolt against the Victorian family. If we pursued this development into the twentieth century it would become in-creasingly dominant and would conclude with the peculiar phenomenon, the Left Book Club of the thirties; after that comes the deluge, represented by the second world war and by George Orwell. Since this is not a history of reading, all that we are concerned with is that at the turn of the century the literature of revolt was still optimistic, and for H G Wells the suggestion detectable in his last work that Mind was at the end of its tether would have been unthinkable. The movement and the type of reading it inspired can be summed up as revolt in the name of reform and the future.

If we take this same theme at half century, the contrast is at once apparent, and reading no longer plays this liberating role except in the Soviet Union, where it is underground. The literature is one of rejection not of revolt. Frank Gardner touched on this point (or another facet of it) in his Presidential Address to the British Library Association in 1964. He mentioned Compton Mackenzie's novel *Sinister Street*, which for many young people helped to open doors to an exciting cultural and social world. This, of course, was not the revolt theme so much as the ' world as oyster ' one, but the relevant point is that Gardner seemed to regret that contemporary young people (including librarians) lack that kind of motivation and do not get the same inspiration from reading.

Whether we regret it or not, the role of reading in this respect, as in others, has changed. If we are thinking of novels, what is the equivalent for the nineteen fifties? Some would at once suggest Kingsley Amis and *Lucky Jim*, but he is a parody of earlier heroes—the academic ' angries ' of the fifties were simply making gestures and faces and rude noises in answer to their predicament in a class society. The real counterpart is Salinger's *Catcher in the rye*, significantly, an American work.[1] Here there is not revolt but total rejection, or ' opting out '; the anti-hero automatically assumes that all adult society is ' phoney ', and that adults are some lower form of life.

For those who share such attitudes (and they are legion) there is no reason to read at all. The current liberating medium is not reading but music. The other strand in this pattern is a curious ambivalence to traditional high culture. It is in the first instance instinctively rejected because it has been appropriated by the ' square ' world in a sterile and reactionary manner. As one of the Beatles has stated it always later comes as a surprise to discover that ' classical ' music has something to communicate after all. The current challenge for traditional culture is not the indifference or hostility of the pop world, it is the need for its own transformation and the incorporation of what is most enduring in pop art.

Meanwhile in the sixties, the literature of protest, as represented by the folk hero Guevara, or the Marxist heretic Marcuse, or the neo-Freudians R D Laing and I O Brown, if read at all does not have the same type of direct influence. Che Guevara for example is mainly a *symbolic* figure, and the important thing is that he failed and was martyred. A more significant figure is Artaud, the theatrical apostle of violence and the absurd. It may well be that the most representative act of protest of the 1968 American presidential election was that the yippies elected a pig as their president. If and when the various group incoherently involved in protest movements should ever come together, a new literature will be necessary.

As far as Britain is concerned reading habits change not with every generation but with each decade. At present they are being influenced by the other communication media, by two world wars and the war in Vietnam, by the increasing tempo of living, by the loss of the empire, and by the collapse of faith in political processes. In addition, the quantity of knowledge or information represented by the vast range of literature makes it difficult both for the specialist and for those caught up in the education process to read beyond their particular disciplines. Within the field of science, and with particular reference to periodicals, bibliographical services such as abstracts are intended to introduce order into this expanding jungle (where lost librarians lurk like distracted beasts who have forgotten who they are). If the role of bibliography is less important outside science, it remains true that all forms of bibliographical and library guidance are increasingly essential. Otherwise the wrong books unfailingly reach the wrong readers at the wrong time.

UNIQUE ADVANTAGES OF READING

It is usually alleged that reading has special advantages compared with other media, and it is claimed therefore that the printed word will continue to be the most important channel for education and cultural advance. The advantages claimed are, firstly, that reading is a personal and secret activity which fosters individual development; secondly, that any kind of literature can be read and re-read until its message is absorbed; thirdly, that reading matter can be carried about, whether the reader is on an escalator or a desert island. The process is not one of instant impact, but a permanent and often a growing influence. Once the material is printed and distributed, no further organisation, gadgets or machinery are required before it can be used. (Nothing is so dead as a tape without its recorder.) Finally, the printed word is not necessarily intended to be read by millions of people at the same time, so that quality can be preserved. If we list the advantages in this way it becomes clear that they cannot be accepted without qualification.

(Students of librarianship, who seem to feel that they are required to show that reading in itself has some inherent valuable quality, particularly stress that films or television cannot be replayed to meet the needs of individuals. They tend to ignore the fact that tape recordings can be used in this way, and it is now certain that within a few years there will be devices generally available to enable users to record and replay television programmes in their homes. Already a ' cassette ' has been produced for this purpose, and there are alternative methods. This will of course apply to the visual programme as well as to sound broadcasts.)

Furthermore, reading *appears* to be a personal activity, and in one sense it is, but it is also very much part of a social process. As we have already noted, printing is one of the mass media, and, like the others, can be used either for private or social purposes. In short, there are so many uses for reading that it is impossible to discuss them all at once, or to treat reading as an activity or process otherwise than in a narrow context.

Marshall McLuhan concentrates on print as a medium which, before the electronic age, produced people who responded to the world in a certain way. ' The book is an extension of the eye ', and western history has been shaped by the alphabet, which caused people to perceive the environment in visual and spatial terms. In such a world rationality was the organising principle of life: ' Rationality and visuality have long been interchangeable terms, but we do not live in a primarily visual world any more '. Now that we are back in our primordial global village, all happenings are simultaneous, and time and space are no more. In fact we all live in a yellow submarine, and from this heritage a few centuries of literacy had divorced us. These claims for the passing role of literacy are noted without comment, except that we do know that illiterate people live in another world. As for those of us who live in developed regions, even if we do now have our nervous systems extended by the electronic media, we are also still literate: much of our communicating still goes on in the medium of the written word, and McLuhan sends out his anti-lineal messages in print.

In trying to analyse the present use of reading and the impact of the new mass media, I have inevitably concentrated on the developed world. It is worth noting, therefore, that roughly seven hundred million people, or at least forty percent of the world's population, are still illiterate. Although this percentage may be diminishing slightly, the total number of adult illiterates continues to increase. The official figures show that between 1950 and 1962 the total number had increased by thirty-five million. They also show that in eighty five countries of Africa, Asia and Latin America the illiterate adult population is growing at the rate of at least twenty million a year. The population explosion is largely responsible.

In most parts of the underdeveloped world the illiteracy figure is fifty percent or more, and in some countries, for example Afghanistan, Ethiopia, Saudi Arabia, Haiti, it is over ninety percent. In the Caribbean islands generally (apart from Haiti), the rate is now down to about twenty-five percent. In some of these countries official efforts to overcome this are slowly making headway, and in others all forms of education cannot keep pace with the growth of population: it is a losing battle.

The most spectacular results were obtained in the Soviet Union between 1919 and 1930—perhaps the most impressive achievement of the revolutionary regime. In 1919 Lenin signed a decree that the entire population must learn to read and write. By the end of 1939 illiteracy had been eradicated. The usual compulsion was present, but in this case it was scarcely necessary as there was a tremendous spontaneous response. A more recent example on a much smaller scale is that of Cuba, where, at a public meeting in 1960, Cuba was declared free from illiteracy, 707,000 persons having been taught to read and write in a few months. The programme has been followed up by post-literacy courses. But apart from these all-out national campaigns with their clear political motivation, the general picture is not encouraging.

I am here taking the view that, whereas in some cultures of the past it did not matter a great deal whether people were literate or not, illiteracy is now wholly disastrous in terms of both social and individual welfare. These 700 million people are living outside time and place as we now normally experience them, and in a sense outside their communities. As a Unesco pamphlet states, ' For two thirds of humanity the twentieth century does not exist '. They naturally cannot read notices of any kind; they cannot find their way about; they cannot tell the time, or know what day it is, or how old they are, or what lies beyond the frontiers of their village. They are at the mercy of swindlers, bureaucrats, letter writers and tricksters of every kind. It is even difficult or impossible to buy tinned or bottled or packaged goods in a shop, because they cannot be identified. I stress these facts because those of us who have been overexposed to print and to advertising at every turn may be tempted to envy the illiterate in his more organic world. We are, of course, slaves to the clock, and to machines, and to an overorganised unspontaneous existence where unscheduled impulses or responses can wreck the social fabric, but the illiterate is no less a slave, and his condition in this century is not idyllic or happy and he would be the last to think it so. The world to him is hostile and terrifying.

Pioneering work in combating illiteracy was mainly done by Christian, more particularly Protestant, missionaries. In the one hundred and fifty years since they began their work, much experience has been gained in methods of combating illiteracy. The difficulties, particularly after Unesco's work, are more fully understood. It is appreciated, for example, that many backward regions are not capable of the sustained national effort that is required. It is also generally recognised that illiteracy cannot be tackled as a problem by itself, but must be part of community development generally. At one time it was thought that if all the children were required to go to school, the problem would solve itself in one generation. But societies are not simple like this, and the same social circumstances which produce illiteracy also produce conditions where there are no free schools and where child labour is universal. This is particularly the case in Latin America: the same social conditions produce over-population and so on. It is because of some of these factors that many campaigns conducted successfully have been allowed to lapse, or else have not been followed up. There is a tendency for ' backward ' peoples to become *relatively* even more backward as the century proceeds. The gap between rich and poor nations is widening; so also is the economic gap between white and black people in the USA; so also is the social gap between the wealthier elements (mostly of European origin) and the poor (mostly indigenous) in South America. Unesco's effort has been particularly valuable in suggesting the best methods for overcoming the problem, but it should be remembered that this work is a small drop in the ocean; as someone has said, ' Unesco's annual budget is less than the cost of one dozen jet bombers '.

4*

Dr. Frank Charles Laubach, who has done more than any other single individual to combat illiteracy in so many different countries, wrote 'Whether literacy is really an important contribution to the lives of a people or not depends upon the material that the people read after they become literate. At least one half of the literacy problem, therefore, is what to provide for new literates to read in the transition period while they are building up a vocabulary to the level where they can easily read and enjoy standard literature '.

In other words, there is a gap between learning to read and reading standard literature: this gap must be filled by the use of appropriately graded texts. The problem is not fundamentally different from teaching growing children to read. Recognition that this is the second necessary stage in overcoming illiteracy does not, unfortunately, mean that the demand can easily be met. In underdeveloped countries there is no simple law of supply and demand, and this is often why, in Unesco's words, ' literacy campaigns have earned more tombstones than monuments '. The publishing programme involved must be a substantial one and must be subsidised. We noted in chapter 11 that the religious stories published by the Society for Promoting Christian Knowledge and other organisations of the same kind are still read in West Africa. These agencies play a useful, limited role, but the main responsibility is clearly that of the state.

In several areas this challenge has been met by setting up what are usually known as ' literature bureaux '. Their functions are: firstly, to publish practical literature for the government, such as leaflets on public health or farming, and secondly, to publish on their own account reading material which is not likely to be available through the normal operations of commercial publishing. Such material may include books and periodicals for recreational reading and translations, and many of the bureaux may have to concentrate on literature suitable for those who have learnt to read and write but are not yet ' functionally literate ', *ie* those in the first stage mentioned above. Often the bureaux are faced with a lack of literature in their vernacular languages, and concentrate on publications to remedy this deficiency. They may also attempt to encourage local publication in English or French or Portuguese—the languages brought by the colonial powers, which are still the official languages of the country. There are many difficulties, not the least of which is a lack of enthusiasm which sometimes exists for literature in the vernaculars, when the route to advancement lies through one of the major European languages. In view of the vast number of vernacular languages in West Africa this is wholly natural. Work in vernacular has been done for many years by the Bureau of Ghana Languages, the Zambia and Malawi Joint Publications Bureau, the South Pacific Literature Bureau, the Latin-American Fundamental Education Press, the Burma Translation Society, and the Regional Literature Agency of Northern Nigeria.

In spite of all these activities it cannot be said that appropriate literature exists, either from the point of view of quality or quantity. In addition, there is always a physical distribution problem, which is one of the main reasons why commercial publishers are reluctant to enter the field. These obstacles do not exist so much in the case of basic material used for instruction in schools, or for adults, but with other types of literature. The rural areas are naturally those where the problem is most acute, and it is here that library services are most important. Where village libraries and mobile library services have been developed, as in the West Indies and Ghana, and some parts of India, literature is brought to the people which can be distributed in no other way.

ILLITERACY IN DEVELOPED COUNTRIES

Brief reference, finally, should be made to the fact that semi-literacy exists on a considerable scale in the advanced countries, notably among the huge populations of the USA and the USSR. In the former, according to the 1960 census, the illiterate proportion of the population was 2·4 percent, or three million. In addition, there were eight million ' functionally illiterate ', or ' undereducated ' people ie those who had received less than five years of school. This underprivileged section of the population suffers from similar or worse disabilities to those in the underdeveloped regions. Their illiteracy or semi-illiteracy is one aspect of their poverty. In the UK adult illiteracy has continued to decrease—but since general standards of literacy are improving, and it is more and more important that everybody should be fully literate—those who are semi-literate fall further behind. The official figures for 1956 was roughly four percent in this category.

NOTE
1 Equally significant for other reasons were Joseph Heller's *Catch 22* (attitudes to the second world war) and *Herzog* by Saul Bellow (the dilemmas of the middle aged). Holden Coldfield, Jossarian and Herzog are typical anti-heroes of our time.

7

the book trade

To the outsider the book trade has never been easy to understand. As the structure is now being modified it is even less comprehensible and not noticeably more rational. One of the difficulties has been that traditionally the trade, or at least the publishing part of it, has been conscious of a cultural role and responsibilities, and has insisted that the publisher is not like other businessmen or manufacturers, but is concerned with other values as well as profit. This claim is not without some justification, but it has produced an ambivalence which has always affected the relationships of publishers with authors, or even librarians.

Quite apart from the publishers' ideals or pretensions, it is true that there are unique features of the book trade which make analysis difficult. Books are ' different ', not only because of their essential cultural role, but because a book is not a commodity in the usual economic sense, and each title is unique. One book costing £1 is unlikely to be comparable in any other way as a product to another book costing the same amount. If one compares book publishing with the other communications industries, the special characteristics of the former are apparent. Unlike broadcasting or newspaper publishing, expensive plant is not required, so that small firms can enter the business. Advertising resources for each book (product) are limited by the short production runs—short in comparison to a mass circulation periodical or newspaper. Books are not necessarily mass media and quite small editions can be produced economically.

The contents of books are not influenced by a dual role of advertising media, as are periodicals and newspapers. Lastly, because of their usually compact physical form and the absence of auxiliary equipment for their use, books have several practical advantages over other media. (Their relative disadvantages, especially the loss of immediacy, are obvious, and have been touched upon in earlier chapters.) These characteristics make it possible for publishers to respond to demands for a wide variety of different material; book publishing is, therefore, a fairly flexible industry which includes many different types of activity in the act of presenting communication.

PAPERBACK PUBLISHING

At first sight it is very odd that a vital distinction in modern book production should be whether a book has a hard or a soft cover—particularly when one considers that in continental Europe books have traditionally been published in paper covers. The difference is that the paperback represents the impact of mass production and mass selling on an industry otherwise geared to the supply of a smaller market.[1] It shows another aspect of the clash between *nouveau* mass culture and that of a conventional minority. It has been estimated that paperback sales in Britain now account for about sixty percent of all book sales.

In chapter 3 I described a communication source as a mass medium when it reaches over one million people more or less simultaneously. If we use this criterion, paperback publishing becomes one of the mass media only in the case of the bestseller—and even then the one million figure is not reached immediately. However, Penguin Books have stated that they have published thirty five titles with sales over half a million. The chief of these are *Lady Chatterley's Lover* (3,600,000), Homer's *Odyssey* (1,600,000), *Animal Farm* (1,700,000), *Room at the top* (1,000,000), Shaw's *St Joan* (1,000,000). Penguin's sales figure has risen from just over twelve million copies a year in 1959 to nearly twenty nine millions in 1968—a little less than a third of the total paperback market. These figures are quoted to indicate firstly how rapidly the paperback trade is expanding, and secondly that, although this can be called a mass market, it does not reach, in volume alone, so large a proportion of the population as, for example, pop records. This growth has been assisted by new technical processes, notably monochrome and colour offset printing.

Even if we regard *some* paperback publishing as a medium of mass communication, a considerable part of the paperback trade now sells books which are neither cheap nor necessarily popular. Prices have increased in proportion more than they have for hardback publications, because a variety of 'quality' paperbacks are being published in relatively small editions. Publishers' own cheap reprints in the old sense have almost ceased to exist; they have been replaced by paperback editions and, in general, fewer copies of them are printed than in the paperback editions of new books. The 'egghead' paperback trade, which first developed in America and has grown in importance with the expansion of higher education, is not directed at a mass market. It takes advantages not of a mass market, but of a *known* market (students) which can be more surely attracted to buy cheap editions. Apart from the publications intended for students, particularly at the tertiary level, it should be emphasised that Penguin Books proved long ago that quality publishing in cheap paperback form can be a commercial proposition, through sales figures which in the thirties would have seemed impossible. This was the key to Penguin's success in the first instance.

The reference to Penguin, which first began publishing more than thirty years ago, serves to remind us that paperback publications are not new in Britain, but the overworked term 'paperback revolution' has been widely adopted because of the extent to which this sector of the trade has come decisively to influence the rest. In fact, many would agree with John Calder (' Some aspects of book publishing ', *Library Association record,* 1967, p 339) that paperback publishing has ' taken over ' the trade. He points out that many hardback publishers can survive only by selling paperback publishing rights in their books as quickly as possible after the contract has been signed with an author. According to Calder, in most cases the only reason for publication in hardback form is to *obtain press reviews* which cannot be had for a paperback, and when paperbacks start to be reviewed in the same way, as presumably will happen, the trade will be ' turned upside down '. For the moment, first publication in soft covers under a paperback firm's imprint is still largely regarded as ' unserious '.

There is the further significant point that most of the large British paperback companies are now American owned or controlled and they are becoming, not necessarily through ' parental ' influence, very much more profit-conscious, with the resulting qualification which this imposes on the material they select to publish. There is, therefore, what might be called a crisis in publishing, and the advent of the paperback is partly responsible. Many publishers have prophesied doom for the conventional hardback trade, though from the point of view of the consumer it may seem largely irrelevant what kind of covers books have, provided that they are produced and distributed in sufficient numbers. The paperback does present special problems for librarians and these are discussed below.

THE END OF THE GENTLEMAN PUBLISHER

Partly because of the paperback phenomenon, and partly for economic reasons which are not confined to the book trade, publishers have had to adopt the attitudes of 'modern' businessmen or perish. They now refer to 'marketing' and not 'selling'; they are using automation in warehousing and distribution; they pay attention to exports; and, most important, they have continued to amalgamate their firms, so that eventually there may be only a few large publishing groups left in control of most of the trade. At present, six of the largest British publishing groups account for about thirty percent of the sales. These are International Publishing Corporation, Collins, Penguin Books, Associated Book Publishers, Hutchinsons, Routledge and Kegan Paul. This trend has caused some concern. It has been suggested, notably by Raymond Williams ('Books in peril', *Library Association record*, January 1963, p 3), that this amalgamation process will affect the *quality* of publishing, and may make it more difficult for works of merit but no obvious commercial value to find a publisher. He stresses that the current emphasis is on *speed of sale*, and this will mean that there will be pressure *on authors* to help serve the interests of rapid selling.

It is true that book production and distribution is now being diversified, and is, to some extent, passing into the hands of people who do not value books in the way the old fashioned publishers did. Paperbacks of suitable market appeal are being distributed in supermarkets and by slot machines, as in the United States. (In this context it is of interest to note Penguin's claim that the American reliance on supermarkets is not really economic, since, although there are vast sales, there is also a high proportion of the stockholding returned unsold to the publisher—possibly as much as fifty percent.) There has also been an increase in the use of direct selling, instead of through bookshops, as is noted below. There can be no doubt that commercialisation and amalgamation have their dangers—publishing's new technocrats are a significant portent, but whether they are a menace to civilisation remains to be seen.

So far there is probably insufficient evidence to show that all Raymond Williams' fears are justified. He has on numerous occasions proposed the setting up of a 'Book Council' in order to keep publishing and bookselling in the hands of those who value books. One of its functions would be to establish (with the aid of a state capital grant) a distributive system for the selling of books. It is certainly true that many of the large companies which are moving into book publishing are not book publishers in the traditional sense at all. Some of them, like the Thomson Organisation, are newspaper publishers. Whether a state agency—like a Book Council—is a better alternative is a matter of opinion.

It should be added that although mergers take place with some frequency, there is still in existence a large number of small independent publishing units (some of the big groups allow their subsidiary imprints some measure of independence), and this is of relevance to the alleged *overproduction* in British publishing. (The figure of new books published rose from 24,617 titles in 1963 to 28,501 titles in 1967). Clive Bingley (in *Library Association record*, March 1969) suggest that the growth is partly caused by publications being put into lists to maintain financial turnover levels while the volume of sale for individual hardback titles continues to fall. Bingley goes on to point out that the long term trend of hardcover sales to individuals is downwards, and argues that there is a causal relationship between this fact and the rising levels of book prices. He analyses the other reasons for price increases in some detail, as does a statement by the Publishers Association in the same issue of the LAR, p 75. This statement admits that price increases are continual, but concludes 'What is maintained is that across the board these increases are not unreasonable and that British books are not highly priced and remain the cheapest unsubsidised books in the world outside the Soviet bloc'.

Many public librarians, bothered by local government committees, fail to appreciate either the justice of the increases or the reasons for them. It may be that publishers should have increased their prices dramatically long ago in preference to the recent steady creep, which has been estimated to be at the rate of roughly ten percent a year during the 1960's. The trade has long been afflicted by social attitudes to books which cause people to expect them to remain cheap even when other commodities continue to rise in price. It is possible, and a point of much debate, that the knowledge that books can be borrowed free, whereas other items cannot, causes even the reading public to feel that the purchase of a new book is a greater extravagance than buying a bottle of whisky for the same amount of money.

THE GROWTH OF EXPORTS

One postwar development has seen books become an important export industry. The Publishers Association, encouraged by the government, responded to the trade's awareness of the importance to its future of expanding export markets, by setting up in 1966 the *Book Development Council* to promote book exports abroad. It appears that none of the available trade statistics can be accepted without qualification, but it may be safe to say that at least half the books sold annually by British publishers go abroad. Overseas markets have become vital, and Macmillan's for example, have made an interesting and controversial innovation by co-operating with several African governments in establishing and developing their state publishing enterprises.

THE BOOKSHOP CRISIS

The outstanding trend in modern bookselling has been a decline in the number of good bookshops of the traditional kind—reflecting perhaps the decline in hardcover book sales already mentioned. Many towns do not now have a good bookshop at all, and even in London many of the best shops have closed down. It has been estimated that eighty percent of the UK bookselling trade goes to ten percent of the booksellers, and that the remaining twenty percent (mostly single copies) goes to the rest. Of all books bought it is probable that only about one half are sold over the counter in bookshops. Chain stores like W H Smith & Son Ltd do not offer a service comparable with that of the traditional bookshop. In the United States, bookshops of the old type are not often found, but numerous alternative outlets exist, and, as Calder notes (in the article already quoted), you can buy a book in about every fifth building in a large town.[2] In Britain, however, the booksellers are declining in number, and the new outlets which might replace them do not yet exist in sufficient quantity; in addition, many people in the trade do not want these new outlets. They are not, after all, part of the traditional book trade at all. Even so, diversification is likely to increase and, as far as booksellers proper are concerned, there is likely to be a move towards the consolidation of existing shops into larger groups to face the competition, and a greater reliance on mail order selling. Those who appreciate the cultural value of a good bookshop in the life of a community must regret their gradual disappearance.

A reason for the decline of small bookshops, and a sound justification of consolidation among them, is that the large number of books now in print has meant that many of the small bookshops are incapable of holding a broad enough range of stock to retain general custom;[3] this is one of the acknowledged functions of the bookshop (the other being the provision of bibliographical information, so that books can be ordered). It may be that it is the marketing difference between the bookshop and the new mass retail outlets that is now a more important factor in the organisation of the trade than the disintegrating distinction (for business purposes) between hardcover and paperback books. (For example, publications first issued in paperback are now often reissued in hard cover editions, instead of vice-versa; also, many publishers, especially the university presses, issue books simultaneously in soft and hardcover editions.)

THE BOOK TRADE AND LIBRARIES

Publishers and booksellers now depend on libraries' custom, particularly public libraries, far more than ever before. There has been an enormous increase in hardcover *reading* in recent years, even though book buying by private individuals has declined. The majority of this reading is through the agency of public libraries, which lend approximately 500 million books a year. One quarter of all books which are bought in the UK is bought by public libraries, representing a spending power of £15 million annually. Because of the increasing importance of the library market, the book trade has increased its contacts with libraries in a number of areas. There has been fruitful co-operation, and inevitably some friction, on particular issues. The following are some of the most noticeable developments.

DECLINE OF SUBSCRIPTION LIBRARIES

Ever since the eighteenth century, subscription libraries have played a significant role in British social life, and throughout the nineteenth century they provided literature for middle class people who did not use the public libraries. With the arrival of the railway age, Charles Edward Mudie established in 1842 what was to become a nation-wide network of subscription libraries, and later the firm of W H Smith followed suit. The early twentieth century saw the establishment of Boots' 'Booklovers Library', the Time Book Club in London, and libraries in a number of department stores such as Harrods. In addition to these commercial circulating libraries, there were in most of the large provincial towns what can best be called 'proprietary subscription libraries', which maintained a permanent stock: these also date from the eighteenth century. The London Library was founded in 1841—a library which for intellectual workers, particularly writers, has provided a service which cannot be equalled by public libraries. It is perhaps for this reason that, in spite of continuing financial difficulties, the London Library alone remains the best known of these ventures. The others have mostly closed down (W H Smith's in 1961, Boots' in 1965, Mudie's in 1937), and the changed twentieth century role of public libraries towards providing a better service for middle class readers is undoubtedly one of the main reasons.

There were undoubtedly economic factors as well. As far as public libraries are concerned, readers who formerly used subscription libraries have increased the demand for certain types of 'middlebrow' literature, and placed a heavier burden on reservation or request systems. These are the kinds of people who arrive in the library on Monday mornings with a list of requests compiled from the review columns of the Sunday papers. This demand has been called 'best-seller pressure', and by some librarians condemned—a curious professional example of the puritanic attitude. The point is worth stressing, because students of librarianship commonly suppose that the subscription libraries simply dispensed light literature, and presume that their demise has transferred the light fiction 'problem' to the public libraries; if this is really a problem, it is one which has always been there. It is true, but only partly relevant, that subscription libraries did provide light novels, and there are still small stationers who run a 'library' service wholly devoted to this kind of literature. What is relevant, perhaps, is that public librarians can no longer employ the argument that those who require light fiction should go to the subscription libraries. Otherwise, the main impact of this situation has been the need to increase the number of copies purchased of books which are currently news. (Some librarians deal with the demand by not reserving new books at all.)

BOOK CLUBS
In the United States, book clubs offering cut price editions of selected titles to a subscribing membership represent a large trade outlet.

Because of quasi-legal agreements concerning the sale of new books in club editions, book clubs in the UK have hitherto been of lesser importance. In 1968, however, the discovery of a technical loophole, and subsequent hasty ratification of it by the trade, made it possible to publish new books simultaneously in trade and book club editions. An increase in this type of publishing seems likely.

JOINT WORKING PARTY

After a conference initiated by the North-Western Polytechnic School of Librarianship in 1965, a Working Party for Library and Book Trade Relations was set up, with Peter Wright, then lecturer at the school, as chairman. The working party was concerned about the fact that, although librarians and members of the book trade have common aims, their attitudes and their methods are frequently in conflict. This was an *ad hoc* informal body which was interested in practical results, and its most important achievement so far has been the introduction in 1968 of PICS, the Publishers' Information Card Service.

This project is a commercial undertaking, with editorial services supplied by Whitaker's, the bibliographical publishing firm. Essentially the scheme provides a centralised information service about new books, with the information presented on standard cards designed eventually to replace much of the diverse publicity material which individual publishers circulate. The service is free to receiving libraries, and the publishers pay £10 for each title for which they wish to have a card printed. The cards are, as far as possible, advance notices of publication compiled from information supplied by the publishers. The information given includes not only the title but scope, contents, readership, a note on the author and the standard book number. The administrative and practical advantages of this service, both for librarians and publishers, are readily apparent; booksellers could also find uses for the cards. As G R Davies points out (*Library Association record,* January 1969, p 8), the book trade had not sufficiently realised that, although forceful publicity may be an appropriate means of promoting sales to private individuals, it is not helpful to librarians. In addition, publicity material is issued at random times in all shapes and sizes, from hundreds of publishers, and it cannot rely on individual attention from librarians. It represents in many cases the production of expensive material destined straight for the wastepaper basket. Davies also notes that the production of PIC cards by publishers themselves is not a practical proposition; a centralised system is required, and in fact costs each participating publisher less than if it were to be done by himself.

At a trade conference in 1969 it was announced that seventy publishing firms were then using the service, and general satisfaction with the working of it was expressed by librarians and publishers. It should be added that, although the usual book trade bibliographical services list all new material, these listings are not (at least in the UK at the time of writing) in advance of publication, and there is, of course, no explanatory information about the book beyond the basic bibliographical details.

STANDARD BOOK NUMBERS

During the early sixties, some publishers introduced computer systems into the accounting and distribution sides of their organisations, and it soon became apparent that the uncoordinated adoption of internal book numbering systems for computer processing, not only by publishers, but also by wholesalers and large bookselling firms, would seriously impede any general trade improvements in distribution to be brought about by computerisation. In consequence, following an investigation by Professor F G Foster, the Publishers Association, in co-operation with the British National Bibliography and J Whitaker & Sons, introduced a scheme for the standard numbering of book titles. Under this scheme all books in print and all books published in future in Britain will be assigned a nine digit code number, which comprises a publisher prefix, a title code, and a check digit. The numbers are recorded at the Central Standard Book Numbering Agency, and it is expected that they will be included in a new Whitaker's list of *Forthcoming books*. The numbers will also be included in the existing Whitaker's lists, and the *British national bibliography*, although they will not, in the first instance, replace the present BNB numbering system.

It is intended that the scheme will become international, and the British Standards Institution is acting as agent for the allocation of numbers for foreign countries. The library applications of the scheme have not yet been fully worked out.

PUBLIC LENDING RIGHT

The long standing discussion on the establishment of a public lending right for authors represents one area where the book trade and librarians have not agreed. Just as a composer or a dramatist receives payment under performing rights legislation whenever his work is performed in public, so authors have sought to establish their right to an analogous public lending right, by which they would receive a payment when books are borrowed by public library readers. There have been a variety of different proposals since 1951, when John Brophy first suggested that for every loan of a public library book its author should receive one penny. These have included the similar proposals incorporated in a Society of Authors' pamphlet *Critical times for authors* (1953), and a memorandum drawn up by A P Herbert under the auspices of a special committee of the Authors' and Publishers' Lending Rights Association. This memorandum, published in 1960, surveyed the practical difficulties of setting up a workable scheme, and noted the objections of librarians. It recommended that a Bill should be presented to parliament, to amend the Copyright Act of 1956 for the establishment of PLR under the aegis of the (then) Ministry of Education. In 1960, Woodrow Wyatt presented the first PLR Bill to the House of Commons. This was based on the penny-per-issue principle, but the government would not support the proposals, and it was decided to abandon any attempt to relate PLR to copyright legislation. A second Bill was drafted, and presented by William Teeling, but the opposition remained too strong and it was duly 'talked out' —in November 1960, and again in March 1961. Meanwhile, the Library Association had expressed total opposition to the scheme, which this time proposed that the library authorities should be allowed an option to charge borrowers. Following this second failure, the campaign continued, and included a motion in the House of Commons (1961) and a booklet by A P Herbert called *Libraries : free for all?*. This last suggested that public libraries should make a maximum annual charge to registered readers of 7s 6d per head. There was also an attempt, which failed, to introduce an amendment to the Public Libraries Bill of 1964.

Further impetus was given to the campaign by the publication in 1965 of the government white paper, 'A policy for the arts', produced by Miss Jennie Lee, minister with the responsibility for the arts. She subsequently showed herself sympathetic to the idea of PLR, but rejected any proposals which invalidated the concept of the 'free' public library. In principle she found Scandinavian practice more acceptable, since these schemes do not involve payment by public library users. (The Swedish scheme is based on books *issued*, while the Danish one is related to *stocks* held.)

The next stage was the setting up in 1965 of a working party by the Arts Council of Great Britain, to consider all aspects of PLR. The initiative thus finally passed out of the hands of the Authors' and Publishers' Lending Right Association (APLA), which had sustained the campaign for six years. During the period it had become evident that proposals which involved payment by the public or by the local authorities could not gain acceptance. This working party sent their report to the Department of Education and Science in 1967, and the scheme which it proposes involves a grant from central government funds, on the basis of fifteen percent of the annual sum spent on books by library authorities. The amount available would then be divided, with seventy five percent going to authors and twenty five percent to publishers (previous proposals have not always included the publishers). The use by libraries would be calculated, not on any figures for the number of times a book is borrowed, but on *stocks held*. To obtain the required information, three representative library authorities would each year be sent a list of all books in copyright, and they would send in a return showing how many of these books were in stock. In the words of a Society of Authors leaflet, the PLR committee to be set up by the Department of Education and Science to run the scheme would then ' gross up these sample returns in the ratio they bore to the total stock of all library authorities in the country '. The leaflet claims that Danish experience suggests that this might yield approximately 10d a book, ' so that, on 2,000 copies of a single title held by public libraries throughout the country, an author would receive £85 a year '. It will be apparent that the scheme is strongly based on the Danish principle.

During 1969, several statements were made by government spokesmen indicating that there was official sympathy for the Arts Council scheme, but that, in the words of Baroness Phillips, ' the government tend to have an open mind but a closed purse '. Later, in reply to a parliamentary question, Miss Jennie Lee, the minister responsible, said that there were alternative proposals to be considered, and that a working party would be set up. It therefore appears that there will be yet another working party report before a solution is found, but the present evidence suggests that eventually some form of PLR will emerge.

There is no need to summarise here the arguments for and against PLR, for during the controversy they have been constantly repeated. Certain comments, however, are called for. What must strike any impartial observer is that this campaign has taken eighteen years to come anywhere near the possibility of a successful conclusion, and one reason for this has been the total lack of co-operation between the Library Association on one hand, and the bodies representing the authors on the other. (Publishers have been sympathetic to the idea, and have, naturally, pressed their own claims.) Many of the earliest proposals, which were impractical both from an administrative and political point of view, might not have been pursued for so long if librarians had shown themselves at once to be more sympathetic or co-operative to the principle. At no time has the organised profession admitted that the authors have any kind of a case, and some of the statements by individual librarians published in the press have betrayed an almost paranoiac antipathy towards writers, for reasons which it would be uncharitable to pursue. The Library Association did at one time meet representatives of APLA (1962), but this has been the limit of professional concern. (The LA stated that it could not accept representation on the 1965 PLR working party because the local authority associations were not represented. In January 1968 the Association of Municipal Corporations announced their unqualified opposition to any PLR scheme, particularly if publishers were to be, in their words, 'subsidized'.)

As a footnote to this topic, and an illustration of the law of rising expectation, it is interesting that on April 30 1969, 500 Swedish authors invaded the central libraries of four major cities in Sweden and removed twenty tons of literature from the shelves, which were left empty: the books were returned the next day. This was a protest action, organised by the Swedish Authors' Association, demanding that authors should receive 4d for every book borrowed, instead of ½d as at present.

THE NET BOOK AGREEMENT
The Net Book Agreement, which allows publishers to establish and maintain the prices at which their new books may be sold, has survived a fair amount of hostile criticism, as well as an investigation in 1962 by the Restrictive Practices Court, which gave judgment in its favour. Public libraries therefore continue to purchase books at the ten percent discount provided for under the Library Licence Agreement, which was revised by the Publishers Association in 1964. The court concluded that, in general, public libraries would not benefit from the abrogation of the Net Book Agreement. Nevertheless, in view of the

continued rise in book prices, many librarians have claimed that the ten percent discount off publishers' prices is insufficient. Some publishers also criticise the Net Book Agreement on the ground that it serves to subsidise inefficient booksellers.

PAPERBACKS IN LIBRARIES

Paperback publishers, particularly Penguin Books, attempted for some years to prevent libraries making arrangements with bookbinding firms to bind or reinforce paperback bindings before they are used in libraries, both public and institutional. This practice, it was alleged, undermined the sale of hardback editions, and reduced the royalties paid to authors, since the libraries were in effect paying for the specially bound books a higher price than the published one. Legal enforcements were sought and some paperback publishers refused to supply their books to the library binders. From the library point of view this state of affairs was clearly unsatisfactory, and Penguins since 1967 have instead experimented with special ' library editions ' which are hardback bound and thread-sewn.

Clearly this is not the end of the matter, and the question must continue to arise. If hardback editions are in future to be produced mainly for the library market, what effect will this have on book publishing? It would appear that many librarians may have to change their present attitudes towards the paperback as a suitable form for library provision. On the continent of Europe, the traditional paper covered book has had to be absorbed by libraries, and in many countries the paperback ' revolution ' never took place. Paperback editions are now provided by libraries, but they are thought of as an extra type of provision rather than the norm. Increasingly, many works will be avaliable only in paperback editions, and libraries will have to adjust their provision to provide for them. This may mean that library book provision will become more expensive, since paperbacks will have to be replaced frequently (assuming that they are likely to be kept in print), or specially provided with hard covers. Both methods will be necessary.

NOTES
1 Marshall A Best, ' In books, they call it revolution ' (*Daedalus*, Winter, 1963) analyses the paperback situation in the United States. He notes that the lower prices of paperbacks are possible not because of the binding—not even mainly from the larger quantities printed, but because of :
 1 The saving in the heavy cost of typesetting and platemaking.

2 The saving in editorial expenses, *eg* ' the cost of finding new authors, nursing and sometimes financing them, guiding the manuscript through the hands of the printer '.

3 The saving in the cost of launching and advertising a new book: this is a major factor.

4 The reduced cost of author's royalties.

These points are quoted because they help to explain why *original* paperback publishing is unlikely to take over completely. The library market is the other important factor.

2 As an antidote to this somewhat misleading reference the reader is referred to ' The bookshop in America ' by Edward Shils (*Daedalus, op cit*). He asserts that the condition of the book trade in the United States is wholly unsatisfactory and is getting worse. In the future it seems probable that ' Good bookshops will be scarcer than hens teeth, and countless youths, middle aged, and aged idlers will have to live without the harmless and permanently enriching experience of a good browse '.

3 In recent years the Booksellers Association has introduced a ' Charter bookselling scheme ' under which publishers have agreed to offer better discount terms to booksellers who send their staff to the association's training courses, have at least a specified minimum number of books in stock, and can provide certain bibliographical tools to answer customers' enquiries. Whether this scheme will produce the required results remains to be seen.

The Industrial Training Act of 1968 also could have a beneficial impact on the book trade (even though there has been some opposition), since its purpose is to extend vocational training programmes.

8

the use of education

PURPOSE: This chapter is concerned with higher education in Britain. This is a field where the challenges of technological society have been met by a response which is massive indeed, but so confused that most laymen have long since ceased to understand the 'system' at all. Since, as the Robbins report pointed out, there is no system, this is scarcely surprising. The cultural time lags which abound in our society include large areas of education, which is to be expected, for education, like librarianship, is partly concerned with preserving the culture of the past.

Educational patterns have, naturally, always been based on (or, more correctly, associated with) certain declared or undeclared aims or purposes, and the emphasis has shifted from one to the other as times have changed and in response to different social demands. It is probably true to say that in all education systems at least four basic aims can be found. First, education prepares the individual for his place in society (social adjustment); second, it provides him with practical skills (the world of work); third, he may acquire some system of beliefs or values or some coherent attitude to life (the world of ideology). In addition to these largely social purposes and often in conflict with them, there are those educational aims which concentrate on the development of the individual in so far as he is considered as a unique or separate personality. In pursuit of these aims psychological conditioning or training is undertaken, and certain qualities are developed according to the type of society or of groups within it. Such qualities include 'character', the ability to judge or discriminate, aesthetic sensibility, the capacity to think logically and so on. These abilities, whether they are regarded as innate or not, can be trained irrespective of the 'subjects' taught, and they are largely a product of teaching *methods*, so that the education problem is not only what should be taught but how. The answer to this problem, it might be thought, is to be found in 'philosophies' of education, but since education is not autonomous, the term has little meaning, except as part of some larger view of the world.

In the culture of today, at least in Britain and other liberal societies, there is no such commonly accepted view, so that educationists find it difficult to formulate educational aims, or else they evade the issue altogether, or present a limited theory which is rapidly proved false. Many educational patterns produce 'lopsided' individuals because they have concentrated too exclusively on some of the aims or some of the human qualities mentioned above. The obvious example is the British public school system of the past, which produced several generations of 'leisure class' Englishmen who never grew up at all. When systems of this kind cripple a balanced individual development there are reactions against them, such as the progressive movement in education associated with A S Neill and others in the past, or the anti-university movement today. These non-systems of anti-education are bound to fail in one sense because they ignore some of the social requirements mentioned above. For example, people who have been to 'prog' schools are often totally unfitted for life outside the school. It may well be that the world outside is in dire need of reform or revolution, but this is not the point here.

The various official reports which are milestones in the history of education in Britain abound in partial or temporary theories of the kind under discussion: these theories are mostly a reflection of social pressures within societies and, particularly, of differences caused by social class. The Hadow report of 1926, for instance, claimed that 'subject mindedness' is a psychological urge which begins at the age of eleven—and as an apparent result of this theory the present selective secondary school was set up. In fact, a passage in this report may be taken as indicative of the extraordinary statements which have been made: 'There is a tide which begins to rise in the veins of youth at the age of eleven or twelve. It is called by the name adolescence. If that tide is taken at the flood. . . . We therefore propose . . . etc.' The Crowther report of 1959 justified the intensive specialisation, which characterises sixth form work in English secondary schools, by similar arguments about the importance of early specialisation, but the report does not attempt much of a theoretical justification. The Robbins report on higher education of 1963, from which all present blessings flow, evaded the theoretical problem in its perfunctory section on the aims of higher education, which simply discusses functions.

Many critics have considered that the principal weakness of the recommendations of the report was that they accepted the ' system ' as it was and simply recommended more of the same.

In view of the poverty of these philosophies the layman may be forgiven for imagining quite different purposes of his own—such as the passing of examinations. Alternatively, other cynics have pointed out that in modern industrial countries young people are not required to work, and therefore the only purpose of education which can be identified is that they should be shut up in schools and colleges to keep them out of the way—and if this is not done hordes of teenagers will totally disrupt social life. (Parents commonly send their children to Sunday School for the same reason.) This may be defined as the custodial function of the school, which can be compared to the custodial function of libraries. Young people, like books, must be preserved for the future.

THE PRESENT PATTERN AND CURRENT TRENDS

STUDENT POWER: As we have seen, one of the traditional functions of the educator is that he should preserve traditions. This role is now being modified or reduced because traditions are nullified by the rapidity of change, and the teacher finds that he no longer has any cultural heritage to pass on, or any system of values or beliefs to impart. He is expected to concentrate on more limited objectives, in spite of the fact that the structure within which he works was intended for more authoritarian purposes. The current leaders of opinion for the young are usually not teachers, since it is impossible for a teacher to be a ' trend setter ' (one of the slogans of the students in revolt at Berkeley University was ' trust nobody over thirty '). There is no sign that the trend towards a concentration on trends can be reversed, and it must be regarded as an inevitable feature of the modern cultural pattern. The meaning of both the past and the future, as they were formerly understood, has become devalued and it is the present instant which is significant. For this and other reasons, the focus in education is shifting towards the student himself, and it is happening that the fourth of the aims noted above (the development of the individual) is increasingly clashing with the demands of the state, or of employers, or with the advancement of knowledge (research). From this point of view (one which the students themselves adopt) it becomes apparent that what is wrong with their universities cannot be put right without reference to the social structure as a whole. This was most evident in the French student rebellion of 1968. Yet in France, and subsequently in the United States and elsewhere (for example, Pakistan), it has emerged that student political movements are producing changes within the universities, but so far have had no constructive impact on society as a whole. Instead they tend to produce a dangerous backlash led by people who wish to preserve both the best and the worst of an older tradition.

TYRANNY OF SUBJECTS

The stress on ' subjects ' was and is an essential part of the traditional academic structure. 'Academic' education involves an intensive study of one subject and conflicts with the ideal of liberal studies, which implies a general education over broad fields, preferably including both science and the humanities. The universities which developed in the late Victorian era and in the early twentieth century maintained this subject orientation, but the eight new universities set up since the second world war have all tried by different routes and in varying degrees to escape from it. Sussex, for instance, is organised in broad schools rather than in specialised departments. Courses include concentrated work in one school and mandatory work in others. Lancaster has created ' Boards of Studies' in addition to the usual academic departments, and allows students to study in at least three fields during the first year of the degree course. The system at the first of the new universities, Keele (1950), consists of a four year undergraduate course with a first year programme of very broad studies. These experiments (particularly the one at Keele) have not been generally accepted as satisfactory but the attempt to achieve a broader education is being made. The first vice-chancellor of Sussex defined the aim as ' the need for disciplined study in depth and the . . . need for the major study to be set within the context of related subjects '. These departures were possible because, unlike their redbrick predecessors or the colleges of advanced technology, these new universities started from scratch as fully-fledged universities.

It is this academic subject tradition at the universities which is largely responsible for the much criticised early specialisation in the sixth form of secondary schools in England and Wales (but not in Scotland, where the universities have always required study on a broader front). This unique specialisation at an early age is, of course, one of the reasons for the two culture divergence.

All the indications are that the move towards a higher education with a broader base will continue as it has elsewhere in Europe, notably in Sweden. Owing to the different social structure and smaller financial resources, this need not follow the same pattern as in the United States, but it will undoubtedly be a move in their direction. There are various possibilities. A D C Peterson in *The future of education* foresees a system of secondary education to end at seventeen years of age, to be followed by a variety of two-year colleges, all of which would give a general education. After this a proportion would continue to university for more advanced studies and the remainder would enter adult working life.

Some alternative schemes are already in existence, notably, the sixth form colleges which students may enter from secondary schools after they have passed the *O* level examination, or even before. About thirty local authorities have either established these colleges or have plans to do so. These are not designed to change the emphasis on early specialisation as yet, but they will represent a new developing pattern. More relevant to the point is the current discussion typified by the 1968 government publication called *Science policy studies no 3* by M C McCarthy. This points out the fact that, whereas in the USA the education system for science and technology produces seventy percent 'generalists' and thirty percent specialists, the corresponding figures for Britain are fifteen percent generalists and eighty five percent specialists. It is suggested that Britain is producing three times the number of specialist graduates she needs. There are many factors which modify the force of this comparison, but a number of proposals have been made to change the proportions. Writing in *Nature*, Professor A B Pippard advocates a two year science degree course for the many, and a four year degree course for the few. He notes that ' The rigid three year course and the tradition of deep learning for the intellectual élite constrain secondary and university science into a strait jacket of specialism which is increasingly seen . . . as menacing our future development, industrial and social '.

In conclusion one may note that although the ideal of combining breadth as a foundation with depth of study later on is generally accepted, it is difficult, certainly for the layman, to assess how success-ful some of these 'experiments' have been. In view of the opinions expressed in chapter 1 about the differences between the sciences and the humanities, it seems reasonable to suppose that those founda-tion courses which embrace several unrelated subjects both from the arts and the sciences are likely to be of limited value and are ultimately educationally unsound. The concept of 'the generalist', so popular in the United States, can easily lead to the required learning of chunks of knowledge from different areas side by side. In such a process the 'subjects' do not relate, and in the last resort it is only the relationship which counts. Such knowledge, if acquired at all, is useless to the state and either distressing or irrelevant to the individual. (It may well be that the 'credit' system encourages this approach.)

THE TRADITION OF THE ELITE

Related to the problem of specialisation is the tradition of providing higher education only to the few. This tradition is now being drastically modified, but the proportion of students who receive higher education is still small compared with the USA. It is reliably estimated that for the year 1970 the proportion of the age group entering universities will be six percent, compared with over forty percent in America. (These figures of course exaggerate the differences, as the systems are quite different.) The British structure in the past reflected the needs of a class society, and even when later modified to provide for merit, it is still based on the idea that higher education should be available to all who can benefit from it—and not that it should be available (at least in some form) for all. It would appear that the Robbins report[1] seriously underestimated the future *demand* for higher education, in spite of the revolutionary nature of its proposals. It seems likely that the future will see a rapid growth of various institutions of tertiary education which are not universities of the traditional kind.[2]

Such institutions may stress vocational or liberal education rather than academic education in the narrow sense. Indeed, this sector of the education system has already vastly expanded. Developments include the creation since 1963 of ten colleges of advanced technology which have full university status (the CATs are at Battersea, Brunel, Chelsea, Northampton, Birmingham, Bradford, Bristol, Cardiff, Loughborough and Stafford). Also, technological and vocational work has been expanded within the universities, for example, at the Imperial College of Science and Technology. Another significant development is the award of degrees by the Council for National Academic Awards set up in 1964. Courses for these degrees are run in a variety of technical and commercial colleges. Finally, a government white paper of 1966 proposed to incorporate sixty or more colleges of technology, building, art and commerce into thirty new polytechnics. All these establishments will provide degrees and they are, in fact, university type institutions. But the universities continue to have their own exclusive characteristics: they have an independent legal existence, which is financed by the University Grants Committee: they concentrate exclusively on full time studies for their own degrees, and they support professors. In view of these differences and the increasing number of students who fail to reach existing university entrance requirements, it seems likely that this type of higher education will continue to expand. Apart from the CATs, these colleges have been divided into twenty five regional colleges, national colleges for specialised industries, and some 500 area and local colleges. In addition, there are art colleges and agricultural institutions and about 7,000 evening Institutes. In accepting the exclusive nature of the universities, the Robbins committee also left out of their orbit the colleges of education, which provide qualifications for teachers. It remains true that both the colleges of education and the various other types of colleges for higher education have not achieved the status of universities and show no signs of doing so.

This summary has been made to indicate how the increase in the *quantity* of higher education (*ie* the much larger numbers involved) is creating problems which methods based on an élitist tradition cannot solve. At the centre of these contradictions is the relationship of teaching to research. Traditionally, although research was considered to be paramount, it was recognised that the two activities were interdependent and inseparable. In practice the needs of undergraduates were often neglected, and much that passed for ' research ' was and is of dubious value. The word is used so that it covers all kinds of activities, including the collection of worms in primary schools. The importance of true research remains, and the rate of change so much emphasised in these chapters must result in an increase in research and probably a change in its nature. What have been deservedly condemned are teaching methods which no longer teach, ' research ' policies which are not research, and a lack of integration between the two.

NEW SKILLS AND MORE LEISURE

Another notable consequence of the rapidity of change, we are told, is that the subject content of everybody's formal education will become out of date within a decade or less, and the same applies to training in technical skills. People will be less likely to stay in the same type of work all their lives, and re-training courses will be essential. It appears that we shall all have to go back to school again at regular intervals. Furthermore, there will be a need to educate citizens for the use of leisure as well as for work, and this again brings in the importance of liberal studies.

METHODS

There can be no doubt that the use of television, videotape and other audio-visual techniques will have a decisive effect on traditional teaching methods at all levels. Programmed learning, with or without machines, has already proved its superiority over earlier teaching techniques in many fields. Most courses of all kinds no longer rely on the lecture form alone, and it will come to be regarded as one possible technique among others, or as a technique to use in conjunction with other procedures. It is, after all, a medieval survival. These other possibilities include the use of team teaching, which is so far mainly an American development and involves the use of auxiliaries as teaching assistants. The programmes which are carried out by teams may, for example, consist of about forty percent of large group instruction or 'mass lectures', twenty percent of small group lecture discussion with classes of twelve to fifteen, and forty percent of individual study supervised by teaching assistants. This can be seen as an attempt to incorporate the well known advantages of the 'Oxbridge' individual tutorial system into a mass education structure.

EXAMINATIONS

The role of examinations in education may be one method or means which could have been noted in the previous section, were it not for the fact that in most systems examinations have become entrenched as an end in themselves. In 1935 Hartog and Rhodes in their work *An examination of examinations* reported on the unreliability and unfairness of the examination system in a school certificate context. They proved their point, but it has always been possible to show that these anomalies arose because there was a number of different examining boards, and that this did not necessarily dispose of the examining process itself. Beyond this the critics have been asked to produce a realistic alternative, which it is assumed cannot be found. The feeling has been that without examinations educational incentives would disappear and human laziness would come into its own. These assumptions about the nature of the educational process are now in question precisely because they are assumptions.

The emphasis on the examination as the *sine qua non* of higher education is part of the élitist or competitive view, and probably remains because of pressures from outside the education structure. It would seem, therefore, that the method is unlikely to be abolished in the immediate future, and in some areas, for example, for university entrance purposes the reliance on examinations may even increase.[3] Even so there will be many courses leading to a degree or a professional qualification where alternative and less artificial methods will be developed. From a social and economic point of view it is obviously extremely wasteful that every year as many as fifteen percent of university students drop out of courses through examination failure, and few would claim that this arbitrary process serves any useful purpose, particularly when the students have already been screened by examination at school certificate A level. One desirable modification is a liberalisation of the examining process itself, so that the element of memory testing is reduced. Most examinations do not test whether an individual has benefited from a course, but simply whether he is good at passing examinations.

Some talented people never learn the techniques. One possibility is the ' open book ' examination, which allows students to use text or reference books in the examination room, or alternatively students may be given time to produce answers so that the artificial test at one time and in one place can be eliminated. None of these suggestions are new, but the ' system ' has been slow to incorporate them. There will also be much greater use of supplementary or alternative methods of assessment, such as evaluation of course work and the use of objective tests where appropriate. The case against examinations rests firmly on the arguments first, that they do not always test ability, second, that their existence distorts and disturbs the educational process, and third, that the failure rate causes a pointless wastage of human potential.

EDUCATION FOR LIBRARIANSHIP
I have chosen to discuss professional education here because recent changes cannot be understood without reference to the general expan-

sion of higher education of which it forms a part. Recent growth has been a response to new pressures and, in particular, to the demands of a larger student population. The labour force in libraries has doubtless expanded, but the increase in numbers and size of the library schools is not due in the first instance to pressure from the employing authorities, or indeed from the library profession at all. Recruitment direct from secondary schools and universities has been an important element in this process.

POST WAR FOUNDATIONS

After the second world war, nine library schools were set up in technical and commercial colleges and conducted courses for the Library Association examinations. It is probably safe to claim that they would not have come into existence had it not been for the need to provide educational opportunities for those who had been away in the war. So it was that almost by accident the old apprenticeship system, which had been taken for granted so long, was gradually abandoned and the proportion of part time students slowly declined.

During these early years of full time library education, the attitude of the profession towards educational matters (insofar as such a thing can be postulated) changed very slowly and most librarians probably still thought in terms of the Library Association Charter, which required the association ' to hold examinations in librarianship and to issue certificates of efficiency ', but made no reference to education for librarianship as such. In retrospect it seems extraordinary that this policy could have gone without question for half a century, but it seemed only natural, for example, in the thirties, when governments were more concerned with the problem of mass unemployed than with providing increased opportunities for higher education. At first, then, the courses run by the schools were regarded simply as one convenient device amongst others to enable recruits to the profession to pass the Library Association examinations. During the first decade, lecturers in librarianship were struggling with problems arising from the external system, which separated examinations from teaching, and where examiners regularly set questions which the teachers regarded as educationally inappropriate. The examiners for their part were anxious to maintain a practical approach. In consequence much time and energy were wasted in Library Association and other committees trying to resolve conflicts about examination policy, and on futile post mortems on individual questions. It is arguable that the years of dialogue between the schools and the Library Association did help to produce the change of opinion which made the later transition to a different system possible. The foundations during this period were laid, and one fortunate factor was that in most cases those who were in charge of the schools were able and energetic people whose horizons had been extended by war time service. Throughout this consolidating period there was no spectacular increase in the number of students, nor in the size of the schools, and it was frequently urged that these should be fewer and larger.

CURRENT EXPANSION

In 1960 there were 300 full time students in the library schools and it was from about this time that the expansion took place. (The Robbins report was published in 1963.) By 1968 the number of students had risen to approximately 2,800, which represents almost a tenfold increase in eight years. At the same time the number of institutions offering courses in librarianship had increased from ten to fifteen. In the post-Robbins era there was the same proliferation of degree and postgraduate courses that took place in other fields. For students who contemplate studying librarianship, it is now possible to take courses leading to any of the following qualifications. (Any attempt to provide an accurate list would become almost immediately out of date.)

1 A two year non-graduate course in twelve of the existing colleges, leading to the Associateship of the Library Association. This can be followed by an FLA which will be obtained by thesis only. Several of the schools are now examining for part one of this ALA course, and a smaller number are examining or about to examine for part two.

2 A one year course for the post graduate diploma of the Library Association, offered by most of the colleges. This is also about to be approved by the Library Association as an internal examination in some of the schools.

3 Diplomas are also offered by several of the university schools (Sheffield, University College London, Aberystwyth, Belfast). These are postgraduate, except at Belfast, which is a one year course for graduates and two years for non-graduates. The North Western Polytechnic school is about to offer a course leading to the University College London diploma.

4 There was at Liverpool College of Commerce a three year course, a 'sandwich course', leading to the ALA, but this is now being abandoned.

5 Courses combining academic and professional subjects leading to a first degree (University of Strathclyde, four years for a BA: University College of Wales, Aberystwyth, three years for a BLS: University of Technology, Loughborough, three years for a BSC). In each case the pattern is different.

6 Council of National Academic Awards first degree courses are available at Birmingham (BA), Leeds (BA or BSC), Newcastle (BSC), and at North-Western Polytechnic (BA). These are either three year or four year courses.

7 Higher degrees, ie MA, MPhil or PhD, are being offered by London, Belfast, Loughborough and Aberystwyth. These follow either a course plus examination, or a thesis, or a combination of both.

IMPLICATIONS FOR PROFESSIONAL EDUCATION
THE CURRENT CHALLENGE: The changes indicated above are so considerable that new problems have emerged and new solutions will be necessary. Some of these are as follows:

1 Educational problems caused by a relatively large number of students.

2 The relation of theoretical courses to practical experience. This was always a difficult matter, but the problem is now more urgent because a high proportion of students come to the professional course straight from secondary school or university, with no previous library experience. The schools in consequence are becoming recruiting agencies for the profession.

3 The changing role of the Library Association which no longer controls all the qualification channels.[4]

4 In common with other fields of higher education there is the need to develop new educational methods.

5 Difficulties may arise in future because of the diversity of qualifications (eg with regard to ' equation ').

6 Technological and other changes need to be responded to by regular revision of the contents of syllabi, and by a new balance of subjects. At the time of writing the Library Association syllabus is under revision.

7 The increased importance of programmes and courses to re-educate senior or experienced members of the profession who qualified in former times which must now be regarded as prehistoric.

It is significant that little attention has been paid to these problems in the professional literature, and it is not difficult to appreciate why. In the first place the education agencies involved in this expansion have been so heavily engaged that there has not been time for theoretical discussion. Secondly, many of the developments are so recent that it is not yet clear what all the implications are. Thirdly, an important factor is that the drives or pressures which generated the new patterns have not come from within the profession or even from the schools. The movement is a national one, and the universities and colleges are responding as best they can to the new challenge. Nobody has disputed that a higher educational standard is required, or that librarianship, if it is not to get left behind, must eventually become a graduate profession.

What could be in dispute (if anyone had time, or considered it a useful exercise to make it) is the *form* which some of the new courses have taken and the direction in which they may be leading. I am not suggesting that the new goals are necessarily wrong or unsatisfactory, but simply that we do not know what they are. I started this chapter by noting the aims of education, and there is a danger that these may become so confused that the entire system will be no more than a self perpetuating *process*. It is generally recognised that a crisis does exist in higher education, and professional education is also involved, although not to the same extent. The new degree courses are a case in point: they have come about not because anyone believes that a degree course of mixed professional and academic subjects has any intrinsic merits but for the very good reason that they became politically possible and the demand was there. Such courses have long been abandoned in the United States (although there have been signs of a revival of interest recently), and they can be regarded as appropriate to a certain stage of professional development or necessary when staff shortages exist. They may also in some cases be suitable for the needs of developing countries. Whether this is a desirable pattern in Britain from an *educational* point of view remains to be seen. Such courses are open to the objection that there can be only a limited amount of integration. The 'subjects' are different, not only in the usual sense, but also because some are vocational and the others are not. The result can be a hotch-potch which is an unsatisfactory experience for the student. From the career point of view, a first degree of this kind is likely to equate unfavourably with a second degree qualification. (The term 'postgraduate', although commonly used in Britain, is strictly speaking a misnomer, and a postgraduate situation is reached only in death.) Similarly, strong objections can be raised against one year courses leading to an MA by examination. They have been introduced solely because precedents for this type of MA qualification exist in other fields.

Having noted this alleged lack of direction, it is only fair to add, firstly, that such criticisms can only be made because the new challenges *have* been met by positive action and, secondly, that there is safety in diversity—and room for welcome experiments—and the opportunity for improvement remains. At such a time of transition the student becomes a guinea pig, it is true, but it is a noble cause—and guinea pigs are happy creatures.

Since the quantity of education has grown so dramatically it should now be possible to concentrate more on quality. It now seems (1968) that the increase in the number of students is halted, and this should provide opportunities to consider improvements in teaching methods in accordance with modern educational requirements. If this is not done, in Kinglsey Amis's notorious words, more will inevitably mean less. In many institutions educational methods are being reconsidered with a view to reducing the dominance of the lecture and of examinations. The alternatives are familiar and were mentioned above with reference to higher education generally.

THE RELATION WITH PRACTICE

Technical or vocational or professional education has been faced with the task of evolving an approach which on the one hand escaped from the factual minutiae which are required in practical training, and on the other does not become confused with what used to be called academic education. In earlier years in Britain there was for a long time a failure to emerge from a factual descriptive method, while more recently the search for 'principles', which are rightly regarded as necessary, has led to a straining after 'academic' standards, which are irrelevant. If there are still those who ask the question whether librarianship is an academic subject in the traditional sense, the answer to them must surely be firmly in the negative. The problem is not to create an academic discipline, but to evolve a type of education which relates to practice.

The same problems exist in other fields, which are concerned with the applications of 'pure' knowledge, notably in the education of

136

teachers. Since the four year degree course for teachers was introduced, persistent dissatisfaction has been expressed on several counts, not the least of which has concerned the methods of practical training. Library education is now, even more than in the past, faced with this problem, which admits of no wholly satisfactory solution.

If we are considering vocational education, another goal must be added to the aims or purposes of education mentioned above. The extra requirement is to establish a satisfactory working relationship with the general practitioners in the field or on the ground, or, in our case, within the library walls. If this is not done, a tiresome split develops between the libraries and the agencies which provide professional education for their staff. The possibility is always there and has fortunately, so far, been more of a danger in the United States than in Britain.

I could deal with this by enumerating the various possible approaches to the ultimate working situation which students will encounter, but since these are sufficiently obvious, I refer here only to two matters which are less discussed. The first is that the attitudes of librarians to the educational agencies may be largely influenced by the public relations techniques adopted by the schools. If these are excellent the librarians may feel that all is well, but it does not follow that student requirements are met. Most students find that their periods of practical work do help to give them a better perspective, but the benefits naturally vary according to their individual experience in different libraries. The teaching agencies can, within certain limits, organise and control the type of programme they will undertake, and (subject to the pressure of numbers) can select appropriate libraries. This may be partially successful wherever practical work is an integral part of a course, and in this context introductory courses are important. The same cannot always be said for practical work which is undertaken because colleges may require library experience before students are admitted to courses.

Visits and study tours are another matter. Naturally they can be of value if they are carefully organised, but many study tours, both in Britain and abroad, have suffered because the organisers have proceeded on the assumption that a succession of visits to libraries is both necessary for educational purposes and enjoyable for those who take part. Neither assumption is true, and some visits to libraries are a waste of everybody's time. A factor of increasing importance is that there are so many parties of visiting students that a severe burden is placed upon the host libraries, a burden they will welcome only if the visits are worthwhile. Finally, the value of these journeys should be considered only in relation to the heavy costs involved, and to the dislocation of teaching programmes, and to the interruption of vacations which could be used for more profitable purposes, both by students and staff.

The second matter concerns the teaching programme itself, with particular reference to library administration. Lecture courses in this subject have been consistently unsatisfactory, possibly because of basic fallacies in the approach. The difficulties are more apparent now that an increasing proportion of students have had no library experience, and hence have no practical or theoretical foundation on which to build. It thus becomes the responsibility of the schools to provide one, and new methods and a new programme are required. It is to be hoped that practising librarians and employing authorities will not expect students to have learnt how to construct estimates or run committees. It cannot be too often repeated that education can only be a preparation for practical experience, not a substitute for it. Training in a specific work situation is the responsibility of the employers and can come later. For the ' mature ' or experienced librarian in a position of responsibility it may well be valuable to attend courses of this kind, and he benefits in a like manner from attending meetings and conferences. Such courses can be and are run by library schools, but their purpose is quite different from that of a first course for students.

Another associated problem is that there usually is, or appears to be, a gap between ideas and ideals in library schools and the absence of these in many libraries. Because of the divergence it is alleged that students taking up employment suffer from cultural shock, and that librarians are afflicted with an extra exasperation. This undoubtedly happens and it is usually assumed that the gap is a necessary one that always exists between the ideal and the real. This is surely a false assumption. Courses in administration should be concerned not only with policies and aims and ideals, but also with the structures within which these goals must be achieved. ' Principles ' can only be applied in practice, but an educational programme should indicate what the practical context is. If this is not done, courses become abstract, lifeless and irrelevant. It is therefore a responsibility of the teaching agencies to prepare students for the type of challenge they may have to meet.

There are, of course, established procedures for this practical approach, including the use of case studies and even of lectures by practising librarians, although it must be admitted that as a rule the more eminent these are, the less value their contribution seems to have. The problem and its solution is familiar enough in management studies. It is also often noted that students who survive courses of librarianship emerge from college or university with an incomplete awareness that there are other things in heaven and earth besides librarianship. This again is said to produce confusion and surprise, and if it does happen, the reason can only be that courses are too narrow and insufficiently related to the world, or that students lack a background of general education.

DULLNESS IS ALL

It remains to mention one other affliction which characterises most librarianship courses. They tend to be thorough, earnest, solemn, worthy, unimaginative and profoundly dull. In this respect they resemble many teacher training programmes. Courses of this type continue not usually because of sadistic traits amongst lecturers, but because many students prefer them; they know where they are and it is more comfortable that way. In any case they take it for granted as a result of experience that this is what the education process is. It may be that there is no particular remedy, since it is impossible to make the gentle art of inflicting boredom a criminal offence. Imagination is not an acquired characteristic—and even when present can be suppressed.

Not to conclude on this flippant note, I should return at this point to the aims of education and to the need for liberalising technical education—a topic on which A N Whitehead seems to have said the last word: ' The antithesis between a technical and a liberal education is fallacious. There can be no adequate technical education which is not liberal and liberal education which is not technical: that is no education which does not impart both techniques and intellectual vision.' Or again, ' Imagination is not to be divorced from the facts: it is a way of illuminating the facts '. He then goes on to make his famous distinction between this imaginative acquisition of knowledge and the absorption of inert ideas. This, no doubt, in these days is commonplace, but it is frequently not acted upon.

The remedy may be sought in ensuring an understanding of the nature of the problem, and in the proper construction of courses and syllabi, but in the last resort it is to be found in the calibre of individual lecturers. This, however, should be qualified since educational planning must proceed on the assumption that almost anybody can teach, but that only a minority can teach well. Programmes can be organised which allow for this and there is no reason why some lecturers should ' lecture ' at all. Education is now a collective enterprise which requires a variety of abilities not usually found in a single person.

CONCLUSION

In this brief survey of some aspects of library education I have tried to consider the topic in relation to higher education generally. It is necessary to return to this background, because professional education cannot be successfully carried out if the general educational foundation is not there. This has always been a problem of fundamental importance for librarians, since they need a broad general education in a way which doctors and lawyers do not. In the past the difficulty was that most librarians did not go to a university at all, but the advantage of this lack of formal education was that the best of them educated themselves by very wide reading. It was perhaps for them a more satisfactory experience than the current one, where four years may be misspent as a result of being caught up in the higher education machine. The most usual criticism of the present British system is precisely that it does *not* provide a general education, and for library education the problem remains in another form. For example, we have always justified the removal of English literature from a dominant place in the library studies curriculum on the ground that this ' subject ' should be part of everybody's general education. What happens instead is that a graduate who takes up a post in a public library may be equipped with a detailed knowledge of Beowulf and that is all. The specialisation does not help, except in certain very specialised posts. To offset this lack of a general ' culture ', some would like to add courses or lectures on such topics as literary appreciation. These could not do any harm, but professional courses are so crowded with necessary subject content that such a remedy would simply scratch the surface of the problem. The real answer is to be found, firstly, in the reform of higher education generally, and, secondly, in a true liberalisation of prefessional courses.

At the risk of appearing banal, I will enumerate the forms which such liberalisation might take. With regard to lecturing methods, it was for a long time a valid criticism of librarianship courses that they paid far too much attention to descriptive detail—to the accumulation of facts which neither the lecturer nor the student could assimilate. This happened because library studies seemed to embrace more facts than a lecturer knew what to do with, and, in addition, most lecturers in librarianship were (and are) regrettably over-conscientious. This trend was particularly noticeable in enumerative bibliography, and it was difficult to persuade lecturers that particular items of reference material were of interest only if they exemplified some point of educational importance. The rest is training and can wait until the student takes over his job. It may well be that courses overloaded with meaningless factual details still persist but it is to be hoped they are in a minority. (The search for 'principles' of sufficient academic respectability has, in some quarters, resulted in high flown lectures which have abandoned the world of facts and things altogether, but this is probably a temporary aberration.) Apart from these elementary matters, liberalisation as a teaching method within particular subjects consists of linking or relating the content (however technical it may be) to the rest of the world—what Wordsworth called the 'pursuit of affinities'.

But the fundamental problem is much more substantial than this. All forms of further or higher education are faced with a vast expansion in the amount of knowledge, in the quantity of literature and in the number of students. In consequence, in order to survive as a truly educational process, the modes of education must wholly change. In the past, what passed for professional or technical education was often either simply training of a misguided sort, or the continuation of teaching courses more suitable for children. In such programmes it was sufficient for teachers not to interpret but to summarise the literature. In such an atmosphere it was appropriate that lecture sessions should be numerous and compulsory, and that lecturers should cultivate methods and manners more appropriate for sergeant-majors or gymnasium instructors. Their own teaching load was often excessive (for example, in London technical colleges, twenty two hours a week). More civilised policies would have wrecked the system and sometimes did.

Fortunately, the circumstances mentioned above are obliging colleges, including library schools, to adopt a new approach. What does this mean in practice? It means less instructing, less examining, less dragooning, less paternalism; it requires more seminars, more tutorials, more participation by students, more insight from the lecturer. When all this happens, and only then, will the student no longer feel he is on the factory belt, a commodity for social consumption. The approach involves greater use of the library for individual work and a more flexible curriculum. This last point is particularly important, because the arrival of internal examining creates opportunities for a total restructuring of courses. What these new structures will be depends on the aims and circumstances of particular institutions. Some of them will in many areas dispense with examinations altogether, and rely on alternative methods of assessment.

The above catalogue of requirements is so apparent that I hesitated to repeat it. What is much less obvious is the fact that these tasks are immensely difficult. A significant feature of the educational scene is that for many years almost everybody who counts in education has insisted that the curriculum is overloaded, that the emphasis on examinations must go, that individual students should receive more attention and should work more by themselves, and so on. As a result of all these changed attitudes, what has happened very often is not a new system but no change at all, or half hearted reforms which may leave the situation worse than it was before. The reasons for this failure to adapt quickly enough are numerous and complex. All educational institutions, by their very nature, are conservative, and academic work is cumulative and based on a slow growth, rather than constant new departures or explorations. Individual teachers who have painfully built up a method of teaching, a body of organised lectures, are naturally reluctant to start again and reshape it all. There is a law of inertia which used to be valuable in the academic world, but may prove to be the opposite now. Other reasons for this slow response to change lie outside the educational sphere, and derive from the expectations of employers and politicians, and an electorate educated in another fashion and in a different and less crowded world. But in spite of these retarding influences, the new patterns will emerge, bringing their own new problems.

NOTES

1 The Penguin educational special, *The impact of Robbins* by Richard Layard and others, gives useful statistics for the expansion of higher education. The Robbins report forecast 63,000 people getting two or more A levels by 1967, whereas the eventual figure was 79,000, a difference of about twenty six percent. Chapter seven gives a brief summary of the arguments for and against the ' binary ' system. In 1962 the universities provided sixty percent of the places for higher education, but by 1967 their share had fallen to fifty three per cent—the increased number of students having gone into the non-university sector. The overall picture is that ' apart from

electronics and natural gas higher education has grown faster than any major national enterprise in the 1960s . . . From 1962 to 1967 the number of students in full time higher education in Britain grew from 217,000 to 376,000 and the increase over these five years was greater than over the preceding twenty five '.

2 In 1965 Mr Crosland, Secretary of State for Education, indicated that this division between the universities and the rest of higher education should be regarded as permanent. The binary principle implies that there should be two systems of higher education at degree level, one in the autonomous sector (the universities), and one in the publicly-controlled sector (the technical colleges, and, for BEd courses, the colleges of education). The second sector would be developed more rapidly than the first.

3 Thus Bantock in *Education in an industrial society* (p 70): ' In spite of all the high sounding aims and claims of educationists, the history of twentieth century education is, in considerable measure, the history of certain examinations; and in an age of still rising expectations emerging from the widespread acceptance of a norm of social mobility and the status seeking it engenders, diploma hunting is likely to increase rather than to diminish.'

4 The arrival of internal examining in the library schools has created opportunities for new approaches, but the retention by the LA of control over the examination structure inhibits any radical restructuring of courses. In consequence the old obsession with examinations and phraseology of syllabi remains. Because of this a Library Association sub-committee has spent hundreds of hours tinkering with papers in a proposed modification of the old syllabus. This work has been overtaken by events in the schools, and it may now become apparent that to take years to construct syllabi which can otherwise be formulated in half an hour is a misguided procedure. A syllabus *by itself* is of no particular consequence, and it is doubtful whether a *national* syllabus will continue to be either possible or desirable. Eventually the Library Association will concentrate on its proper function of ensuring appropriate standards in schools.

9

social background

The other chapters in this book are intended to deal with the social and cultural context in which library services are embedded. This section is an examination of certain factors which are everywhere operative and which can be applied to particular situations. The treatment is inevitably cursory—partly in the interests of brevity, but also because much of the relevant evidence is not easily available. Most of the examples of 'impact' refer to British circumstances.[1]

CLIMATE

Montesquieu, who in the *Spirit of the laws* explored most of the regions which are now known as the social sciences, maintained that social institutions in different places differ from one another largely because of environmental factors, and the greatest of these is climate. He could not have foreseen that modern scientific developments would go some way towards controlling the environment and mitigating the rigours of climate, but the point is still valid. Climate particularly affects all forms of reading and academic pursuits. People in temperate regions tend to read more than those in the tropics, because they live indoors. For this and other reasons the responsible Englishman's home is, for better or for worse, his castle, and he spends much of his leisure time shut off from his neighbours and the world, except insofar as television has provided a new kind of window and another dimension. People in hot countries cannot exclude the outside world in this way, and reading then becomes something of an anti-social activity. The sub-tropical lands, such as those of the Mediterranean, represent a half way house, but there also the sun is an enemy of books and is partly responsible for the fact that public libraries have not fully established themselves.

There is, too, the inevitable link with religious ideologies. The Lutheran and Calvinistic traditions have favoured the development of individual reading, except where religious fundamentalism has produced a new authoritarianism based on the *Bible*. It is well known, however, that when these or any other doctrines are transplanted to new climates, for example those in Africa, they soon take on new forms. Among the Presbyterians, for instance, the grim concepts of original sin and predestination tend to dissolve, and God becomes less terrifying. Climate, of course, is only one element in these syncretic transformations, but here we are isolating its impact, which operates in tropical areas all the time. In Britain the results are less constant, since there is no climate, only weather—which can be used to explain away almost anything—and particularly the statistics of public lending libraries.

The impact of climate on library architecture and administration in developing countries is discussed in chapter eleven.

GEOGRAPHY

The ideal library service as a national plan is most easily thought of in a country where there are no vast distances between centres of population, where the population itself is not too thinly spread, where there are no physical barriers such as unbridged rivers or lack of roads to limit easy movement, and where the country itself is not too large and not too far away from those focal points of civilisation where literature is produced and published. In the UK there are no really formidable geographical obstacles save in parts of Scotland and Wales, but there is an uneven pattern of public library development, not only because of the peculiarities of the local government structure, but because of considerable social diversity and real differences between different types of community, each with its own characteristics and traditions.

Distance: The *distance between libraries* affects library co-operation. Thus with regard to academic libraries, the *Parry report* on university libraries states (p 8) that ' In comparing university libraries in the United States it is necessary to remember that generally there are much larger distances between libraries in America. For instance, the distance from London to Harvard is about the same as the distance from Harvard to Los Angeles. This distance factor makes it necessary for American university libraries to aim to be more comprehensive. Partly because of this and partly because of the effect of distances on the time required to make inter-library loans, the volume of loans in America is relatively much smaller than in this country.' This distance factor is naturally a feature in all large countries, such as the USSR or the USA or Australia, and library planning must be modified accordingly. Even in the UK special library provision in some of the research associations is conditioned by the fact that they are situated in isolated localities and cannot easily obtain fringe or general material.

Islands: Other geographical factors such as the existence of islands (Indonesia or the Caribbean) obviously create a situation where special types of library provision are necessary.

Rural and urban life: When the county library service in Britain was being developed, it was often assumed (as in the *Kenyon report* on public libraries of 1927) that rural readers are likely to be interested mainly in recreational reading. Insofar as there are now few wholly rural counties, and Britain has become increasingly suburban, this distinction between rural and urban provision is no longer valid (if it ever was).

Rapidly changing population densities are now a challenge for public libraries, and a good example of the problems involved is provided by the creation in Britain of the new towns. Ken Jones, in a Library Association fellowship thesis, has analysed the current situation. He points out that library planning was not possible in some of the new towns, owing partly to difficulties in obtaining loans and partly to building restrictions. He concludes ' The unevenness in standards of provision which has characterised the development of the public library service has unbelievingly been carried forward even into communities which have otherwise been planned with a particular care for educational, cultural and recreational provision '. What is interesting in our context is that the earlier new towns were planned as a number of more or less self sufficient residential neighbourhoods, and this presents peculiar problems for library provision, since the establishment of several small branch libraries is not sufficient, and library resources tend to be dissipated. The neighbourhoods are separated from each other and there are transport difficulties. On the other hand, the six ' second generation ' new towns now being planned have a looser structure, with more emphasis on the centre, and easier access from one neighbourhood to another, so that library provision should be less difficult. As Baguley has pointed out (in LA *Conference proceedings*, 1958, p 68) the numerous ' overspill ' housing estates present a quite different pattern and a different type of library service is needed. There is a much higher proportion of unskilled and unqualified workers and a lower proportion of professional people. In the new towns, on the other hand, the majority of the population consists of skilled workers.

In addition to new towns and new ' overspill ' estates, various other types of urbanisation in Britain have produced different problems. For example, in many parts what were originally village or small town areas have expanded and coalesced; some of them have retained their political autonomy and some have not; some have been absorbed by the counties and some by the large cities. When the Royal Commission on Local Government Boundaries' recommendations (1969) are implemented many local authorities will be amalgamated, and many of the smaller public library authorities will cease to exist. In some areas, for instance Surrey, a number of districts or towns each with a population of over 40,000 have already become autonomous library powers, as they are entitled to under the Public Libraries Act. In short, the administrative pattern of public library service will be totally changed by the time the reconstruction of local government boundaries catches up with the movement of population.

It has often been stressed by surveys and reports that the existence of so many small authorities has produced an uneven library system with many inadequate services. The professional consequences have been less often noted. In the past the ambition of many public library assistants was directed towards becoming ' chief ' librarians, and most who succeeded in their aim became ' chiefs ' of small systems, and inevitably spent the remainder of their careers as ' little librarians '. This process, together with the apprenticeship system of qualifying (which took up most of their energies over a number of years), tended to produce librarians with limited horizons, and with preoccupations which were professional in the worst sense. They lived in their own small worlds, which to the outsider were not attractive. Their attitudes were often reflected in the deliberations of the committees of the Association of Assistant Librarians, and in the pages of the *Assistant librarian*. It is a comforting thought that recruits of the library profession will, in the Britain of the seventies, no longer be likely to feel that they must carry a chief librarian's baton in their knapsack.

In the United States there is a formidable social problem caused by the decay in the centre of the great cities and the creation of Afro-American and Puerto-Rican ghettoes. This represents a difficult challenge for libraries, and population growth and shifts have provoked several state and national surveys. The challenge has to be met, not only in the cities, but in the suburban areas to which the middle class people have moved. Guy Garrison, in a study of Chicago (in *Illinois libraries*, 1965, p 79-89), suggests that between 1950 and 1960 there was an overall decline in library capacity in relation to the population to be served. In *Library quarterly* (34), 1964, p 163, Ennis deals with this ' suburbanisation '. He notes that one aspect of decentralisation of the metropolitan city is the fragmentation of outlying suburbs into autonomous localities: ' The resulting tangle of local pride and prejudice makes it practically impossible to create larger library districts,' and the result is a proliferation of small inadequate libraries. Bookmobiles are an expensive alternative, and there is bound to be a conflict between the needs of central libraries and this type of provision.

This is the suburban situation. The problem in the city centre is, of course, quite different and no satisfactory solution seems in sight. In the report of a symposium called *The public library and the city* edited by Ralph W Conant, 1965, a number of librarians, sociologists and educationalists considered the possible reading needs of the American poor. One contributor pointed out that in New York, Washington DC, Philadelphia, Chicago, Cleveland, Detroit, Los Angeles and most southern cities about *seventy percent* of the pupils in the public schools come from working class families, and half of these were from ' slum ' families. (Americans distinguish between the lower and the working classes.) All the contributors agreed that, by and large, libraries are for the middle class and of the middle class. It is significant that they do not agree whether libraries can do anything at all about the lower class. It is repeated several times that their needs can be met only by other agencies and more radical programs, since the lower classes do not wish to be assimilated into the working and middle classes: they do not desire the kind of self improvement which was a common aim among the immigrants in the past; most of them are functionally illiterate. Some people have taken a more positive line, and advocate special library programs and new types of service, for example to distribute books to the mothers of Afro-American children so that the children can benefit. (In many places children are the principal users of the public library.)[2]

148

It will be apparent that this widening gap between the affluent and the (mostly black) poor in the United States has no *exact* parallel in Britain, yet there are library problems of a similar kind. For example, there is evidence to suggest that the public library is now even more of a middle class institution than it formerly was. There is evidently no equivalent to Hoggart's *Uses of literacy* for the United States, and Howard S Becker (in the Conant symposium), when discussing non-College youth, makes the statement (p 55) 'We do not know what goal of adulthood motivates lower class youth . . . what they are striving for . . .' etc. In a land of sociologists, this, if it is true, is a most significant omission. It is only fair to add that Hoggart was dealing with a British working class tradition of a different order.

EDUCATION
The development of higher education is discussed in chapter eight. Here it should be noted that one of the main influences on current library services has been that of changes in the educational system. This has always been so and it is important to bear in mind how small, in former times, the number of library users was.

University libraries: The growth of higher education has resulted in an increased demand for libraries and librarians in these institutions. The expansion of university librarianship has produced new buildings and an increase of staff without which an improved service cannot be given. At undergraduate level there has been a new emphasis on the provision of multiple copies of books, especially in the new universities. (At York there is special provision for undergraduates in the colleges.) At research level expensive special collections and special study centres have become necessary. More attention is being paid to the role of recreational reading, and the need to provide instruction for readers in the use of books and libraries is at last being taken seriously. Similarly, reference service is being fully developed in many universities and colleges, and this can fairly be regarded as a new departure from the history of university libraries as a whole. For example, at the University of Lancaster senior library staff act as academic subject specialists: they advise readers and instruct them in bibliography. The new libraries in particular have emphasised exploitation and use and they have provided open access for all. In this context the increase in the number of tutor-librarians is most significant. The expansion of technical education, in the colleges of advanced technology, has produced libraries which are true information centres, where there is a close link with industry which is ' built in ' because of the sandwich courses offered by the colleges, and where there is an emphasis on liberal studies. In the technical colleges professional qualifications for librarians may be preferred to an academic degree, and in most universities there has been an improvement in the status of non graduate staff.

All this can be regarded as a welcome growth of professionalism among librarians who in the quite recent past did not always consider it necessary or worthwhile to modify an older and more amateur tradition. This professional indifference is indicated by the fact that there has been no comprehensive new book on university librarianship published in Britain since before the second world war.[3]

However, in spite of this response, there is another side to the story. University library development has by no means kept pace with the general expansion of higher education, and many libraries remain unsatisfactory. It has been frequently noted that the Robbins report said little about university libraries—but this was to some extent remedied by the appointment of the Parry committee by the University Grants Committee, and by its report in 1967. The section of the latter devoted to the functions of a university stresses that probably the basis of all other changes is the large increase in the student population. It mentions also the rapid growth of specialisation, and the fact that the increasing use of tutorials in preference to lectures (as recommended by the report of the Hale Committee on University Teaching Methods) means that much greater demands will be made on the library service, since students—even undergraduates—will be expected to read extensively on their own. Thus (para 23) ' the adoption of the tutorial method of teaching, together with the tendency towards broadly-based courses, makes it imperative on university libraries to have in stock and easily available an adequate supply of books specifically for undergraduate use '.

Many libraries are still not geared to this and other developments, and the conclusions in the report are not encouraging. For example (para 617), ' There is some evidence that there has been a decline of expenditure on libraries in relation to other expenditure on staff and students '. The report also notes that the special amount made available by the UGC for each of the seven new universities libraries was not adequate. Evidence submitted by the Library Association and by SCONUL suggested a basic stock of not less than 250,000 volumes, whereas the UGC grant would purchase only about 75,000 volumes. In the case of the colleges of advanced technology, the amounts received from the UGC were also insufficient to support a broad range of studies. Since 1967 there is no evidence that the situation has improved—and many well designed and well equipped buildings continue to receive inadequate funds for books. Michael Beloff in *The plateglass universities*, 1968, notes that the total annual expenditure on books in the University of California exceeds the grants to all the new British universities put together. He also states that if offered a choice he would not go to a ' plateglass ' university because of their inadequate library services. It is noteworthy that many of the student protest movements have included objections to alleged unsatisfactory library provision.

School libraries: School library development in Britain has always been uneven. The 1919 Public Libraries Act brought books to the schools and homes of village children, and between the wars there was steady progress in the provision of libraries in public and grammar schools. The 1944 Education Act opened the way for provision in secondary schools generally and, particularly since 1960, in primary schools. There has been an increase in the number of professional librarians in secondary schools, for example, in the Inner London Education Authority, Stirling, Hull, West Sussex and Nottinghamshire. In 1958 the Teacher Librarian Certificate was set up jointly by the Library Association and the School Library Association. It cannot be said, however, from an educational point of view, that this is a satisfactory syllabus, and of the relatively small number of teacher-librarians who have taken this paper there has been a high degree of wastage—in some years only one half of the candidates have passed. Meanwhile, an increasing number of students at library schools have studied library work with young people as part of the Library Association syllabus. The 1964 Public Libraries Act has brought about a closer link between public library services for children and the school library service to the extent that the Department of Education and Science now has responsibility for both.

Public libraries: For the last ten years or more in the UK the annual reports of public libraries (both municipal and county) have commented on the demand for a higher level of literature, and this phenomenon is usually linked with the expansion of higher education. It is also commonly noted that public library readers now expect more of their library services, and are not content with the negative library responses which were often accepted in the past. Apart from the fact that a better standard of book provision is expected by the public with higher education behind it, there remains the problem of provision for current students which makes an impact on public as well as university and college libraries. We have already noted that public reference libraries have been faced for many years with student demand for study rooms, and that various attempts, particularly in London, to deal with this problem have met with little success. For example, in 1963 a meeting of interested bodies was held under the auspices of the Ministry of Education to consider this by-product of the student ' explosion ', but little result can be reported. It would appear that the only answer is for the libraries themselves to provide study rooms, but usually this is not an economic proposition, and many librarians are not in favour of such a policy anyway—students do not pay rates, even if their landladies do! In 1962 a survey of reference library use in the London metropolitan boroughs discovered that half the students concerned were from overseas. Those who have to deal with this competition for seating accommodation in London libraries often find that the colour problem has entered their world. With regard to provincial libraries, a comment from Bradford's report in 1962/63 has been quoted: ' College students, always the main body of reference readers, tend more and more to monopolize the accommodation; the more mature and established users, who quietly follow their individual lines of study or research, no longer occupy our tables. When the young students have passed their examinations, the library tends to see them no more, and *this is the measure of our failure to make and cultivate real readers* ' (my italics). Where then have all the ' established ' users gone? And who were they? The answer to this rhetorical question—if one could be found—might illuminate some of the obscurities with which this book is concerned.

In the United States the problem has been even more urgent and special arrangements were made to discuss it at the 1963 Conference of the American Library Association. A comment in the chapter on American public libraries in *Five years' work in librarianship, 1961-65* (p 283) indicates another facet of the situation: ' High school students, looking for material for term papers . . . are apt to disregard all common barriers to locating information '. This is either a comment on the decline of public morality, or on the failure of library services to ' keep up ', or both.

It does appear, then, that the challenge of new educational patterns has been met by a variety of new library responses and these have been noted above. Inevitably this response is insufficient in many areas of library service and it is perhaps impossible to judge how typical some of these developments are. (Surveys such as *Five years' work in libarianship* always distort what is happening because they are largely based on published accounts. Not every event is reported and some reports relate to non events or dreams of things to come.)

It may well be that this trend in academic libraries towards a wholly different type of service will emerge as the most important single professional development in librarianship today. The library implications of a student centred method of education are now generally understood but they have not yet been fully carried out in practice. The process has gone further in some colleges in the United States, and particularly significant is the library-college movement which dates from the mid-thirties. Since the second world war there have been two conferences (in 1965 and 1966) devoted to the library-college idea, and there is now a specialist journal, *Library college*. The term is used because, instead of a college library where the library is subordinated to the college, it is claimed that the college should be built around and largely within the library or 'learning resource centre'. In such a system each student has his own study carrel within the library, with dial access to the 'resources' through his own personal viewing screen. The teacher's main function is to guide the student through the appropriate sources. The original concept in America was and is intended to deal with the special problems arising from the credit system of education, but the tutor-librarian movement in Britain has similar aims which are not dependent necessarily on computerisation but on a new approach generally. The implication is that the college librarian should become the most important agent in the liberalisation of education. Thelma Bristow at the Institute of Education, London, and Frank Hatt at the Canterbury College of Art, have shown what can be done, although neither of these libraries can be regarded as typical. The significant point is, of course, that this type of service is perhaps possible only in institutions of formal education and that in these colleges the role both of tutors and librarians is fundamentally changed. It is a response which the new educational developments require.

TRANSPORT

Library planning is influenced not only by distance and population densities, but also by transport facilities. If these are good, or if a high proportion of families possess cars, then it is reasonable to suppose that library service points can be planned further apart. The Branch and Mobile Libraries Group of the Library Association conducted a limited survey in relation to the use of private cars, which roughly confirmed these expectations. It has long been realised that in planning service points for city libraries, allowance must be made for the fact that most people regularly travel inwards to the centre, and that branches must be sited accordingly. Similarly, it is now usually agreed that central libraries should be built in or near the shopping centre of towns and not in secluded parks.

Without adequate means of communication library co-operation in a national system is impossible. This involves using a postal or telephone or a telex system, and good rail and road networks, not only for dispatching material, but also for the library services themselves in the case of mobile libraries. Motor transport is most common for this purpose, but there are book trains and book boats (Svendborg in Denmark). An important monograph remains to be written on the role of the camel in spreading Arabic literature throughout Africa; (admittedly, this is not a library development).

With regard to reading habits, the various possible means of transport have had an important influence. Reference has already been made to Charles Mudie and W H Smith and the railways. At the present time Britain is a nation of newspaper readers because of the commuter way of life of a large proportion of the population. Cases have been reported (usually in the courts) of people who read while riding bicycles, but more significant is the use of radio communications in motor cars. No doubt as video-tape develops, automobiles will also be equipped with visual media unless it is legally considered unsafe to do so. Other means of transport induce their own type of reading : for example, those travelling by sea are often dependent on the eccentric contents of ships' libraries and many lives have been changed by this unusual exposure. It is more doubtful whether reading in aeroplanes ever makes a similar impact.

SOCIAL CONDITIONS

The basic characteristic of social conditions in our time is that they are constantly changing, and the rate and extent of the change varies from country to country and in different areas within countries. All we can do is note that library planning is influenced anywhere by a number of social factors. These include the general social and political structure, the employment situation, housing conditions, lighting and heating, the size of families, leisure opportunities, the education system, the existence of minority groups. Most of these factors particularly condition public library provision, and they are inevitably interdependent. Their influence is decisive and at the same time difficult to analyse in relation to libraries, because they are so often simply *there* and taken for granted by those who live there. For instance, many librarians have wished to stress the educational function of libraries, but in so doing they have to admit that their effort can succeed only if the education system produces the readers, or the right kind of readers, in the first place. Perhaps a less obvious but significant example is the use of public reference libraries, which, particularly in university towns, are often full of students using them as study rooms because they have no other convenient place to study; this particularly applies to students from overseas. The same pattern has been repeated in underdeveloped countries, where there is an urgent need simply for a room where students can study for examinations.

In the UK the traditional public library newspaper room, now disappearing, is a legacy of less affluent times when the unemployed (particularly in the nineteen thirties) had nowhere else to go. This was of course an unstated social function, although the official purpose of this service was quite different. At the present time some public reference libraries, particularly those near old people's homes, are occupied by the aged, and here again the library is performing a social service which should really be performed by some other agency. (The problem of course is that old people do not wish to be *segregated*.)

There are numerous other factors which directly affect public libraries. The pattern of reading which characterises areas where people are predominantly middle class or professional, or where there is a large student population, is clearly different from the pattern in a working class region. In some communities people live mainly in flats and there are few children; in others almost the entire working population are commuters, and this affects the nature of library provision both in the suburb and the city. The impact on charging systems has already been noted, and the new public library of the city of London has many administrative features caused by the peculiar concentration of readers at particular times.

Urbanisation has already been considered. Since world population is increasing at such a high rate, it is relevant to note that a high population density produces living conditions where reading becomes almost impossible. Apart from overcrowding there is the problem of *noise*. Some cities, for example Naples, are notoriously noisy. One consequence, also a result of social *mobility*, is the decline of the private library.

People in the affluent society, apart from the submerged sector of the socially deprived, have more money to spend on leisure pursuits. One can only speculate to what extent this affects reading habits. On the one hand, individuals have more money for a variety of activities which they otherwise could not afford, and this may well reduce reading in some cases. On the other hand, the increase in the variety of leisure time pursuits may act as an incentive to reading. The evidence is no more conclusive than it is about the use of television. All that can be said is that there has probably been a reduction in some kinds of recreational or compensatory reading, but the fact that the number of books borrowed from public libraries has increased rather than declined suggests that this particular factor is only one among several. In the United States it seems correct to say that the proportion of the population which habitually reads anything except magazines and comics has always been smaller than in the UK, and much smaller than in the USSR. Again, affluence may be partly responsible, but there are other causes.

THE 'SHUT-INS'

Elsewhere in this chapter I have referred to special groups of readers. Some attention should be paid here to groups of people which the Americans have called 'shut-ins'. These are the deprived who are physically confined by choice or force of circumstance, temporarily or permanently beyond the pale of normal existence. They are particularly those in hospitals or prisons; some are in ships or in lighthouses; others are physically handicapped, such as the blind, who are shut out of the sun and of many advantages taken for granted by the sighted, or those in old people's homes who face the last confinement of the grave. They are mentioned here because in varying degrees they represent a special challenge for librarians. For them books may be an important aid to recovery, or a solace or salvation, and sometimes there is little else for them. Their environments require that the nature, and in some cases the form, of their reading must be provided with particular care. (In passing it may be noted that the Americans use for these people the euphemistically abstract description 'socially disadvantaged'.) Library work with children also shares this extra dimension, but there is the difference that the condition of childhood is not usually regarded as one of deprivation or abnormality, except possibly by children themselves. Even so, the problems in book selection, or in the writing of children's literature, are not dissimilar, since the providers are trying to communicate with beings in another world. This raises the question whether they should be encouraged to stay there, or whether, out of envy or (as in Victorian times) moral rectitude, they should be led or driven hurriedly on to reconciliation with their ' lot ' in the adult world.

To return to the shut-ins, it is not necessary to describe the mechanics of prison or hospital library administration, but my concern here is the peculiar nature of the librarian's role. To borrow an academic parallel, one may suggest that this kind of work takes place in the gaps between disciplines. The hospital librarian is a special librarian, not because he deals with a special subject, but because he is providing a service for special people who may have nothing in common except their disabilities. So it is that the administrators of prisons (in spite of the existence of the educational library at Wakefield, and of public library prison services) are not necessarily acquainted with the use of literature for rehabilitation purposes; similarly psychiatrists rarely study bibliotherapy. If, alternatively, these matters are left to the public libraries, how can a librarian have sufficient knowledge of the emotional effects of particular maladies or of criminal psychology to be able to provide what is in fact a kind of social service? As far as librarianship goes, the answer is partly to be found in special training, but this is a world where professional librarians must encounter the work of other professionals. These include not only doctors or prison education officers, but administrators as well as professional philanthropists. In consequence, a harmonious association of the various elements is not easily achieved but this is now being attempted in most fields with some success.

From the institutional point of view, these services are interesting, since they require this combination of traditional social welfare organisations with the activities of the modern welfare state, and also a contribution from professional librarianship. In most other fields the state has taken over such services long ago, but in this area voluntary welfare services still have a part to play. Often, for example, they have the financial resources to conduct expensive experiments which the state would or could not carry out. In any event, they were the and do provide training courses. Yet the contribution of their workers is, rightly, not wholly professional, and they are not likely to specialise, for example, in the study of English literature. On the other hand, public librarians who supply books to hospitals may not appreciate that the selection criteria are not those which they would normally use. The inhabitants of hospitals represent a cross section of the community, not of the normal reading public. In addition, those who do read in their normal healthy circumstances may need to read a different, and probably a more recreational, type of literature. For these reasons the arguments against light literature are no longer relevant.

The voluntary bodies have other limitations. They are necessarily paternalistic in their attitudes, which have survived from an age when charitable good works were part of the responsibilities of the more fortunate social classes. This has led inevitably to some degree of control over the type of literature which is made available. This tendency is still not wholly absent from the Braille books provided by the National Library for the Blind, or by the Royal National Institute for the Blind. It is only fair to add that one of the difficulties is that those who transcribe the books may object to the transcription of ' dubious ' works. It is also relevant to note the difficulties which arise in the provision of books in large print for the partially sighted. The Ulverscroft publications were not, at least in the first instance, a profitable venture. They have been dutifully supplied by public libraries, but an adequate service may require special methods to get them into the hands of suitable readers.

It is reasonable to conclude, therefore, that at present professional expertise is being added to services which were effectively pioneered and developed by voluntary workers who possessed the necessary qualities of enthusiasm and dedication. In these areas a direct welfare function is added to normal library provision.

RELIGION

The attempts of religious institutions to control publication are dealt with in the chapter on censorship. It would be possible, and was at the turn of the century fashionable, to depict historical progress as the result of a long struggle between the free spirit of man engaged in intellectual enquiry, and the religious forces of fanaticism, ignorance, superstition, obscurantism and violence. Such a dramatic view of history can be found in the pages of Wynwood Reade's *Martyrdom of man,* or in a less lurid form in some of the works of H G Wells, a writer who at one time dreamt of an encyclopedia free from human prejudice. The interaction of religious forces and freedom of publication is generally considered to be a much more complex process, since many movements of human liberation have been rooted in religious revolts. Such a movement can be seen in the Protestant Reformation, which ultimately led to an emphasis on individual liberty, even if it also led to a stress on the *Bible* as an alternative authority to the Pope.

If we go back to the beginning we find that in pre-Christian times the earliest libraries were associated with temples, and the first librarians were priests. (It is perhaps not too fanciful to compare the modern role of the librarian, as an intermediary between the reader and understanding, with that of the ancient role of the priest who was a *necessary* intermediary between the individual and God. Originally the two roles were identical.)

In later times, the Christian church was, of course, the only organisation which provided libraries, and the Benedictine Order, from the tenth to the thirteenth centuries, preserved the heritage of Greece and Rome and made possible the production of the monastic chronicles, such as that of William of Malmesbury. When the monastic system was finally dissolved by Henry VIII, some Anglican antiquarians managed to preserve an unknown proportion of their library collection. Irwin in *Heritage of the English library* notes that ' It was mainly owing to Archbishop Matthew Parker's interest in historical studies and his anxiety to establish the continuity of *Ecclesia Anglicana* from Anglo Saxon days, that some at least of the contents of the dispersed monastic libraries were rescued and preserved—ultimately to find a home in our national libraries '.

Again, in the late seventeenth and eighteenth centuries, thousands of charity schools were founded for the education of the children of the poor, and a large number of endowed libraries were established as part of the same movement. So the dustjacket of Thomas Kelly's work *Early public libraries* shows a photograph of the old library at Kings' Cliffe Northamptonshire, and over the door we can read that ' Books of Piety are here lent to any Persons of this or ye Neighbouring Towns '.

The various non-conformist movements, narrow and bigoted though many of them have been, have also promoted the spirit of individual enquiry, and hence of reading and the use of libraries. Some of the

159

earliest experiments in rural library provision, such as that of James Kirkwood in Scotland and Samuel Brown in Yorkshire, were concerned with library provision for the clergy. Similarly, Dr Williams' library was set up in the eighteenth century specifically to cater for the needs of nonconformists who were educationally deprived.

Quite apart from setting up libraries or preserving the literature of the past, those religions, such as Christianity and Islam, which have or did have a basic missionary drive have naturally played a major role in the spread of literacy all over the world. They have taught their flocks to read, and provided literature which they regard as appropriate for them. Millions of their followers have in this manner been exposed to literature for the first time. These efforts overseas have been matched by educational and missionary work at home. Altick in the *English common reader* has shown how the Evangelical movement in nineteenth century Britain did much to bring about a literate society, while at the same time endeavouring to control the type of reading matter available. Inevitably there have been perversions, and one can still encounter the fundamentalist idea that there is only one ' Book ', be it *Bible* or *Koran,* and where such influences prevail libraries are largely irrelevant, since all other books are anathema and the earth is flat.

We have noted in chapter 6 that reading for devotional purposes is a particular kind of reading which may not encourage intellectual activity or scientific enquiry, but that at its best it may represent a profound and beneficent cultural influence. It sometimes takes the form of repetition by rote, without an understanding of rational meaning. Children read religious works in this way, both in Christian and more particularly in Muslim countries, where a daily regular reading from the *Koran* is a religious duty strictly observed by all. In this way catechisms and creeds are repeated, and possibly become forms of meditation. If this is so, obscurity may be appropriate, which is presumably why the Roman Catholic Church used the Latin language for so long.

It remains to add that the public library movement has inevitably been adversely affected in countries where religious conflicts, notably between protestants and catholics, have resulted in separate Library Associations and separate provision. Such has been the case in Holland and Belgium. Elsewhere the public library movement has not developed because the Roman Catholic Church has become closely identified with the state, and the result has been control of publication and a lack of enthusiasm for libraries. Such has been the case in Spain and Eire and Portugal.

POLITICS

Ideology: Political beliefs influence reading habits and the pattern of library development in a similar fashion to the religious attitudes with which they are often associated. The excellent work of UNESCO on behalf of the public library movement obscures the fact that this movement, as developed in Scandinavia, the USA, and the British Commonwealth, was an integral part of the historical trend leading to liberal or capitalist democracy. Elsewhere there are public or ' free ' libraries, to be sure, but they are institutions of a different kind. The search for a library ' philosophy ' and for adequate official support has from time to time in the United States led to a stress on particular purposes, such as the prosecution of wars, or the Americanisation of immigrants, or simply on education. Nevertheless, the political impetus behind public library development has remained primarily democratic in a broad sense, even if on occasion it has been interpreted narrowly as education for the voters in public affairs. In the UK, the attitudes of public librarians have been almost wholly determined by this nineteenth century liberal tradition, as can be seen in the admirable writings of Lionel McColvin. The open society requires an autonomous independent system of libraries, which in turn implies ' open access '.

This pattern cannot be found in closed societies, where inevitably libraries and reading are wholly or partly controlled in the interests of a ruling party and its ideology. The *Soviet encyclopedia* is quite explicit in stating that the purpose of librarianship and libraries, like all other cultural institutions, is to produce good communists. With aims of this kind, some degree of ' guidance ' is essential. There is, of course, a distinction between those societies, such as the present socialist examples, which make libraries an *active* agency within the appropriate frame of reference, and those like Spain or Portugal which do little to develop libraries for the people at all. Nazi Germany inevitably used libraries as propaganda agencies, and developed the *Volksbucherei* for this purpose. There was in any case a German or Prussian authoritarian tradition which was exemplified at Leipzig between the wars. Readers were issued with *Lese bücher*, or cards, which recorded what they had previously read, so that the omniscient librarian could advise them what to read next. To the ' western ' liberal mind this practice must seem obnoxious, but it is commonly

161

overlooked that the introduction of ' open access ' into public libraries introduced new problems which have never really been solved.

The main one, of course, is that the majority of readers in a public library are usually ' advised ' or helped in an indirect and limited fashion only. Many librarians, possibly an increasing number, would consider that their responsibilities in this direction must and should be limited. If this is so, we are back with a ' freedom ' for readers which is not real, since one of the freedoms required in the modern world is freedom from avoidable ignorance.

Political organisation: The other type of political impact is, of course, the practical one. The method of control or organisation of libraries is a political matter. Most of the limitations and well known peculiarities of the British public library system derive from the pattern of local government control. Most of the weaknesses of the national library system derive from the fact that there has never been a co-ordinated national structure, and once vested interests have grown up it is difficult to create one. A result of this proliferation of overlapping library and information services is that, although professional bodies have thrashed about, there has never been any *official* consideration or report on the pattern of libraries, *as a whole*. Meanwhile, responsibility for these services continues to be split between different ministries or different departments of the same ministry. If anyone should consider this matter unimportant, let him count up the number of different agencies which are responsible, either for providing scientific information, or for promoting more effective dissemination, and then examine this diverse collection of people in relation to the results obtained.

Party politics: It cannot be said that either of the two main British political parties has a record which distinguishes it as the special friend of libraries. When in power at a national level, both parties have showed interest in library services in fits and starts, and a recurrent feature has been a ban on public library building (as in 1961), which has been one of the consequences of the ' stop-go ' nature of the postwar economy. At the time of writing, the Labour Party Minister responsible for the Arts, Miss Jennie Lee, has shown a genuine enthusiasm for what is now usually called the ' quality of life ', and the Open University, which may have a great impact on library services, is one of the results. A political moral for librarians may be drawn from the fact that the Public Libraries Act of 1964, which was introduced during the last months of the Tory administration, made a rather sudden appearance, and it arrived on the statute book at a time when more controversial measures would have been politically difficult.

At local level the record is equally 'spotty', and variations in the standards of provision for public libraries can often be attributed to factors other than purely political. Tory councils are often mainly concerned to keep down the local rates, which inevitably affects library provision adversely, while Labour councils (more notably in the past) tended to concentrate on the reading needs of what were then the working classes, which often resulted in a low level of service. Local councillors of both parties often displayed that anti-intellectual bias which is part of the Anglo-Saxon heritage.

Central government activity: However, what the central government *has* done affects the library system at many points, and, with regard to statutory law, its actions are and have been decisive. I have already remarked that the nineteenth century public libraries Acts largely determined the development of the public library services in Britain, and the same applies to the Public Libraries Act of 1919, which extended the service to the rural areas and lifted the penny rate limitation, and the Act of 1964, which brought in a measure of state responsibility for the first time. But within the statutory framework it was and is the local authorities who have built up the services indifferently or well. In a comparative context (as compared to France, for example), it is worth noting how significant is the strength and variety of local community life in Britain. Traditionally, much of the local resistance to central control is healthy and valuable, but unfortunately in the sphere of library provision there have been well known disadvantages. Recently, of course, there has been the increasing public call for more *regional* autonomy, and this is another matter. There can be no doubt that in Wales, for instance, if there had been one public library system embracing the principality as a whole, there would have been better opportunities to build up individual library services.

At this point it is relevant to refer to the activities of individual library benefactors, and particularly to Andrew Carnegie and the Carnegie United Kingdom Trust which carried on his work. In an article in the *Library Association Record* in February 1957 I suggested that it is not enough simply to remember his services with gratitude, but that the real significance of this tremendous contribution to the development of all kinds of library services in Britain was, and is, that the Trust, and Carnegie before it, were really doing what state agencies should have done. This is a pattern which is much more familiar in the United States, and was more common in nineteenth century Britain, for example, in education. It is reasonable to conclude, therefore, that the state did not assume national responsibility for so many aspects of library services for so long partly because Carnegie and the CUKT were doing so much of the work.

The taking over by the central government of services pioneered by voluntary or private bodies is, of course, a familiar pattern in many areas of the social services. The process gathered momentum after the second world war, and the welfare state is the result. The point I am making about libraries is that this development took too long to come about, and is incomplete even now. The opposite view of course is that the CUKT acted as a stimulus and a pioneer (for example in the establishment of county libraries), and promoted projects which the government would never have set up by its own volition. This cannot be proved either way, but if one believes in the necessity of nation-wide library services, then presumably state responsibility must eventually have come. The other factor, which is perhaps less significant, is that Carnegie's policy of setting up those monumental buildings did distort public library programmes.

It remains to note that major changes in public library provision in recent years have been brought about by legislation. It is still too early to assess the results of the 1964 Public Libraries Act, but so far they have been largely negative, in the sense that many public libraries, because of the implications of the Act for them and possible loss of local government control of their systems, have increased their expenditure to the level required. In addition, partly as a result of the Act, the number of public library systems which a few years ago was nearly 600, is now down to approximately 400.

The most drastic changes were a consequence of the London Government Act of 1963, which followed the report of the Royal Commission on Local Government in Greater London of 1960. The Act caused the transformation of sixty nine library authorities—with parts of four counties—to thirty two. The operation caused an upheaval which personally affected many librarians, and resulted in opportunities for the standardisation of administrative methods and the introduction of mechanical systems, particularly in computer-produced printed catalogues. Meanwhile, the work of the local government commissions affected other library authorities, notably in the

West Midlands, where in 1965 eighteen authorities were merged into five new county boroughs. In 1968, the *Report* of the Boundaries Commission for Wales envisaged the amalgamation of a number of Welsh public library services.

In the long run, library services will mostly benefit from local government reorganisation, but two points seem relevant. The first is that local government changes in general are at least twenty years overdue, and the second is that they are naturally not primarily concerned with library services as such, and the result for libraries may be for better or for worse.[4]

At the central government level, library services have been modified by the creation of new agencies, such as OSTI and the new Ministry of Technology, and by the merging of libraries, such as those of the former Colonial Office and the Commonwealth Relations Office and the Ministry of Overseas Development.

INTERNATIONAL AFFAIRS

Beyond the UK, international and strategic considerations have made their influence very much felt. The publication explosion is an international one, and this is partly responsible for the continuing stress on bibliographic organisation. Since much of the technical information is of strategic importance, governments since the war have been more conscious of the importance of technical information being readily available. There can be no doubt that the setting up of the American Farmington Plan for the collective acquisition of foreign material was partly or mainly a consequence of America's new global responsibilities in the postwar world. The same impetus probably lies behind the more recent project for a National Science Library, and for a vastly increased foreign materials acquisition programme for the Library of Congress. In Britain a similar motivation (for example, an awareness of the Russian space programme) lay behind the creation of the National Lending Library of Science and Technology. I have already referred to some of the computer information programmes in the United States, which are so heavily financed for military reasons.

If preparation for war stimulates some library activity, the great world wars have done the same, at least in Britain. The impact of war has been most noticeable in Germany, where so many of the great academic libraries were destroyed, and where, following the end of the second world war, a planned revival had to be instigated, including a scheme for the co-operative provision of foreign research material.

In other countries destruction was on a smaller scale, and in Britain, perhaps unfortunately, many of the nineteenth century buildings survived bombing.

The withering away of the British empire is now almost complete, but the library consequences of it, in the form of unique collections relating to former colonial territories, are still with us in London, and for most of these countries the historical source material is thus still with the former mother country. The same applies to other former imperial powers: the libraries are all that they have left.

The international scene cannot be left without mentioning the growth of international librarianship, and the activities of the International Federation of Library Associations (IFLA), the International Federation of Documentation (FID), and UNESCO. All these bodies have stimulated development in countries where library services were formerly weak. Their impact on the more advanced countries is less noticeable, but is still considerable. Schemes and methods of international co-operation (such as interlending) have continued to grow. Furthermore, the more advanced library countries, such as the USA and the UK, have helped in the field of library education and training for overseas librarians.

LANGUAGE

Language in communication, and as a decisive element in culture, is discussed in another chapter. Here it is appropriate to note that the absence of an indigenous written national language, and the existence of bilingual and multilingual communities, cause problems with regard to literacy, publishing and education in general. Until these problems are solved, library services can scarcely operate at all. India is plagued with these difficulties, as are most countries in Africa. Examples nearer home of the bilingual dilemma can be seen in Switzerland and Belgium, Eire and Wales. Many countries, particularly the smaller ones, have national languages which are relatively 'minor' from a world point of view, and this means that their libraries must provide a high proportion of works in the major foreign languages.

The existence of bilingual or multilingual societies, or of 'pockets' of foreign language speaking communities, raises the question of the responsibilities of the librarian. Most public librarians would agree that they should provide literature and information to linguistic minorities, but in countries where the clash of cultures occurs, many would go further and maintain that the librarian's cultural duties should include an active responsibility for a minority national culture threatened by outside influence. This is the situation in Wales. Librarians in many parts of Africa are, or will, be caught up in the same dilemma. As is indicated in chapter two, this may be a forlorn attempt to hold up the tide of supra-nationalism, but there is much that can be done, and if a folk culture is really on the way out, the preservation of records and relics becomes the last gloomy responsibility. Other agencies and individuals commonly carry out many of these activities, since the records are often not written ones. Even so, the librarian should be involved—and I am suggesting that this kind of cultural concern should be at the core of professional belief.

NOTES
1 Ralph Conant in discussing sociological changes in American life (ALA *Bulletin op cit*) identifies the following as the most important current trends:
  1 Population growth and urbanization.
  2 Increasing levels of knowledge.
  3 Technological advance.
  4 Decreasing poverty (affluence).
  5 Institutional centralization and development of ties among similar institutions.
  6 Increasing governmental pressure for inter-governmental co-operation and inter-institutional planning. (The reference is of course to state governments.)
  With reference to the UK and in relation to librarianship, I suggest that the first four are particularly relevant, together with the growth of mass communication media and changes in the system of higher education.
2 This reference to the American library situation does not do justice to the degree of *concern* which has been expressed, or the practical experiments which have been undertaken by some American librarians. The bibliography by Carla F Stoffle published in *Library journal* listed 162 items which appeared on this subject between 1964-1968. There is also a special programme initiated by the School of Library and Information Services at the University of Maryland and vividly described by Eric Moon in *Library journal (op cit)*. High John is a library, situated in a deprived area, run by the library school with money mostly provided (for three years) under the research section of the Higher Education Act. High John is also a research project of the library school. The organisers, Paul Wasserman and Mary Lee Bundy, noted at the outset ' If library education is effectively to bridge the gap between theory and practice, it must be prepared to experiment in the field and so provide its students with a laboratory in which to observe, to participate, to study and to learn '. Where no laboratory exists the school should create one.
  Eric Moon's account reinforces doubts as to whether libraries as such, even if they can shed their middle class approaches, can do anything about these appalling social problems. But it is inspiring that there are librarians who are willing to try.
3 James Thompson has, however, just completed *An introduction to university librarianship,* to be published by Bingley early in 1970.

4 Recent Federal legislation in the United States is potentially more significant. In 1956 for the first time the US government initiated a financial assistance programme for library service: since then aid programmes have been added for other types of library service. The Library Services Act of 1956 was extended by a Library Service and Construction Act of 1966 ' to help the states fulfil their obligations '. In addition to providing funds for the extension of public library services and the construction of buildings there is provision for the establishment and operation of systems for inter-library co-operation and for specialised services for those unable to use regular facilities (hospital libraries etc). It is claimed that these programmes have substantially increased public library circulation figures, but a minimum standard for an adequate service is far off in many localities. The mushrooming suburban sections of the great cities are a major problem. Other Acts relevant to the development of libraries are: the Higher Education Facilities Act of 1963 (university libraries); Elementary and Secondary Education Act, 1965 (school libraries); Higher Education Act, 1965 (university and college libraries). Each of these Acts has an authorised existence of five years. The federal government has therefore accepted national responsibility for library services, but, as with other welfare programmes, their assistance may well be too little and too late. A long term financial remedy is required and inadequate services are likely to remain.

Since this was written James Ollé, in *The library world (op cit)*, has produced detailed evidence to show that the majority of Carnegie's grants went to the smaller authorities (224 out of 292 mentioned in the Adams report had a population of less than 50,000). These were the authorities which could not afford to pay for an adequate service. He also notes that proposals put forward at the turn of the century by James Duff Brown, and subsequently by the Library Association, for the establishment by Carnegie of a bibliographical centre, a school of librarianship and a headquarters for the Library Association, were summarily turned down.

5 Since 1966 the National Library for the Blind has also issued large print books which are intended to complement Ulverscroft. These titles, produced by xerography, are mainly classics for which there is a minority demand.

10

the impact of technology

The remainder of this book deals with changes brought about directly or indirectly by technology, and in this section I am simply noting the direct impact on libraries, mainly in the UK. The most straightforward and noticeable changes include the following:

1 *Aslib:* What is relevant about Aslib in our context is that, particularly since the second world war, it has increased the range of its activities to include a much greater emphasis on research. The other aspects of its work have also continually expanded, for example, the library advisory service and the training programme and the growth of the Commonwealth Index of Scientific Translations. The Research Department was not established until 1959, and since 1963 there have been annual government grants for research projects, such as an investigation of mechanised methods in documentation work, published in 1966. There have also been important conferences, such as those on information work 1964, classification 1962, and co-ordinate indexing 1963, the last of these leading to the formation of a new Aslib Co-ordinate Indexing Group.

2 *Government Activity:* National concern for the needs of science and technology has been reflected in the creation of major new library systems and the reorganisation of others. The most significant development was, of course, the setting up of the National Lending Library for Science and Technology in 1962. It is noteworthy that it was considered by the government, if not by the library profession, that an entirely new library service was necessary. It is also of interest that

169

Dr Urquhart, its director, has always been free from traditional pre-conceptions of what a library should be. It has been stated that the NLL has taken over considerably more than a third of the inter-library loan activities of the country, and that by 1966 well over eighty five percent of requests were being satisfied. Even more important is the fact that the delay in obtaining loans—so long a grave drawback in scientific library work—has been reduced to two days or less.

Another major change was the establishment in 1965 of the Office for Scientific and Technical Information (OSTI) within the Department of Education and Science. Its functions, as stated by its director, are that it may stimulate, or, if necessary, undertake almost any activity that can contribute to a better handling or utilisation of information, in both the natural and the social sciences and their related technologies. OSTI is concerned to *co-ordinate* the efforts of other organisations in the information network, and the published brochure makes quite clear that it was the slow and haphazard growth of information activities which caused it to be set up as a promoting body. The leaflet *Why Osti?* states clearly the nature of the problem: ' It has become increasingly difficult to use the published literature as a quick source of information, and over the years various ways have been devised for bringing it under control. At one extreme there are " invisible colleges ", small groups of scientists with common interests, who keep each other informed of progress. Then there are titles and abstracts journals and other guides to the literature; also reviews and data compilations for which useful information is extracted from the literature and arranged in a concise and convenient form. Finally there already exist, at different stages of development, complex mecha-nised systems for disseminating or searching particular sections of the literature.' Whether and in what way a body such as OSTI can possibly ' co-ordinate ' all these activities remains to be seen: the national bodies in other advanced countries are on a much larger scale. OSTI and its Advisory Committee for Scientific and Technical Information also became responsible for the National Lending Library for Science and Technology and for the grants-in-aid to Aslib.

OSTI took over some of the functions of the old Department of Scientific and Industrial Research, which was abolished in 1965. Some of the constituent research stations and associations became the respon-sibility of the new Ministry of Technology, and others were trans-ferred to other departments. The ministry represented official recogni-tion of the importance of technological progress, and is responsible for the National Research Development Co-operation, for the UK Atomic Energy Authority, for the British Standards Institution, for ten research stations and forty eight research associations. In our context the industrial liaison programme is of particular significance. There are nine ministry regional offices throughout the country, which, *inter alia*, co-ordinate the work of industrial liaison centres, based mainly on universities and technical colleges. The aim of these centres is, by personal contact, to stimulate local industry to make more use of existing scientific and technical knowledge. This programme recognises that there has always been this relative failure to use technical information sources, and it is well known that the problem is intensified by the nature of the organisation of British industry, with its high proportion of small firms.

The remaining important step in this national field was the setting up (if that is the correct word) of the National Reference Library of Science and Invention, which, together with the former Patent Office Library, is to be integrated with the British Museum. The developments to date are not inspiring, since the building, which was to be completed on the south bank of the Thames, in London, in 1965, is still not yet begun. Meanwhile, the NRLSI does exist and preparations continue in temporary premises in Bayswater. Plans are also being implemented to decentralise the Patent Office itself.

To complete this picture of reorganisation, it should be noted that the old Science Library in South Kensington continues to function with a charged role, and it is now possible for the library to concentrate mainly on serving the needs of the staff of the Science Museum and the staff and research students at the Imperial College of Science and Technology, while both lending and reference services continue for the general public, although, with regard to lending at least, this is complementary to the main service offered by the NLLST (a figure of fifteen percent of the loan requisitions which the NLL receives is quoted in the literature).

To sum up, it is difficult at this stage to evaluate the effectiveness of this new pattern since it is still evolving. So far, one is left with the impression that, apart from the clear policies of the National Lending Library, there is still confusion and overlapping and that the overall co-ordination is weak. From the point of view of *bibliographical* organisation the problems remain much as they have always been.

3 *The development of special libraries:* Inevitably the need for scientific information has led to the rapid growth of special libraries, both in numbers and in the importance of this work. In certain areas, for instance that of the learned societies, there has been a decline in importance, but the increase has been marked in the industrial field. The new situation has also resulted in the reorganisation and co-ordination of the great engineering libraries—a change which became necessary both for economic and service reasons.

4 *The profession:* The advance of special librarianship has con-siderably modified both the organisation of the profession and of library education. In 1962 the Library Association was reorganised, partly to allow for more adequate representation for all types of libra-rians. Furthermore, in 1963 the association set up an independent Scientific Library Services Committee to review special library services and to make recommendations. The committee reported in 1968. Three sub-committees were also appointed. In library education, the 1961 LA syllabus paid more attention than in the past to the needs and importance of special librarianship, although Aslib had with-drawn from the joint responsibility which was first intended. The new emphasis on full time education did, however, cause difficulties for industrial and other special librarians—difficulties which to some extent still remain, although the setting up of a Library Assistants Certificate by the City and Guilds Institute in 1966 was some mitiga-tion. Also relevant was the foundation of the Institute of Information Scientists Ltd in 1962. This body caters for the needs of highly qualified information officers and classes are held for the institute's examinations. A further proposal, for a programme for 'mature entry' qualifications to the LA for special librarians, came to grief at the 1968 Annual General Meeting of the Library Association, but it is reasonable to suppose that some provision for the needs of a small but important category of special librarians will eventually be met. From the point of view of professional unity it is extremely desirable that it should. Finally, it should be noted that the postgraduate library school at Sheffield University has oriented its work towards the needs of science graduates.

5 *The subject approach:* The increase in specialisation has led to the fact that 'general' librarianship, at least in its older unmodified forms, is less satisfactory from the point of view of use—particularly in large libraries. There has been an inevitable tendency in the UK to follow the American pattern of subject divisions in large public libra-

ries as in Bradford, Liverpool and Manchester (where in 1964 the central library was reorganised into nine specialised departments). Most towns with populations over 200,000 now have commercial and technical departments.

At a national level it has become increasingly apparent that libraries with national responsibilities, and in particular the British Museum, were individually so organised and collectively so unco-ordinated, that the structure at the apex of the nation's library system would have to be rebuilt. Ever since the end of the second world war, discussions have been constant as to whether there should be co-operation for the acquisition of foreign material (at present not guaranteed) on the lines possibly of the American Farmington Plan, or whether national libraries in subject fields should be concentrated on, or whether there should be a national library for the humanities in addition to the existing one for science. In 1968 (for other reasons) the Dainton committee was set up to reconsider the functions of the British Museum Library. At the time Mr P Gordon Walker, then Secretary of State for Education and Science, said in the House of Commons that the present pattern of library services was ' a patchwork which had developed piecemeal over the years under different institutions '. The committee would ' examine the functions and organisation of the BM, NCL, NLLST, and Science Museum Library in providing facilities. The committee would consider whether in the interests of efficiency and economy these facilities should be brought into a unified framework. Also they would have to consider how the needs for the storage of material should be met '.

6 *Library co-operation:* As is indicated by the establishment of the National Lending Library for Science and Technology, even within the field of interlending, it had been found that for special libraries the system based on the National Central Library and the regional bureaux was too slow and cumbersome. Other patterns of co-operation existed, such as the Aslib network and that of the former DSIR and the research associations, or the Science Museum Library. In addition, within the national interlending system, subject specialisation schemes were developed to improve coverage of the literature, and when this proved partially successful, a national structure of subject specialisation was superimposed on the regional systems.

Quite separate from this, a number of local schemes developed which linked together libraries in a particular area for an information service to industry. These arrangements follow a pattern set by Sheffield

(SINTO) before the second world war. In every case a public library became the centre of a scheme to link up information services, and there are now more than a dozen in areas including Liverpool, Hull, Acton, Manchester, Coventry, North Staffordshire, Mid-Staffordshire, Huddersfield, Nottingham, Hampshire and Bradford. They are co-ordinated by a Standing Conference of Commercial and Technical Library Co-operative Schemes.

7 *Technical colleges:* As is noted elsewhere, the technical colleges and colleges of advanced technology became increasingly important, and their library and information services now often extend beyond the colleges. For example, Hatfield College of Technology provides bibliographical and technical information to the County of Hertford-shire and beyond.

8 *The bibliographical crisis:* The technical explosion has caused a bibliographical crisis which continues, and it is generally agreed that, at least with regard to scientific and technical literature, present arrangements in most countries do not meet the challenge. The possible uses of machines are discussed below, but the solution also has to be found in the sphere of organisation. In the USSR a large organisation was set up—the All Union Institute for Scientific and Technical Information (VINITI). Since 1963 the enormous abstracting service Referativnyi Zhurnal (1953) has been expanded to include a large number of more specialised fields. In 1964 about 17,000 periodicals, 90,000 patents and 5,000 books were abstracted, and the abstracts were done by 23,000 scientists working outside VINITI. In spite of this centralised bibliography, it is admitted that in the Soviet Union there are many gaps and deficiencies. It does not appear that there are plans for large scale mechanisation as in the USA—plans which are mentioned below.

THE IMPACT WITHIN THE LIBRARY
Library processes, by their nature, lend themselves to mechanisation, and those who have worked in libraries have often performed tasks which appeared more appropriate for machines. In view of this it is at first surprising that mechanisation on a large scale is by no means always possible, or even generally accepted as desirable. What follows is a summary of the most significant developments.

Copying and communications: The improvement in copying techniques, especially the use of electrostatic processes, particularly Xerography, has helped to raise the level of library services, but as far as public libraries are concerned, developments have been more slow than might have been expected. For example, *Five years' work in librarianship 1961-65* reported that in 1964 only eighty one public libraries in the UK reported photocopying services. The position may have improved since then, and the smaller and less expensive electrostatic machines may have become more common in smaller public library systems. National and academic libraries continue to expand their copying services, which means that interlending can be reduced. The use of copying (for example by the National Lending Library for Science and Technology) is a more satisfactory method than lending for the dissemination of periodical articles. The American project for a National Scientific Library is based on this principle.

Improvements in communication methods, particularly the use of telex, have made it possible for the dissemination of information and the lending of materials to be speeded up. Telex services now link many of the larger public libraries, and by 1962 Buckinghamshire County Library had extended the provision of telex to all full time branches. Hertfordshire County Library has developed a similar programme, and telex is now used by most public and commercial reference libraries. Telex requests are normal practice for the National Library of Science and Technology, but the National Central Library and the regional systems have been unable to use it as a standard medium, since they are geared to a system of circulation forms. It is, however, used by them for general enquiries and is generally more effective than telephone or postal communications.

Microforms: Just as exaggerated claims were made initially for mechanised information retrieval, so it was at one time thought that the use of microforms might totally transform library practice—and solve the space problem. Fremont Rider's *Scholar and the research library*, drew attention to the serious situation in the great academic libraries of the USA, where stocks were expanding at an exponential rate and the microform was seen as a possible solution. Since then it has been more generally appreciated that micro-records are more likely to be complementary to existing library services than a substitute for them, and within this more limited scope the impact has been considerable. During the present decade, the production of microforms, and in particular microfiche, has greatly increased, especially in the USA, where government departments have been using microfiche to circulate unclassified reports. (Other government publications are available in Microprint, the opaque form.) In addition, the

National Library of Science project in the USA involves the use of microfiche to reproduce quickly information from the file at the centre. Various other bodies, such as NASA, AEC and OTS, have already adopted similar methods. This increasing emphasis on the microfiche for library purposes has happened in America because the roll microfilm does not lend itself to segment duplication, and the opaque microcard is also less suitable for making ' hard ' copies.

In Europe the microfiche had always been preferred, although its use has not been on the grand scale which is now occurring in the USA. The importance of microforms led to the formation in 1960 of what is now the Microfilm Association of Great Britain, which includes various groups, including one for library users and which publishes the periodical *Microdoc*. In 1965 OSTI made a grant to Hatfield College of Technology to evaluate the use of microforms. The use of micro-records for charging systems and information retrieval is noted else-where. The publications of University Microfilms Ltd have made familiar the role of microforms as a publishing intermediary—filming rare books which then become replicas of the original. To sum up, we may note that microforms may be used to save space with little used or bulky material, or as a medium of publication to make available rare or out of print material, particularly periodicals, or to provide copies of periodical articles in lieu of loan, or to preserve material, such as newspapers, which is in danger of deterioration or destruction.

Possibilities of mechanisation: Data processing or computerisation can be used for most technical processes in libraries and also for information retrieval. The distinction is not clear-cut, but if there remain doubts about the possibilities in informational retrieval (for reasons which are noted below), it is otherwise possible *under certain circumstances* to set up fully mechanised library systems and this is being done. Indeed, there are advantages in total mechanisation as compared with data processing for certain areas only. This is because once data has been recorded it may be used many times again—whereas in manual systems the same data has often to be retyped. For example, an acquisitions record prepared on punched paper tape, or punched cards, or magnetic tape, can be used for all forms of record, including accessions, catalogues, book lists and for a circulation or charging system. The most comprehensive integrated data processing system for an academic library in the United States is at Florida Atlantic University, where an IBM computer has mechanised all procedures through to the printout of book catalogues. It is worth noting that this was possible because this was a new library, and it is likely to be efficient in a way not possible in a smaller library.

However, it should be noted, particularly with reference to the UK, that mechanisation, for example with punched card applications, can be made for individual separate processes. In general it is apparent that machines when used properly are more efficient than man, work at a much greater speed, and that there is a reduced reliance on human judgment. On the debit side there is, of course, the cost factor, which often rules out mechanisation altogether. Some libraries are too small and others are too large to be able to change over from manual methods. There is frequently the difficulty of access to machines which are not used solely by the library. There is the further difficulty that there is a certain rigidity about machine systems, so that once they are introduced at considerable cost, the routines cannot easily be changed or modified for exceptions and variations. Another hazard which must be provided for is possible breakdown, and this usually means that provision has to be made for a temporary switch-back to manual methods. Finally, large scale mechanisation, particularly when it is first introduced, alters the structure and nature of an organisation and its management. This will inevitably cause stress and involve readjustment on the part of the staff. (These problems are examined more fully in chapter two of Paul Wasserman's *The library and the machine*.)

Charging systems: In the UK, for reasons which are not wholly clear, the traditional Brown system was regarded as satisfactory for public libraries between the wars, although it resulted in queues at the 'discharging' point of service in rush periods. During the last twenty years, however, various alternative systems have been applied with reasonable success, even though there are some limitations, such as those involving reservations or overdue procedures. From the point of view of the user, most of these methods save time and there is usually a staff economy. Several libraries now use a cheque book system (although this is a manual process subject to error); others have introduced 'Bookamatic', or explored the possibilities of computer charging (Camden). In general it would appear that in British public libraries photocharging is gaining ground, although one London borough (Kensington) has successively abandoned the token system, the cheque book method and photocopying to return to the Brown system. The main reason appears to be based on the reactions and behaviour of Kensington readers who are difficult to control! In special libraries, particularly in the USA, there are various computer controlled circulation systems. Wasserman has noted that the mechanised charging systems can be divided into two types: those using transaction cards and those using book cards.

Periodical circulation: A great deal of experimental work has been done on the control of serials by mechanical means. Many systems are in operation in the USA, the best known example in academic libraries where data processing equipment is used being at the University of California at San Diego. Because of the notorious complexity of this task the difficulties are apparent. It is not economic to have a large amount of computer input which will only be used once. One method is to programme the computer to print out each week a list of the serials due the following week, and these are checked manually as they arrive. Another (used at Purdue University) is to use cards which are automatically punched with the necessary information in anticipation of the arrival of the next issue. When the serials arrive, the cards are used to print out lists by destination and alphabetically. Cards remaining in the file indicate non arrivals.

The production of catalogues: It is at least established that computers can now produce a fairly effective catalogue. In central London the borough of Camden has produced a catalogue by computer, copies of which are kept up to date by cumulation, superseded issues being discarded. Similar computerised catalogues are being produced at Dorset County Library, West Sussex and Barnet. It is of interest that at least one of these programmes (Dorset) followed an OM investigation. In the field of special libraries, IBM's library operations are now entirely computerised, but for most special libraries in the UK the cost has been too great. In the USA the picture is different, and several academic libraries have mechanised wholly or partly, for example, Pennsylvania, Hawaii, Florida Atlantic, Maryland, Massachussetts Institute of Technology. In Canada, there is a project ONULP (Ontario New Universities Library Project) involving five academic libraries.

All these projects are based on the fact that cataloguing data can be typed on to punch tape, which is then computer processed to form magnetic tapes, from which both a master record and duplicates in various forms can be produced. The use of computer produced catalogues has brought about the return of the *book catalogue,* which most users probably prefer to card catalogues. It is also possible economically to produce *supplements* regularly, but not total cumulations. In addition, the system can be used to prepare bibliographies, acquisition lists, union lists and special purpose lists. These, however, may be restricted because it is again not economical to review frequently the entire file. For the production of catalogues there are, of course, other mechanised processes. Several institutions in the USA, for example University of Illinois (Chicago Undergraduate Division), Florida Atlantic University and (jointly) the medical libraries of Columbia, Yale and Harvard, have produced punched-card catalogues. This last, which is a union catalogue, in book form, is of particular interest because it is also a retrieval system. The catalogue employs a random access memory device to answer enquiries from each of the three libraries within a matter of minutes. As in the case of MEDLARS (see below), it is possible to use more subject headings than with a manual system, and there is a reduction of costs for each library. It is noteworthy that if this procedure were to be adopted more widely in university libraries, then the reference function and role of large academic libraries would change, and they could provide an anticipation service for periodical literature as the catalogues of the past did for books. Hitherto, intensive reference service has not been thought possible in large university libraries.

Other libraries are using various types of photographic catalogues, and the achievements of the British Museum and the Library of Congress in publishing their catalogues by photographic means, are sufficiently well known.

The most far reaching developments are likely in the field of national centralised cataloguing. In 1967 the MARC I project became operational in the United States, and a selected group of American libraries were receiving, from the Library of Congress, machine readable catalogue records of current books, on magnetic tape. This project shows every sign of success, and after OSTI supported feasibility studies in the UK, the British National Bibliography started in 1968 a similar scheme, MARC II—the immediate aim being the supply of catalogue records on magnetic tape to co-operating libraries. This project is not a system in itself, but a record designed to be used in any number of ways in library computer systems. The result is that a *total* record will become possible, and the form in which it is produced will allow for total flexibility. The project will also rely, firstly on the Standard Book Number scheme (promoted jointly by Whitaker's, the Publishers Association and BNB), secondly, on a new publication called *Forthcoming books* from the Standard Book Numbering Agency, and thirdly, on indexes provided by BNB.

The implications of this venture have probably not yet been fully appreciated, and its realisation depends on co-operation from the publishers (already forthcoming), and from the libraries that will use the tapes. It is, however, already clear that these developments could mean that the old dream of a universal current bibliography is, for the first time, within the realms of possibility. The American and British projects are already co-ordinated, and the system could extend to other countries. Apart from this, the scheme could be the beginning of a centralised national system which could go far beyond the scope of the existing *British national bibliography*, and could help bring about total automation in many libraries. It should be added that the need for comprehensive listing is only one of the problems of bibliography, and that the greater the quantity of publication, the more important becomes the other main problem, which is selective guidance.

Production of bibliographies: It is no longer possible clearly to distinguish catalogues from bibliographies from information retrieval systems in this context. Several important projects combine these functions. Perhaps the best known and the most significant is MEDLARS (Medical Literature Analysis and Retrieval System), from the National Library of Medicine in the USA. Since 1964 this system has used computer processes to produce *Index medicus* and *Cumulative index medicus*, both of which can now be published more rapidly and in an enlarged form. In addition, the computer can carry out bibliographical searches much more quickly and effectively than by using manual procedures.

The significance of this project is that it has shown that it is possible to set up in one large subject area a national bibliographical system capable of high speed searching. Once this has been done, it is now possible, by several means, to link up with other libraries in the field and to provide a centralised co-operative bibliographical service. Several new types of mechanical indexing have been developed. Of these KWIC (keys words in context) indexes have become familiar; they simply list alphabetically all the words in the title of the articles by machine. The advantages in speed are obvious and no real subject indexing is required, but the limitations of using title words only are sufficiently obvious. SLIC is a KWIC index based on a selective principle.

As the volume and flow of articles increases, the relevance and importance of the selective principle becomes more and more apparent. Experiments have been made, particularly by NERC (National Electronics Research Council) along selective lines with SDI (selective dissemination of information) to correspond with the declared interests of users. SDI systems have been developed by IBM for large organisations. The computer input consists of abstracts of articles, books and documents. For each document a profile of key words taken from the ' Thesaurus ' is read into the computer, together with the interest profile of individual clients. When there is enough of a match, the details of the document are printed out for the individual user. The significance of these mechanised SDI systems is that they attempt to undertake the equivalent of a personal service which is normally not possible for a large organisation. The machines, therefore, are not *substitutes* for the librarian, but undertake tasks which are impossible for him. However, the process still depends on the classification used— and this cannot be too strongly emphasised. A thesaurus, in fact, represents a recognition that subject analysis remains the key problem.

Another development, which many have considered to be of great significance, is *citation indexing*. This system links all the source articles, referred to in an article, with the article. The user checks on a particular paper and the citation index then tells him what papers written since the one in hand cite *it* as a reference. *Science citation index* is a monumental work: it does not require skilled indexers to produce it, but its value is probably still in dispute.

National Science Library (USA): This vast project envisages that all scientific journals will be made available through a national network, based on regional centres and involving other major national libraries (such as the National Agriculture Library). The scientific literature will be converted onto tape and eventually to microfilm. It will be a mechanised copying service to make all scientific journals available, and is really to complement existing library services.

INFORMATION RETRIEVAL

The above applications of the computer deal with the listing or catologuing of material, but none of them (even the indexing systems) are intended as a complete answer to the explosion of information and its retrieval. There exist in addition a number of computer techniques which are based on traditional methods. For example, experiments have been carried out to see whether it is possible for classification schemes on a given subject to be generated by computers. This is done by the statistical association of words in a given document, so that the machine builds up the scheme itself. Similarly, it is feasible to use UDC as an indexing language in a computer retrieval system, and, finally, co-ordinate indexing can be done by computer operations, where there is a comparison of items under each of a given set of terms. In the case of Imperial Oil Ltd in Canada, the co-ordinate system actually includes a description of the document, so that there is no need to refer to another file.

There remains a number of systems and proposals of much more ambitious scope. Ever since the first claims were made for electronic searching in 1945 by Dr Vauneva Bush, in an article in *Atlantic monthly*, many information retrieval specialists in the United States have worked with the hope, or the assumption, that *ultimately* the computers will produce the required results. Many (quite rightly) have attacked the chaos, duplication and waste in present library and bibliographical services, and some have gone on to declare that libraries as we know them today will be obsolete by the year 2000. This is implied in the gigantic proposal for the computerisation of the Library of Congress. The complete plans involve two main stages. The first recommended that the library catalogue should be computerised by 1972, and this would allow an extensive production of bibliographies, and beyond that the *reproduction of texts*—this last stage to be realised by the turn of the century. The report concludes that this programme is feasible. The system would eliminate the catalogue and replace it by consoles, where an electric typewriter would feed readers' enquiries into the system, and the relevant contents would be displayed on a screen in front of the reader. If the request should produce too large a number of titles, the enquirer would be asked to rethink the question. It will be noted that the reader would, in fact, conduct a limited kind of dialogue with the computer.

Apart from this project, other prophecies of a similar kind have been made. The Council on Library Resources sponsored a two year project on this problem and J C R Licklider, in *Libraries of the future*, 1965 (the final report), recommended a 'meld of library and computer' which he called a 'procognitive system'. The book will no longer be a central feature. ' By the year 2,000 information and knowledge may be as important as mobility. We are assuming that the average man of that year may make a capital investment in an " intermedium " or " console "—his intellectual Ford or Cadillac—comparable to the investment he makes now in an automobile . . . the concept of " desk " may have changed from passive to active; a desk may be primarily a display-and-control station in a telecommunication-telecomputation system—and its most vital part may be the cable (" umbilical cord ") that connects it via a wall socket, into the procognitive utility net.' If such a prospect seems repellent or remote to old fashioned procognitive systemisers, they should be reminded that at least one university (Western Michigan) has installed cables to all student dormitories to be used eventually for consoles requesting information. Furthermore, at the Grand Valley State College, the library was designed for 256 carrels, each with a microphone, two loudspeakers, a television picture tube and a telephone dial. After group learning activity, the student will go to his carrel for individual learning. ' There, by simply dialling a code number, he will be able to get a repeat of the lecture, excerpts as they apply to his assigned lesson, a list of problems. He will use the microphone to record his answers on tape, erase and correct them, if necessary, then dial his instructor. He then plays the tape for his instructor.' (This quotation is from Dr Sol Cornberg's article in the May 1964 issue of *Architectural forum,* entitled ' Building for books— are they obsolete?': the answer, for Sol Cornberg, is ' yes '.)

There is no doubt that systems of this kind can be constructed even now, and the Massachussetts Institute of Technology has produced INTREX (INformation TRansfer EXperiments), which is based on this same principle of long range browsing by television.

These are the more grandiose prospects. Meanwhile, information retrieval by computers continues, and more sophisticated systems are being developed. In view of the hopes that have been raised concerning the performance of machines, it remains to note that, so far, the evidence for their value over older conventional systems remains inconclusive. Even in the USA, many competent authorities are critical of the mechanisation projects; on this side of the Atlantic it has been consistently pointed out (for example, by members of the Classification Research Group) that the basic problems remain unsolved, and many would go on to claim that the American concentration on the computer for information retrieval purposes, has evaded the real issues. Certain limitations have always been admitted, even by the IR specialists themselves. For example, Licklider himself eliminates as beyond the scope of mechanised retrieval works of art and works of literature, although ' within the scope lie secondary parts of art and literature, most of history, medicine and law, and almost all of science, technology and the records of business and government ' (*op cit,* p 2). Similarly, Andrew Osborn, in *Library planning for automation,* edited by Allen Kent, p 61, notes that ' The world of the imagination lies outside the exigencies of the computer to a high degree '. He goes on to make a plea for a clear limitation of the areas of responsibility for IR and library science respectively. This sounds sensible, but implied in this distinction is the view that IR and library science are two separate activities, and that the arts and the sciences as far as libraries are concerned must go their separate ways. The two cultures are here to stay.

This may eventually prove to be the case, but it is possible that the dichotomy is arising because of an ill-founded faith in computers. Some of the difficulties are being overcome. For example, considerable improvements have been made with the development of the use of language by the computers, whether natural or artificial. But it is surely significant that it constantly emerges that the fundamental obstacles are still the same as they are with human information retrieval. The problem has been traditionally stated that it is difficult to find out what the reader or user really wants, and exactly the same thing occurs in dialogues with computers. The definition or description of the reader's needs does not correspond with the language system of the computer. For instance, in the case of the NERC project mentioned above it was found that the stated interests of the researchers (which is the basis of the system) did not correspond with the articles they found useful. Other objections are mentioned by Stein in a much quoted article from *Library journal,* July 1964, where he concludes that a ' reading of the literature does convey the impression that these systems (*ie* electronic computers) have not yet achieved a remarkable advance over conventional methods '. Stein particularly notes the economic and practical difficulties, with special reference to large collections. Also there is the obvious fact that the computers are still based on human judgment, either in the screening of computer answers, or in the system of subject analysis on which they operate.

In other words we return to the fundamental problems of classification, which are still there in spite of the machines. One important point which Stein makes is that these difficulties are inherent in machine retrieval systems, and that it is *not* a question of improving the machines. He also quotes Professor Bar-Hillel's reference to the ' great crudeness of the semantical views exhibited by many information retrieval specialists '. With regard to the cost factor, which has presumably limited the use of computers for IR in Britain, it is surely significant that the only existing totally computerised library on a large scale is that of the American Central Intelligence Agency, where WALNUT is a photographic-electronic library system which retrieves bibliographical data in about five seconds. It has been suggested that the cost of machine retrieval can be justified in such high pressure areas, but not otherwise. Presumably, because of the nature of this intelligence material, the system is effective, but from a wider cultural point of view it is difficult not to regard it as a sinister phenomenon. The computer plays this same role in the war games of the Pentagon.

To conclude, I have emphasised the question of the possible obsolescence of the library as we know it because it is of fundamental importance. There are, of course, the traditional humanistic objections to mechanisation from book-lovers or book-oriented librarians. As A C Foskett remarks in his chapter in *Five years' work in librarianship 1961-65*, p 463, 'who wants to curl up in front of the fire with a console?' But valid though these misgivings may be, I do not think they are central to the discussion. There is, particularly in this country, a prejudice against mechanisation, which is not unconnected with the fact that many of us do not fully understand the processes involved or the literature which describes them. There can be no doubt that the information crisis does exist and that traditional reference or retrieval methods have not solved it. There *is* chaos, duplication and waste. What I have tried to suggest here is that on the evidence to date, we cannot yet be sure that machine retrieval is the answer. Beyond this, there are factors discussed elsewhere in these chapters which render communication of all kinds difficult, and these wider social and cultural problems are outside the scope of the information retrieval specialists. This does not mean that they are irrelevant in our context.

11

underdeveloped societies

Almost everything worth recording on this topic has been said already by Lester Asheim in his book *Librarianship in the developing countries*.[1] What follows are some background notes conditioned by personal experience. They particularly relate to English speaking West Africa, but these countries can be regarded as typical of ex-dependent territories in many respects.

THE ROLE OF LITERATURE

In most African countries literacy and education developed as a result of the European advent—and in consequence the people were drawn into an alien culture which disrupted their own. The literature of the earlier missionaries seemed to tell them to despise their own way of life; on the other hand, the literature of the modern scientific world led them to ignore it as irrelevant. In British dependencies the schools taught the same things that were taught in the UK, except that little bits of local colour were grafted on. So long as the formal education system included the British curricula and examinations this was inevitable.

With the coming of independence, indigenous education structures have been set up through to university level. This change is a slow process and the problems need not detain us here. The implications for literary culture in the wider and deeper sense are, however, more relevant to our theme. Nationalists everywhere appreciated that the colonial culture should be replaced, but the obstacles were and are formidable. For one thing they were faced with the fact that almost all the literature dealing with their countries or with the world has been written from the outside by outsiders, and the result is a cultural imperialism which affects the people on many levels. Both in traditional and non traditional societies, people's attitudes are largely determined by the imaginative arts. The artist's vision of the physical and social environment provides coherent and significant patterns. In one sense the painter or the poet or the novelist actually *creates* the environment. Most of the literature about the tropics was produced by writers who grew up in another place. The result is that the local people can see themselves only in mirrors which heavily distort.

Nobody is quaint or picturesque to themselves, but only for tourists, and one's environment is not exotic but normal. Because of this alien cultural heritage, local artists have been forced to look at their world through borrowed spectacles, as it were. It is not just a matter of content, but of form and style, so that poets have tended to write in the manner, for example, of Alfred Lord Tennyson.

It is notorious that in tropical places people do not know about their own fauna and flora, but they are familiar with robins which appear on Christmas cards, or with the swans and nightingales of the poets. This tendency is carried so far that the frangipani tree, for example, which is found in the tropics all over the world, is in West Africa popularly called the ' forget-me-not '. In Jamaica somebody told me proudly (and incorrectly) that they have no wild animals or snakes —the implication being that this is a token of civilisation. It is only fair to add that this ' pre-scientific ' attitude is characteristic of all peasant societies where animals exist to be eaten, not classified.

But much more than nomenclature is involved. There are folk tales everywhere, but our consciousness (or, if Jung is correct, even the deeper levels of the mind) are dominated by primeval myths. Much of European mythology relates to the four seasons, and represents a cycle of birth, growth, decay and death, and again rebirth. A sense of time and urgency and change is partly a result of this seasonal rhythm. But in the tropics the seasons are static and one season simply seems to replace another. ' If winter comes can spring be far behind?' Substitute dry and wet seasons for winter and spring, and the meaning, if not wholly lost, becomes something else. These examples are quoted in order to indicate how the clash of cultures causes confusion and loss of identity. Many black West Indians insist that they are Europeans, and one can see what they mean but clearly something is wrong. In

South Africa the whites regard themselves as Africans, as indeed they are, yet their towns are plastered with notices saying ' Europeans only '. Something is even more wrong here.

READING HABITS

All observers have noted (and usually deplored)[2] the fact that in developing countries reading is largely utilitarian in the narrow sense, or what Landheer has called ' achievement' reading. For academic purposes, reading naturally follows the set pattern laid down for school and university curricula, as it does to an increasing extent in developed countries also. Outside the institutions of formal education, vast numbers of people read with some immediate practical purpose, usually concerned with the acquisition of skills or qualifications. These include many who have fallen by the wayside in the struggle to obtain higher education, and who are still trying to pass examinations. Imaginative literature is not read very much, and it is often suggested that if there were more local novelists, reading habits would be different.

There is some evidence to support this: for example, the Nigerian novelists are popular in West Africa. Similarly, the modern West Indian novelists are read in their own islands, although some aspirants to middle class status find them not respectable. In spite of this, it is my view that at this stage of development this utilitarian emphasis is natural and appropriate. Often novels are read in order to improve the readers' command of the language, and it is very relevant that in West Africa English and French are second languages. This slows up not only the process of learning to read, but also the reading rate. Those who lament the existence of this pattern forget that reading serves different purposes at different times and places. In Europe, and to a lesser extent in America, the reading of novels is a characteristic leisure pursuit of middle class elements in society. In Africa the social structure is not the same and women, for example, play a different role. The pattern reflects circumstances, some of which are mentioned below.

In spite of this practical emphasis, there is, of course, some ' culture ' reading, and in ex-British territories it is not wholly clear why certain British novelists are universally known. The obvious example is Marie Corelli, who is now forgotten in her own country except perhaps in some parts of Wales or the Outer Hebrides. In West Africa another favourite is Bertha Clay, a writer of old fashioned romances whose novel *Beyond pardon*, about a fallen woman who takes the veil, is part of every young girl's education.

Evidence which would show how certain works achieved this position is probably not available, but some influences can be discerned, and one of the most important is the historical impact of Christian missionaries. This may account for the ubiquitous presence in Ghana of a children's book called *The basket of flowers*, written by a German in the late eighteenth century—a nauseating story of religiosity and feudal values. The appeal of such works and of Marie Corelli reflects a social climate which in certain respects can only be called Victorian. Apart from such hardback literature, there is the usual popular demand for periodicals which offer cures for inferiority complexes, or information on the occult, or what the stars foretell.

The other factors which determine reading patterns in the tropics are well known. The most notable social influences are probably housing and lighting. (It is important to remember that near the equator it is always dark at six o'clock in the evening.) In many parts of the underdeveloped world one can still see young people studying in the evenings at the foot of a street lamp. We have already referred to the constant visitations of the extended family and the lack of privacy. In such circumstances children are not encouraged to read, and in any case in peasant societies children are a source of cheap labour and are required to help in the home. A tropical climate reduces the likelihood of solitude, and in addition to this it must be faced that heat, and particularly humidity, are enervating influences which affect mental activity and leisure pursuits. It is debatable to what extent this inhibits academic growth or material progress, but the impact is there, even if modern air conditioning techniques can improve matters for a minority.

In most ex-colonial territories the presence of an authoritarian tradition affects intellectual life. In schools and universities students expect their teachers to provide the answers, and books are not used for individual enquiry. This attitude naturally extends beyond the schools, and does not lead to the growth of wide reading.

I have mentioned so far outstanding environmental influences. These are so pervasive that some librarians have claimed that there is, or should be, a separate activity called 'tropical librarianship'. This seems to me to be an unnecessary, even a dangerous concept. Most of the social factors are, or have been, present in other countries. Special methods and techniques are indeed required, but the need is felt mainly within a technical area, which includes architecture and the preservation of materials. These, however fundamental they may

189

be, are professional problems only in the narrow sense. There is the further point that, apart from climatic similarities, tropical areas and their library requirements may vary in many respects—for example, language problems, or ethnic pluralities, or cultural levels.

Nevertheless, certain library planning characteristics and requirements which relate to developing areas can be tabulated as follows:

1 As in other fields, the central government must formulate plans for a national library service, and there should be some co-ordinating body for this purpose. This is considered below in the political section. Such plans cannot be based on the policies of older countries without severe modifications. A good example of this need for re-thinking is afforded by the national library problem. There is now general agreement on the functions and responsibilities of a national library. One of the functions, if not the main one, is to collect and preserve the national literature. If the national literature mainly consists of state documents, does this require a special institution to collect them? Another function is generally understood to be the collection of the most important literature of the world as it is published. Usually this is being done insofar as it is necessary or possible by university and other libraries in the country. Is another library required?

2 There is usually a need for a national bibliographical centre, since this work is not done by other agencies as it so often is in developed countries.

3 Because education has priority, the library movement should be linked closely with other cultural and educational movements, including mass education and literacy campaigns. How this is done is a matter for local initiative, but it may well be that, as far as public libraries are concerned, the British model, which tends to separate libraries from formal education, is a most unsuitable one. As I have already implied, the educational function of all types of library is paramount, and Unesco's policies have always recognised this. For example, in some countries the most suitable public library policy might be to set up libraries in schools, rather than to develop a wholly separate library system.

4 The notes above on reading habits imply that any sane library policy (with particular reference to public libraries) would be based on some kind of investigation or assessment of reading needs. This could be done without too great an emphasis on assumptions concerning what people ought to read.

5 In most developing countries it is apparent that what is required are *reading rooms* for a vast student population. This has nothing to do with the provision of reference libraries for information purposes. (This lack simply of a place to study is noticeable even in the cities of the UK. The nineteenth century fog which still hangs over some libraries in Britain is indicated by the fact that even now the regulations of some public reference libraries state that users of reading rooms may not take their own books in to the library.)

6 A fundamental policy problem in public libraries concerns the methods of taking books to the people. Should reliance be placed on developing properly organised branch libraries, or on mobile libraries, or on placing collections of books in other organisations all over the place, or a combination of these methods? Miss E Evans in her book *A tropical library service* states 'The Library Board made a wise decision . . . that no library should be opened unless there was a member of staff with some professional qualifications to take over'. And again, 'It was decided that book distribution to anywhere in the country was preferable to a pilot scheme, no matter how efficient'. This is an example of one policy which brought results. In different circumstances there may be others. There is the possibility of a kind of shock programme, where service is extended by a massive campaign to place deposit collections in every kind of institution—clubs, factories, trade unions, community centres, political party organisations, and so on.

This was done at one time in the Soviet Union, but it remains open to doubt whether such a policy is desirable, since these collections cannot be controlled and do not add up to a library service. They are uneconomic and wasteful, but it may be that in some circumstances such 'waste' could be justified on the grounds that this is the only way by which the mass of the people can be exposed to books. A new factor here is the increasing prevalence of paperback books, which might make it possible to undertake such a programme, or at least to supplement other types of service.

The other aspect I have considered worthy of note here is library provision for children. This is very important, if only because many of the reading obstacles mentioned above do not operate, and there is always such a tremendous response from children themselves that it is a most rewarding experience to provide a library service for them. The proportion of users of the public libraries who are children is immensely higher in developing countries than, for example, in Britain.

The difference is fundamental, and it is another instance where the British model is probably not the best, since library provision for children in that country has not yet been carried to great heights. In America library services are more 'child orientated', perhaps because a much smaller proportion of adults use public libraries than in the UK. American experience, therefore, may be more relevant. Returning to the new countries, the fact remains that the demand for reading matter from children is such that it cannot be met.

So far I have been discussing public libraries. The school library problem is perhaps more intractable. Unesco has paid attention to this need and there has been a pilot project in Lagos, Nigeria. Elsewhere, attempts have been made to build up libraries in secondary schools on the British or American pattern, but as a rule conditions are not propitious, and all that can be said is that usually some kind of library collection exists. There are of course outstanding exceptions to the norm.

ECONOMIC FACTORS

Since developing countries are, by definition, economically backward, it might be assumed that the amount of money available for library purposes is a decisive factor: poor countries must regard library services as a luxury. Yet as Asheim points out, the situation is much more complex. We are back with the problems of cultural change, and what it is that causes an economic take-off or breakthrough. Some societies do not develop even when they seem to have sufficient resources. The explanation can be found in the nature of the social structure, and the attitudes of the ruling classes, groups or factions towards relinquishing their privileges for the general welfare. This is most apparent in Latin America, where the gap between classes is so great, and where religious beliefs are still the opium of the people.

Underprivileged members of a community accept an inferior role partly because they are rooted in a static traditional way of life. Governments lack the will to provide social or educational services because it is not in their interests to do so. In the United States no solution is in sight for the social problems of the Afro-Americans, because in the last resort white Americans are not prepared to pay the taxes which would be necessary to finance an adequate social programme.

With regard to libraries, all that need be said is that if, for whatever reasons, libraries are not required or provided, then obviously those which do exist will not exemplify the canons of librarianship. If sufficient money is spent on libraries, there is a necessary emphasis on the preservation of those materials which they happen to have acquired and the librarian is primarily a custodian; the books must be locked up. In unpropitious times (and many countries have not known any others) the preservation of things, like personal survival, becomes a virtue and a duty. A foreign adviser in such circumstances may go wrong in recommending that old and out of date library materials should be discarded, or that access to books should be as open or liberal as possible. This may be a mistake even in university libraries, where material cannot be replaced. In school libraries, where there is usually a high rate of staff turnover, the main task of those responsible for the library is to prevent the dispersal of the collections.

THE BOOK TRADE

In all the countries we are discussing, bookselling and publishing operate under difficulties, one of which is lack of sufficient local demand. This means that libraries must import material from overseas —from the developed countries where publishers and booksellers and printers flourish. The problem of publishing in minority or vernacular languages is mentioned elsewhere, and we are concerned here to discuss the difficulties, which can be tabulated as follows:

1 Even when money is available, there is a time lag caused by the distance from the main world centres of publishing. Some items, notably periodicals, can be obtained by airmail, but the bulk of library stock must be obtained by sea transport. It is claimed by some public librarians that the demand for new books is ' snobbish ', or not quite respectable. This is an untenable view anywhere, and one which could not be held in an underdeveloped area where this time lag impedes intellectual and professional progress. For this and for other reasons there is a psychological climate which makes people feel that they are running in order to stand still: as in nightmares they can never catch up. Life is impoverished, since in the modern world a high proportion of new literature meets an instant need. In scientific and technical fields, and in the social sciences too, a book which is two months old may already be irrelevant—a periodical will transmit not news but history. Incidentally, it is here that the mass media of information have a special importance, since their impact can be so much more immediate.

2 The absence of local or national publishing must result in some

degree of neo-colonialism. The absence of adequate bookshops affects the laws of supply and demand in library provision, since the stimulus of demand is weak or absent. Often the only satisfactory bookshops are in the universities, and the mass of the people are not exposed to a variety of literature to stimulate their interest.

One answer which suggests itself is that national or public libraries should themselves undertake either publishing or bookselling or both. In some countries state publishing centres have been set up: these are possible and partial remedies. A feature of African life in the towns—one which fascinates the curious tourist—is the presence of small stationers' shops which display a heterogeneous stock of literature to meet local needs. Most of the books are textbooks and primers, but there are devotional works and political pamphlets.

3 There is also the problem of acquiring older material. New libraries anywhere may not be able to obtain standard works which are out of print. Micro-records and photocopies can, of course, be provided, and there exist the usual channels for the acquisition of earlier literature but there will always be some important items which cannot be obtained, particularly for research libraries. For example, in ex-colonial countries historical research can seldom be carried out at home because the archives, or a proportion of them, are held by the late mother country. Sometimes—particularly if various European powers have trampled to and fro—sources of information may be scattered all over the world. This affords the researcher welcome opportunities for travel, but hampers speedy results. (Apart from several million people who speak the English language in addition to their own, all that now remains of the British Empire is a cluster of extensive collections of official documents in London: the librarians are the last of the imperialists!)

4 The above difficulties occur either because books are new or because they are old. There are further trading barriers which impede the acquisition of *any* type of material—and the main one is probably the existence of financial controls caused by the shortage of foreign exchange. Most developing countries are deficient in this respect; in Cuba, for instance, there is, for the usual ideological reasons, a will to provide advanced library services, but books from the so-called Western world are unobtainable. The Unesco book coupon scheme was introduced to mitigate these difficulties, but it can have only a peripheral effect.

Exchange controls not only limit the amount of material which can be bought, but they also clog up the channels of provision, as overseas booksellers are reluctant to supply books or periodicals on order: they fear, often with good reason, that the payment of bills may be delayed for years. In addition, controls cause internal delays, and harassed librarians, before they can spend overseas, have to fill up forms and badger trade departments. It is worth noting in passing that economic controls usually work in a more orderly fashion if and when there is an honest bureaucracy. In most countries there is not, and bribery is a way of life. It is unfortunate that librarians are not well placed (or may even be psychologically unfitted) to respond to this challenge. Societies which are commonly called 'corrupt' offer splendid opportunities to the privileged or the enterprising to get things done by cutting through red tape with unofficial scissors. In some transitional mixed economies, the unhappy situation arises that neither bribery nor bureaucratic processes produce any results at all, since applicants do not know which approach to use. However, as already indicated, librarians, at least with regard to book provision, are rarely faced with these alternatives.

This relationship between reading habits and the book trade is a typical example of the manner in which the interaction of social and economic forces proceeds in a circular and vicious manner. The book trade cannot easily establish itself because the reading public is small, while reading is affected by the lack of stimulus from booksellers and publishers. To redress the balance and avoid misunderstanding, I should conclude this section by noting that, in spite of all these handicaps, the use of books continues to increase at a surprising rate.

POLITICAL FACTORS

New countries are bound to be politically unstable. This is in itself a symptom of growth, and all nation states in their earliest stages of development have suffered from severe internal political disorders. With regard to library provision this is one condition about which it is impossible to generalise. Where disruption is extreme, as in war, libraries obviously become irrelevant. At the time of writing the former Eastern Regional Library Service based on Enugu in Biafra has presumably ceased to operate and its future is unpredictable.

Many ex-colonial countries which have never known democratic government now have authoritarian systems of various kinds. Some degree of censorship is likely in such circumstances, and library provision may well be restricted, although press, radio and television usually bear the brunt of government controls. With some exceptions, these dictatorial régimes operate in a somewhat old fashioned manner, and should not be lightly equated with modern European totalitarian systems. The tyrannies of traditional despotism are mitigated because they are arbitrary, inconsequential and inefficient. The evil is there but redeemed, if that is the word, by a comic opera element. For this reason, any impact on libraries and other communication media may well be temporary and subject to the same fits and starts which affect all institutions.

In any event, from the point of view of political change, the advantages are not all with the advanced countries, which often combine stability with stagnation. The challenges of the present are not met because of the vast ramifications of out of date institutions; also, the developed countries tend to be run by old men, whose responses are at best inadequate. In this context both France and Britain in recent years can be quoted; in these countries the fixed patterns and frozen postures of the past have been broken only by two world wars. It is possible that they may not be broken again except, as in the United States, by a condition of near civil war. In this respect, then, the developing countries offer opportunities for rapid advance which are not available elsewhere; circumstances are disorderly but not torpid.

As a footnote to the above it is perhaps relevant here to compare the setting up of a library school in Ghana with a similar process in Britain. After the second world war the library schools in the UK were created in order to provide professional education for returning ex-servicemen. When this task was completed the schools remained, and developed into the system of full time education which exists today. In Ghana the library school was founded in the first instance following a sudden inspiration, or whim, of ex-President Nkrumah. (Those whose interests include comparative librarianship or social planning may draw their own conclusions.) The contrast is obvious, but the common element in these happenings is that both were accidental, in the sense that they took place owing to unpredictable events beyond professional, or indeed any logical control. One is tempted to suggest that this is how things always happen, but to develop the argument might subvert our faith in the social engineers or in rational human endeavour. Perhaps the moral is really that there are desirable limits to the possibilities of social control.

Reference has already been made to the fact that in new countries central government planning is essential. There are, for instance, insufficient resources to finance social services at local government level. In the sphere of library provision it thus becomes possible for blueprints to be drawn up for a national library service which stand a chance of being implemented, at least in part. In ex-colonial countries of the British Commonwealth there are excellent examples of national public library services, such as those in Ghana and Jamaica and (formerly) in Eastern Nigeria, but it cannot be said that these national plans have embraced all types of library provision, so that often the plans for special libraries or for a national library are inadequate. In the public library sector the question arises whether the national service should be run by the ministry of education, or by a separate department, or by an independent statutory board. Unesco in its official recommendations has usually favoured the last alternative, and successful library boards were set up in Jamaica, Ghana and elsewhere. This is a characteristic problem, because in some countries boards which are not subject to direct public control become weakened by financial corruption.

In other fields many of them have been abolished for this reason. Yet if we consider solely factors which favour the rapid development of an efficient service, the independent board seems the obvious answer. It might be imagined that the experience of European socialist countries in providing national services would be relevant for this purpose, but this is not proven. There is no evidence to suggest that the developing countries should in fact use any of the institutions of more developed countries as a model, and it is probably dangerous to assume that countries like those in Africa will follow on the same paths. Even so, it has happened that in countries where industrialisation is new there is the same tendency for special libraries to develop in the wasteful and unco-ordinated manner that was evident elsewhere. In view of the fact that nearly all special libraries are directly or indirectly financed from central government funds, this is all the more regrettable. It has often been suggested that at least all government departmental libraries should be co-ordinated, but departmental pressures usually frustrate such a process.

Plans do not always materialise; indeed many of them are simply accepted and then filed away. The projects fail to ' get off the ground '. India is a country prone to this circumstance, and any attempt to study the growth of library services in India, particularly if one does not go there, is impeded by the fact that it is difficult to discover whether plans which are described in the literature have in reality been implemented.

THE PROFESSIONAL SITUATION

The criteria which are mentioned in chapter 12 below cannot be fully satisfied in countries where the profession is new. The most obvious limitation is the small number of qualified librarians on the ground, whose efforts are bound to be clogged by frustrations and setbacks. However, in any comparison with more developed countries, not all the differences are on the debit side.

In the first place it is immediately noticeable that the division of labour and the creation of specialists have not gone so far as in more industrialised countries, so there is no ' image ' of a librarian as a certain ' type '. It follows that recruits to the profession are often of a relatively high calibre. This may be a temporary phase only.

Another obvious difference is that most of the people in key positions are young. This has clear advantages; those who hold important posts have not exhausted themselves in arriving there. But unless the expansion rate can be sustained at a high level sooner rather than later, the senior positions remain filled and there is no room at the top for too long a time.

The adverse factors which operate against library staff, or indeed against most new professional groups, tend to be similar in all the countries under review. Asheim commented on the lack of professional co-operation which seems to be inherent in their situation. Since the profession is small and opportunities are few, colleagues become rivals who are mutually jealous. Library co-operation can work only if it embodies joint self-interest, and if this does not exist the will to co-operate is absent.

The public library scene in Trinidad and Tobago exhibits in a rather extreme form several features which are characteristic in this and other respects. The service includes two entirely separate organisations—one for Port-of-Spain and another for the remainder of the two islands. It is obvious even to the most superficial observer that the two services should be amalgamated, and in 1959 a British librarian, Mr W B Paton, submitted an officially sponsored report which included recommendations for a unified service. As far as I know, this report has never been published, and its proposals have not been implemented, mainly because of the personalities involved. This kind of atmosphere influences the structure of services, the mechanics of library co-operation, such as union catalogues, and also the development of professional associations.

These last are in any case affected by the size factor already mentioned; if one considers that in any country probably only ten percent of the whole take a really active part in professional affairs, the difficulties are obvious. In these activities the question of incentives arises. In Britain, for example, librarians write for journals of librarianship either from professional zeal, or because they have something to say, but at the same time they are not unaware that their contributions may further their career prospects. In developing countries the last incentive may not be present at all, and it is correspondingly difficult to obtain articles for a professional journal when it is by no means clear that such contributions will help either the writer or the profession. What is more likely to further both personal and professional interests is political ' pull ' in the broadest sense.

If these social forces operate in the wider professional field, they can be identified also on the management level within organisations.[3] It has often been asserted that plans of all kinds get bogged down because of poor management techniques. This is emphatically not due to any inherent lack of talent or ability, but arises because of these same social factors which themselves are the result of rapid change. Partly because of personal insecurity and partly in response to authoritarian traditions, those in positions of responsibility behave in a despotic manner, so that full co-operation from staff is not obtained. At the same time and for the same reasons, those in subordinate positions lack due respect.

Perhaps the most fundamental staffing problem in starting library services from scratch is that of training and education. In the first instance librarians from overseas have to be recruited to set up the services and to train staff. Simultaneously, or at a later stage, the future leaders of the profession are sent abroad to obtain their qualifications, and so gradually a professional core is built up. If progress continues and the library system expands, it may be possible to set up a local qualification, preferably organised by an institution of university level. National circumstances will determine how and when this should be done, if at all, but certain generalisations are valid for most countries. From an educational and cultural viewpoint, the sooner a basic national qualification is set up the better. Overseas qualifications have the advantage of secure status but they derive from courses which ignore local problems; they are also, compared with national programmes, relatively uneconomic and slow.

Needless to say there are on the other hand formidable arguments in favour of continuing the overseas nexus as long as possible. Firstly, there is always local opposition to an indigenous qualification because there is the feeling that the qualification may find internal recognition slow, and external recognition non existent or reluctant. Secondly it is natural that students themselves usually prefer to study abroad—and a library school at home may seem to rule this out. The answer is to ensure that the necessary overseas experiences should be gained *after* the basic qualification—although it may be difficult or even undesirable to arrange a trip abroad for everyone. Thirdly, it may well happen that it is difficult to *guarantee* continuous development for a national library school. Breakdowns may occur because of difficulties in obtaining lecturers, or the libraries may reach saturation point with regard to qualified staff. In smaller countries the demand for library personnel is so limited that a national school cannot be supported.

One further outstanding staffing problem should be mentioned. The pressure of events may contrive to produce sufficient qualified staff, but the process does not necessarily provide for the middle levels. In emergent countries it is generally noticeable that they are run by a very able ' élite ', and this is one of the reasons why progress continues. Below this rather thin layer at the top, there is, however, an army of functionaries of all kinds who are inefficient, lacking in appropriate motivation and often half educated; they are evident in shops and offices and public services, and cause many of the frustrations of daily life. It is scarcely necessary to add that it is not their fault and they are not well paid.

This constitutes a staffing problem for most institutions and libraries are no exception. There are various possible remedies which involve recruitment, training and adequate incentives. The problem is mentioned here not to indicate the appropriate methods to solve it, but to stress its importance. If, as often happens, the middle or lower middle elements in organisations are not offered sufficient incentives —status or rewards—then there is a degree of personal discontent, and too many people waste too much effort in trying to reach top posts for which they are not qualified.

Any account of this kind is incomplete without reference to the role of expatriates from abroad in providing vital assistance for development. Given certain pre-conditions, foreigners commonly play an important part in building up institutions (in this case libraries), or in an advisory capacity, or in educational and training work. (Incidentally, it is in this educational field that the last expatriates are likely still to be found when the other key posts have been filled by national staff.) In most politically ex-dependent territories there are now many more foreigners than there were before independence—the main difference being that their national origins are more diverse. The contribution they make naturally varies with circumstances and with the individual concerned. They have a built-in advantage compared to local people, that they can often wield more influence through experience and a not always well-founded 'expert' status. This is particularly useful in dealing with political bosses. Because they are not involved in the play of social and psychological forces within the country, they are often in a position more easily to get things done. Their motives need not be suspect, and they are usually preparing to hand over their post to a national of the country, so that they are outside the competitive structure. (The problem here of course is not whether they should leave but *when* they should leave. If they leave too early the service suffers; if they leave too late unpleasant frictions develop.)

This is on the positive side. There are of course various limitations to this type of foreign aid which are only too well known. The more blatant forms of racial prejudice are now rarely to be found, but individuals who take up service abroad are not always the best people available. In some cases they are obviously unemployable in their own countries: as Asheim points out, the 'ugly American' in this role is not always American. Those who notably suffer from what Charles Lamb complacently called 'imperfect sympathies' may fail to shed their cultural assumptions, and their contributions will be limited in consequence. Some of the psychological aspects are mentioned in chapter 2. There are also culture barriers in reverse, and it may take a long time for an outsider to appreciate the significance of local practices, prejudices and taboos, which may be deliberately kept from him.

On a more practical level it happens that many foreign experts insist on trying to transplant from home methods, policies and systems with which they are familiar but which may not be suitable. Surprisingly few people can transcend their own experience, particularly if they are no longer young. There is the other difficulty that many foreigners do not stay long enough to understand their new environ-

7*

ment, even when they may wish to do so. Many Unesco or American appointments are for two years, and it is only at the end of this period that the visitor begins to ' belong '. This can be a hidden factor in personal relationships, since the local people have an awareness, born of inherited experience, that *they* will still be there to pick up the pieces after the brief spasms of the visitors have subsided. As a corrective to this emphasis on the disadvantages of short term assistance, one should also mention that long residence may bring its own dangers. If the outsider becomes integrated in the community, then his peculiar contribution as an ' expatriate ' may come to an end because he has ceased to be one.

I can agree with Asheim that outside assistance is in the last resort secondary in its impact, and that it cannot operate if the preconditions are absent, or the combination of circumstances is unpropitious. It is for this reason, no doubt, that so many foreign experts have laboured in vain, and that of all their efforts little trace remains.

CONCLUSION

The foregoing comments have concentrated on some of the troubles which the emergent countries face. I have used this approach because much of the literature produced by expatriates describing their work emphasises the exciting opportunities—the ' never a dull moment ', ' myself as a pioneer ' theme. This is all very well and true as far as it goes, but the subjective element is too insistent, and the writers are really considering themselves in relation to the people back home, rather than as part of another environment which has its own validity. (The writings of the missionaries used to exhibit this tendency, which was at least consistent with their aims.)

A balanced perspective is not easily reached; many expatriates form a love/hate relationship with their adopted countries which causes them to oscillate between optimistic euphoria and hopeless gloom. These attitudes depend on the critical criteria used or the terms of reference adopted. When the former colonial territories became independent, sympathetic liberal observers were over-optimistic about their futures; they were still carrying on the debate with the colonialists, who claimed that these people had only just come down from the trees and could not govern themselves, etcetera. More recently the pendulum has swung the other way, since there has been mounting evidence that the much discussed economic gap between the industrialised states and the underdeveloped countries is growing wider with every passing year. We hear much of the population explosion and so forth.

Perhaps a more valuable perspective can be gained if we try to look at this situation not from the outside and not by constant comparison with advanced countries. If we consider these places with reference to their own pasts, the rate of advance is astonishing. In view of the daunting difficulties and social confusion it is often remarkable that in fact things do happen, and new institutions do come into being where there was nothing before. The advances are particularly noticeable in all educational areas, and this is why library activities are important and rewarding to all those who are involved in them.

NOTES

1 John Dean, reviewing Asheim's book in *Unesco bulletin for libraries* 22 (2) March-April 1968, criticises Asheim on the ground that developing countries do not have a common identity: he notes the difference between British and French ex-colonial countries. It is true that these differences exist, especially within particular areas like librarianship, but there *is* such a thing as 'underdevelopment' and a vast literature exists about it. Asheim quite rightly attempts to interpret librarianship against this background.

John Dean also states (in conclusion) 'Dr Asheim's strictures apply quite as appropriately to much of Europe . . .'. For some countries in Europe (Albania, Portugal Greece?) they might apply but for others, *eg* Great Britain, quite other 'strictures' are required.

2 A good example of this approach is provided by Frank Gardner 'Unesco and library services in Africa' *Unesco bulletin for libraries* 22 (5) September-October 1966: 'Probably the most important long term, and certainly the most rewarding task, despite its difficulties, will be the fostering of the role of libraries in the creation, or the re-creation of an African culture. At the present time . . . the user of public libraries in Africa looks on them mainly as a service of supply of non-fictional material of textbook type, for study and formal education. Their cultural role is secondary'. What is meant by 'cultural' in this context is a matter for conjecture, and the suggestion that culture might be created or revived by librarians involves additions to their burdens which one dare not contemplate.

3 It is significant that Adam Curle, in *Educational strategy for developing societies,* searching for a common characteristic, states (p 69) 'If therefore I were compelled to define underdevelopment, I would do so in terms of failure to make adequate use of human resources'.

12

the professional idea

The professional idea is a cluster of ideals and attitudes which well illustrates how traditional values are being partially adapted to new circumstances. In the literature of librarianship, and of many other activities, there recurs this tendency to ask not 'Who am I?' (the search for personal identity), but 'What are we?' (the quest for group affiliations and collective importance). This is perhaps the inevitable consequence of the division of labour, which has continued to subdivide since it was first glorified by Adam Smith.

Whether professionalism as it is commonly understood is a desirable phenomenon is a matter of opinion, but those who believe in the significance of the 'worldly hopes men set their hearts upon' may consider that a professional person is socially more valuable than one who is not. Certainly from a sociological or statistical point of view, it is useful to classify people into groups and to give them labels, but when we attempt to grade these groups according to value judgments concerning their relative importance, it is clear that we are on shifting ground. The evaluations are not constant, and possibly for this reason there is a struggle for professional recognition, with some groups going up and others down. This, as we shall see, is largely a matter of status, but status in turn depends on a number of other factors.

ORIGINS
The various elements which, taken together, constitute professionalism are themselves changing in significance, and many of them have a

long history. For example, the element of mutual protection, which is common to all such associations, dates back to the medieval guilds, which included all those who were engaged in specialised crafts in a particular town. Similarly, the idea of the *specialist*, which is now modifying professional structures, was first noticeable at the beginning of the modern scientific era in the seventeenth century, and in this context Francis Bacon is usually quoted. In his sense the professional was one who had mastered certain specialised intellectual techniques, and it was the intellectual content which came to distinguish the profession from the medieval craft (or the modern trade union). Finally, it is important to note that the modern ideal of professional service is rooted in the former concept of the *gentleman*. This was, of course, a class concept, characteristic of the period before the rise of the modern middle or business class. The humanistic educational tradition had always fostered the idea that certain occupations were fit for gentlemen, while others could never be so, and this emphasis was particularly noticeable in eighteenth century Britain. Before they were absorbed, the *nouveau riche,* who had made their money in business or ' trade ', were inevitably regarded with contempt by the landowning gentry. (It has often been suggested that one of the reasons why the people of African descent in the West Indies rarely entered commercial occupations was that they had absorbed these gentlemanly values from the ' plantocracy ', which had imported their forefathers as slaves.) Once again we here encounter one of the sources of the two cultures division, because this ' classical ' ideal certainly excluded scientists and technicians as well as the businessmen and industrialists. Surgeons and apothecaries were certainly not gentlemen, while teachers were regarded as appendages of the church. It is likely that the modern British distinction between barristers and solicitors (now under attack) has similar class origins.

THE TRADITIONAL PROFESSIONS

Until the Industrial Revolution there were only four fully recognised professions, although changes were becoming apparent in the eighteenth century. These were: the church; the law; medicine; the officer ranks of the army and to a lesser extent, the navy. Of these four, only medicine and law retain their traditional place unchallenged today. So, for example, Carr Saunders and Wilson in their comprehensive survey of the professions, omit the church altogether, because they consider that its functions are now mainly spiritual, while other agencies have taken over its former activities. They also exclude the army on the grounds that ' the service which soldiers are trained to render is one which it is hoped they will never be called upon to perform '.

THE MODERN SCENE

Since the beginning of the nineteenth century there has been an increasing proliferation of new vocations. For instance, the engineers brought about large scale industry, and society required accountants, secretaries, bankers and insurance brokers. The new use of land required surveyors, auctioneers and estate agents. The activities of the state have continued to increase, and the ' institutional ' professions, such as the civil service, developed. This process has continued and ' expertise ' has become essential.

SURVIVAL OF THE AMATEUR

The elements which we have already noted as historically part of the professional ideal were not always compatible, and the cultural clash has continued to this day. The nineteenth century managed to preserve the concept of the gentleman mainly by the development of the public school tradition. As Thomas Arnold of Rugby wrote: ' It is not necessary that this should be a school of three hundred or even one hundred boys, but it *is* necessary that it should be a school of Christian gentlemen '. These institutions helped to make the Victorian age what it was, but the limitations, even then, were recognised by hostile critics. In spite of this, the idea survived that a person who had been to the right schools and knew the right people, was best fitted for the key posts in society. It is now usually considered that this legacy was an unfortunate one, and is still a drag on the ' modernisation ' which Britain needs in order to compete in a world where she is no longer a world power, and where the ' leadership ', once so important in a far flung empire, is of little relevance. From the point of view of economic efficiency this is undoubtedly true, and the amateur ideal could not survive in its original form. Yet in spite of (or perhaps because of) the fact that one generation of these people were almost wholly wiped out in the first world war, they and what they represented still remain as a significant force in modern British society.

Recently the traditional amateurs have been receiving support (which they would certainly repudiate) from unexpected quarters. As the emphasis on specialisation within professionalism increases, the limitations of the professional idea become more apparent. Carr Saunders remarked that 'Every profession lives in a world of its own'. He did not follow up the implications of this statement, but others have done so and it seems possible that if all the key groups in society do live in a world of their own, then culture must disintegrate. Marshall McLuhan has persistently attacked the entire concept of professionalism, which causes the individual to classify and to specialise and to accept uncritically what he calls the ground-rules of society. He objects to the expert as 'the man who stays put'. The case may be overstated but it is not without validity, and it is true that 'experts' are seldom trusted because they have ceased to be 'human' in approach to their occupations.

In fact, it is doubtful whether any group can wholly live 'in its own world', but this negative aspect is mentioned because the organised library profession in Britain and elsewhere often displays these ingrown tendencies and the results are uncivilised and disturbing.

LIBRARIANSHIP AS A PROFESSION

The American Public Library Inquiry which was carried out by sociologists came to the conclusion that if we use the generally accepted characteristics, librarianship is a 'semi-profession', or potentially a profession, at least in the United States. The same is probably true in most countries, but there is usually evidence of growth and development. What follows below is an examination of some of these characteristics, with special emphasis on areas where the foundations are weak.

ASSOCIATION

Professional people are organised into associations, and in Britain the Library Association has established itself as a highly organised and thoroughly representative body. This has happened partly because the association (unlike the American Library Association) has been the student examining agent, and in consequence most librarians belong to it in order to preserve their qualifications. Whatever criticisms might be made about the role of the association, what is relevant is that in Britain it can be relied upon to watch over professional interests. This is not so everywhere, and many national library associations are only half alive because they have no adequate headquarters or paid officials. Also, in many countries there is no satisfactory professional 'umbrella', and there are separate associations for different types of librarians or documentalists. Elsewhere the associations are too small to be effective.

Even so, it must be admitted that the strength of a professional body is not only to be measured by its size. It should have sufficient influence to ensure that posts are occupied by qualified people, and a group is not fully professionalised if some of its members lack qualifications or training: the professional idea must be recognised by employers, and in some libraries this has happened only recently, in others not at all. Some university and special libraries and the national library have not regarded professional qualifications as paramount or even necessary. In the case of government departmental libraries, professional recognition did not come until after the second world war. However, the situation continues to improve, although many consider that the strength of the Library Association will be sapped if its examining function passes wholly to the library schools.

EDUCATION

The second requirement is an adequate structure of professional education. This (in a very uneven fashion) has existed in the USA for more than half a century, and in Britain since the second world war. In other countries the situation is less satisfactory. In Britain one limiting factor has been that full time education (apart from one small school at University College London) came so late and the empirical tradition was so strong that the apprenticeship system operated instead for a very long time. One result of this was that library schools were established in technical colleges, but not until recently in the universities. The current trend, which is producing a proliferation of courses and qualifications, will create new professional problems, but an educational structure does exist and it compares not unfavourably with that of other professions.

AN INTELLECTUAL CONTENT

Professions are based to some extent upon a corpus of theoretical discipline or technique which can be taught. This requirement in practice means that the subject area (bearing in mind the existence of full time education) should be capable of treatment as an academic discipline, and also that the professional work itself should be of an intellectual nature. There are many, both within and without the profession, who have doubts on both these counts. With regard to education in general, the situation is confused by the undoubted distinction between those subjects which are purely ' academic ' and those, like library studies, which are vocational. In the latter case there is the peculiar problem raised by the need to work out, for educational purposes, a satisfactory relationship between theory and practice. Very often the content of library studies has been flimsy, disconnected or pretentious because a satisfactory answer has not been found. Much remains to be done, but there is no reason to suppose that the theoretical foundations cannot be refined so that they are at worst no more unsatisfactory than other professional systems of education.

The doubts about the intellectual nature of library work arise because librarianship is not a primary but a secondary process, in the sense that it organises other people's intellectual activity. It has been referred to as something which belongs not to the core but to the fringe of culture. In this sense it is not ' creative ', but whether creativity is an essential element in professionalism may be doubted. It will be claimed quite rightly that many librarians are in fact creative, as is at once apparent in their library services, but this is perhaps a statement about the librarian as a person rather than as a professional. The other difficulty in this context is the one noted elsewhere that many library tasks are decidedly not intellectual in substance, and it is not always a satisfactory answer to insist that these are not or should not be carried out by professional staff.

PERSONAL SERVICE AND A CODE OF ETHICS
Because professional people deal with the needs of individuals in a particularly fundamental fashion, certain minimal ethical requirements must be met. (The same is, of course, true in most human transactions, for example, buying and selling, and this alone does not distinguish the professional person.) But unprofessional conduct is socially considered—quite rightly—to be a more serious offence than profiteering by a businessman who is merely carrying his normal activities to excessive lengths, whereas for reasons already mentioned purely commercial attitudes can be justly condemned in a professional context. The theoretical distinction is quite clear, but in concrete situations the Devil has his own effective devices. There are, for instance, so many subtle forms of bribery, particularly in countries where ' indirect remuneration ', or graft, is a way of life. Other abuses are possible with regard to personal confidence : priests, lawyers or doctors are responsible for preserving their clients' secrets, and civil servants must not betray the ambiguous behaviour of statesmen.

In the case of librarians these obligations may often exist but they are less apparent. In the last resort what a person reads may be the most intimate thing of all, and this should be a professional secret. Many librarians worry about their social obligations when readers, or ' patrons ' as the Americans call them, seem to want to break into banks, or corrupt young persons, or poison themselves or their wives. There is a responsibility here, particularly in public libraries, when people try to consult books instead of the appropriate professional persons, but it is not one which should keep librarians awake at night. Similarly, if a cookery recipe chokes a family or a chemical formula eventually blows it up—this is not the librarian's concern.

Unprofessional conduct naturally includes all the usual ways of breaking whatever laws of the land there may be—but that is irrelevant here. In Britain it also includes applying for posts which have been ' black-listed ' by the Library Association because of inadequate salaries: this is something which is disallowed by any trade union.

In librarianship the essentially professional activity is personal service to readers, which requires both an association with individuals and specialised knowledge and techniques. In this respect librarians are not indispensable in the same way as doctors or lawyers, who specialise in *crisis* situations, but they are required for the long haul of life, and culture could not survive without them. I should also emphasise that ethical responsibility is present in a wider sense, because of the cultural role discussed in other chapters of this work. It operates in several spheres and at various levels—but the key element is the traditional pursuit of liberal values by the collection, organisation, preservation and dissemination of *all* human records.

If anyone considers this a simple matter he should bear in mind that the majority of cultures do not permit this to happen.

A DEGREE OF INDEPENDENCE
It has usually been claimed that a professional person is, by definition, a freelance. A profession, therefore, should possess a degree of freedom from interference from outside, whether from private organisations or from the state, but this autonomy is relative only.

If we examine librarianship from this point of view we encounter a weakness. It is here that claims are somewhat hollow. A large percentage of librarians are either civil servants or local government officers. In the case of the former, Carr Saunders and Wilson exclude them from professional status on the grounds that they are employed by the state *for* the state. Civil servants might disagree, and Nalgo (the union for local government employees) has always asserted that local government officers belong to a distinct profession—similar in status, but different from the civil service. Whether state and local government officers should be denied professional status on these grounds is a matter of opinion, not without importance since everyone obscurely feels that a 'bureaucrat' is in many respects an undesirable person. If, in modern large scale organisations, the bureaucrats are taking over, then it might be concluded that pure professionalism in the old sense is on the decline. In developing countries a disproportionate number of students seek to become lawyers because this is one of the few careers which is not controlled by the state. (The fact that the law may be lucrative is not the point.)

In librarianship it remains true that almost *all* librarians have a *dual* allegiance which limits their autonomy. Sometimes the 'other half' helps their position: sometimes it hinders. Many special librarians benefit as a result of the salary scales obtaining in the employing organisations; similarly, the salaries and conditions of service of university library staff are linked to those of their teaching colleagues, which may or may not be advantageous, according to circumstances or the level of the post. But whatever the position, these dualities inevitably limit professional autonomy. If and when the parent organisations are weak or deficient in some respect, then librarians suffer through no fault of their own. Local government in Britain has its peculiar virtues, but imagination and vision are not often present among them. The result is an uneven patchwork of public library services, partially redeemed by national voluntary co-operation, somewhat improved by the Public Libraries Act of 1964, and now (1969) about to be scrambled up again by the recommendations for the reform of local government boundaries.

To redress the balance it should be emphasised again that the modern state inevitably restricts professional independence on behalf of the public weal. In Britain, doctors, although they retain a degree of public autonomy, are part of a national health service, and there is increasing pressure for the reform of the legal profession, which has hitherto existed as an independent empire not amenable to social control.

STATUS
The final criterion for estimating professional legitimacy derives partly from all the others. No pretensions, from a social or cultural point of view, can mean anything if other people do not accept them.

211

Public recognition or prestige is, of course, one aspect of *status* which has inevitably invoked much discussion. This is a trend noticeable throughout modern society, and the terms ' status ' and ' role ' are often used in such a loose fashion that it seems advisable to start from the definitions provided by the sociologists. In its strict sense status is simply a position or rank, and role is the manner in which different personalities carry out the requirements of a particular position. In social anthropological writings there is a distinction made between *ascribed* status and *achieved* status—the former being applied to positions which are held without reference to personal qualities, *eg* male, female, adult, child. In most tribal societies initiation ceremonies are performed to mark the progress of an individual from one status to another. They are also called ' rites of passage ', and in industrial societies we have our equivalents in such ceremonies as those for baptism, marriage, funerals and the coming out of debutantes. On another level most factories have shop-floor ' initiation ' ceremonies (often directly obscene) to welcome new recruits.

With this type of status we are not concerned: in most cases it is not in dispute. The second type of status which is achieved is the possession of qualifications—and this again is quite simple; they are either possessed or not possessed, and if they are not then the individual has not achieved this form of status. The insistence on the qualification varies in intensity according to the society or the profession concerned, but in all societies where the division of labour has become universal, and where educational opportunities are open to individuals of ability (without reference to the capacity to pay for them), there is an increasing tendency to deny recognition to those who are unqualified. In the professional sphere such ' paper ' qualifications usually depend on examinations. The system is very much open to criticism, since it is obvious that many able people may be lost or crippled in the process; those who defend it usually declare that there is no fair or valid alternative, and this may well be so, but if the world should become entirely full of 'specialists', then clearly this represents a cultural decline. It is difficult for anyone to love a specialist, except perhaps another identical specialist. (This is one of the reasons why they so often marry each other.) ' For the specialist is one who never makes small mistakes while moving towards the grand fallacy ' (McLuhan: *Understanding media,* p 124).

But here we have to deal with the prestige aspect of status: it is so important that this is what most people think of when they use the word. Any society is—among other things—a *system of status relationships,* and in this respect we are no different from the animals with their ' pecking order '. It is evident that in a culture such as that which obtains in most of modern Europe, where class divisions are apparently dissolving and where hierarchies are no longer clearly defined, people generally will become more and not less conscious of status: they are in search of an identity; they need to be told *what they are* in relation to other people. The old comfortable order, when each man knew his place, has gone, and within the cultural heap there are disturbed areas where precedence has given way to confusion. ' Who do they think they are?'

The subject, as part of a larger one, cannot be pursued too far. At first sight it seems that status in this wider sense is mainly determined by the remuneration which society pays for services rendered. But further examination reveals that this is far too simple. What is the status of a stockbroker *vis-à-vis* a docker, both of whom may be relatively well paid? Some people get high *wages*; others get a low *salary*. Clergymen and teachers have always been poor, but in an unlettered world their status was nevertheless secure; now this may not be so. In fact, this is another chicken-and-egg syndrome—which comes first, the pay or the recognition? In some societies even now people may be respected because they are *not* well paid, and the respect is their only reward. Yet sainthood is not a profession.

Part of the confusion derives from the muddled values which we all share. Sociologists differentiate between ' overt ' and ' covert ' culture; between them there is always a gap. Where *large* gaps occur, the overt manifestation is that of ' lip service ' to high ideals which are too far removed from what actually happens—the covert situation. These gaps were very much present in Victorian England and are notorious in American society today. It is this mechanism which enables people in general, and businessmen in particular, to be high-minded and cynical at the same time. One common result is senti-mentality.

This circumstance is mentioned because librarianship, like the teaching profession, is recognised as being of great importance until the time comes for the provision of money for it. Our *real* values are reflected by what we spend our money on. With regard to librarian-ship, or any other profession, there are naturally several levels of reality. First, what the world says about the profession; second, what the profession says (officially) about itself; third, what librarians think about each other, and fourth, what they actually do. If these levels could be added together, the result might be the formulation of a status for the librarian—as distinct from a particular librarian in a particular place. But since this type of analysis is not an addition sum, we cannot arrive at a simple solution.

Students are often asked in examinations about the ' role ' of the librarian, and the answers are usually confused because the term itself is vague. When we discuss the role of the librarian in society we simply mean his social function in abstract terms, and this is not quite the same thing. If a ' role ' is the part played by a particular person in a specific situation, then an abstract role is a contradiction in terms. It is a *relational* term and implies first that an individual is conscious of the part he is playing, and second that other people can respond. In the sense used here, role is usually defined as ' a set of socially expected and approved behaviour patterns, consisting of both duties and privileges, associated with a particular position in a group '. It is the ' socially expected ' elements in the concept of role which link up with status.

Any individual carries out a number of different roles at the same time, or at different times, and some people break down because they are unable to change from one role to another. This may happen when soldiers return from the wars, or when individuals go to live in a foreign country, or when they return home again. ' One man in his time plays many parts ', but the range of most of the actors is limited, and some never get beyond one or two parts. If status is fixed and clearcut, as for example in a military type organisation, the individuals within it experience no difficulty in playing their parts. As far as librarians are concerned, the role of a university librarian may be more straightforward than that of a public librarian, for reasons which emerged in our discussion of social function and purpose. According to the nature of his personality, a town librarian may choose to behave (and look) like a minister of religion or the borough treasurer or Dylan Thomas, and in every case he may yet be a good librarian.

Partly because of television, we are at the present time very much concerned with the ' image ' of librarianship, which is the impact which our role playing has on other people. In a social and non-personal sense, a collective image arises. What results is, of course, a *type* and not a person. It is not without interest that in ' new ' countries, such as those in Africa, where the division of labour is a relatively recent process, these professional images do not exist in the same way. In consequence, whether a person becomes a lawyer or a doctor or a librarian is a matter of chance rather than temperament. This probably results in some loss of dedication, but specialisation has not yet gone so far that it results in 'peculiar people'. (A 'peculiar' person after all is often a person forced into too rigid a mould.)

Finally, we should not ignore the fact that professional status is adversely affected by feminisation. It is possible (although a matter of conjecture) that the status of librarians in the United States is lower than in the United Kingdom because of the much higher proportion of women working in American libraries. From the status point of view this is undesirable, not because women make less capable librarians, but because in a world where women are still underprivileged and likely to abandon a career in favour of marriage, a profession which does not attract men in sufficient numbers inevitably suffers in public esteem. In Britain there has been a steady decline in the percentage of men joining the profession, a trend which seems likely to continue, and presumably nothing can be done about it.

TYPOLOGY

So far it has been implied that the 'image' of the librarian needs bringing up to date. Potential recruits are likely to be influenced by whatever the contemporary image is, and apart from this may naturally wonder whether they have the qualities or characteristics required. Qualities needed for library work include accuracy in thought and action, sound judgment and a sense of order, intellectual curiosity and an interest in people, a strong sense of social service, and above all sufficient imagination to relate the world of recorded knowledge to the world of living people. (It is the last which is so often conspicuously absent.) It is obvious that these attributes are rarely found in the same person, but a library of reasonable size can naturally accommodate a variety of human types.

There is a pseudo-problem which is often raised as to whether librarians should be a 'bookman' or an administrator, as if the two functions were disparate and incompatible. This contradiction is for us much less troublesome than in the teaching profession, where it is not unknown for headmasters to be appointed who have little or no teaching experience. In universities many able professors do not take kindly to departmental administrative responsibilities. Some 'bookmen' are good administrators; others are not, according to individual abilities. Because of this alleged conflict, it is often deduced that the task of organising and administering a library system is exactly the same as running a department store or any other organisation. This is a fallacy which presumes that in a managerial society all the managers are faceless bureaucrats who can be happily transferred from one sector of society to another. It is mistaken because the principles of organisation, administration and management must include what is called ' policy ', which really determines everything else. Policy in a librarianship context must derive from professional ideals, and these can be understood or put into practice only by librarians; (for this reason organisation and methods investigations have sometimes produced ludicrous recommendations for libraries.) Both administrative principles and administrative abilities have to be applied in a particular situation. The application takes place within a wider professional framework and management is not an end in itself, but a means. The suggestion is often made that the end is *efficiency*; this nihilistic approach can lead to any kind of barbarism. One can only ask ' efficiency for what?'. The role of the librarian as administrator cannot be carried out effectively unless he shares the spiritual values which ' bookmen ' are presumed to have.

To redress the balance it should be made clear that the above remarks do not rule out the possibility that some ' non-professional ' people may be successful in librarianship posts. As Graham Jones has pointed out (in the *Encyclopedia of librarianship* article ' Librarians '), ' In three successive decades the London School of Economics, the Library of Congress and the Massachusetts Institute of Technology, among other great libraries, have afforded prominent examples of outsiders succeeding professional librarians. None of these libraries suffered conspicuous breakdown '. A man of outstanding ability can, of course, succeed in several capacities, and it is one of the more unfortunate results (in this context) that the increased professionalism prevalent today makes the appointment of persons from outside the profession less likely. The essential need is, however, that the body of the profession should attract able people in the first place and at the outset of their careers.

To return to the ' image ' problem, we find that a persistent image is the negative one: recruits to librarianship are often ' shy ', ' retiring ', ' quiet ', ' reserved ', ' withdrawn '. These and similar adjectives regularly appear on references for library school candidates, with the implication that such qualities are appropriate Some recommendations go further and state confidently that the applicant should do well in a secluded life. This is the traditional 'library as womb' concept. Certain posts in some libraries are, perhaps, sheltered, but library work generally is much more positive and outgoing than it was in former times. Robert Burton quoted Heinsius of Leyden as stating 'I no sooner come into the library, but I bolt the door behind me, excluding lust, ambition, avarice and all such vices, whose nurse is idleness, the mother of ignorance . . . and in the very lap of eternity, amongst so many divine souls, I take my seat . . .'. But today the door cannot be bolted and the happy extrovert must return to his vices and those of his readers.

A few generalisations may be ventured concerning noticeable personality types which have been prominent (or not so prominent) in the profession in the past. Even a cursory examination of the careers of earlier outstanding librarians reveals an unexpected prevalence of autocratic traits. Instead of the gentle scholars we might imagine, we find rather alarming tyrannical persons. One explanation is that the custodial function must have required a certain amount of severity if not ferocity. The habits of readers since time began are such that nothing but brutish fear will restrain them. Sir Edmund Craster's admirable history of the Bodleian Library, 1845-1945, contains a description not only of the extraordinary character of Edward Williams Byron Nicholson—one of the greatest of nineteenth century librarians —but also of Dr Bulkeley Bandinel, who was librarian from 1813 to 1860 and is less well known. As Craster remarks, 'the great Dr Bulkeley Bandinel was a law unto himself'. He was a learned man and an accurate and industrious librarian. 'Other librarians since his day have been as autocratic but none so terrifying. The library's treasures were his treasures, jealously guarded as his private property.' As always happens in such a case, it was the staff who suffered most, and 'Bandinel could lash with his tongue and had learned vigour of expression on the quarter deck of the Victory'. A daguerreotype reproduced in Craster's book shows a man of truly alarming mien.

Nicholson, who was librarian from 1882-1912 and one of the founders of the Library Association, had similar qualities on a more monumental scale. He was a reformer who thoroughly reorganised the Bodleian, and was impatient of tradition. 'In Bodley he was a tornado, the billowing sleeves of his MA gown scattering the papers of library readers as he dashed down Duke Humphrey'. His career was one continual conflict with the world in general and with curators in particular. Eventually he communicated with his sub-librarian Falconer Madan only by formal written notes. These two examples might be multiplied, and perhaps an even more splendid prototype is Panizzi himself—the autocrat who reshaped our national library at the British Museum. But he must be disqualified, since had he not been a political exile from Italy who chose librarianship, he would undoubtedly have made his mark in some other sphere.

I have suggested that these characteristics may have derived from the custodial role. Another possibility is that aggressive people came to the fore because librarianship was still striving to establish itself as a respectable (in the academic sense) profession. If this process was difficult in the university jungle, how much more formidable must it have been in the stunted undergrowth of local government, where public librarians were doomed to pass their days. Subject peoples everywhere develop tiresome authoritarian habits, and those who were chained to the parish pump had everything to lose but their chains —and reacted in the only way open to them: they indulged in truculent gestures. We should pay tribute to their success, since although academic librarians (like Nicholson) were prominent in founding the British Library Association and in its earliest years, it was the public librarians who came to the fore later and did much to build up the profession. (The Association as a whole during the period 1900-1919 was not particularly successful in its efforts, but that is not relevant here.)

There is the further possibility that these authoritarian manifestations owed nothing to librarianship as such, but were simply characteristic of the Victorian age, which produced such types in large numbers. Nobody supposes that libraries were entirely dominated by petty tyrants, and in any case even they were often opposed by their counterparts of radical temperament, whose aggression is directed upwards and not down. The outstanding prototype here is Edward Edwards, the father of the public library, but otherwise not a father figure at all. His encounters with Panizzi were often both absurd and painful. At one time Panizzi (symbolically) ordered him to cut off his moustache. In 1848, as Munford relates, Edwards refused to be sworn in as a special constable against the Chartists and signed the Charter instead. A year later, after various incidents he was dismissed from the British Museum staff.

It may also be mentioned that Chairman Mao was once a librarian: his interest in cultural matters is well known.

The two psychological types I have chosen are neither quiet nor reserved. A third and less troublesome group is noticeable. Library work has always attracted people with *obsessional* tendencies, and were it not for them (often toiling away in obscurity), so many libraries would never have become the national monuments they are today. It is perhaps wiser to be obsessed by processes rather than ideas, and those who are blessed with this kind of temperament make excellent cataloguers, and were adept at the many library tasks which required attention to detail and an ability to deal with one thing after another in an endless progression. I have put the last part of this sentence in the past tense because at least some of this work can now be done by machines. But enough remains for man, and it should be emphasised that these labours were never wholly clerical, because judgment and professional expertise was and is required. No examples can be quoted, since it is an essentially anonymous group, and those who belong to it make an indispensable contribution. They tend, however, to collapse when given managerial posts as they are unable to *delegate authority*. Nicholson was obsessional in another way, and frittered away much of his time by pursuing boys on his staff who had forgotten to take off their goloshes, or students who improperly left their bicycles in the quad.

It seems that so far I have accidentally proceeded on Adlerian lines, and perhaps I should pay greater attention to the law of averages. Bernard Palmer says that his ' private code name for the librarian when he is at his most dynamic is " Little friend of all the world ".' The reference is to Kipling's Kim, and this seems to me unfortunate, for it sets up an image lacking in dignity. In ancient times librarians, like scholars generally, were often slaves whose lives were at the mercy of some whimsical potentate.

It seems inappropriate to regard the librarian in this light, yet the concept is important. The best librarians have usually been moved by a passionate interest in the contents of books, and a missionary desire to extend the areas of light further into the darkness which surrounds us all. The term ' cultural missionary ' is, of course, an embarrassing phrase which no self respecting librarian would now use, but it does suggest the dynamic role of the librarian in the recent past. It refers, in fact, to motivation not total behaviour, and the implications are democratic in the nineteenth century liberal sense. The librarian as secular priest may have been inspired by ' progressive ' assumptions which are now less easily made, but this kind of motiva-

219

tion is still important. On another level, it may take the form simply of a humanitarian wish to help people. Those who lack this attitude may find many types of library service unrewarding. Whether this service ideal is sufficient to form the core of the librarian's ' creed ' is discussed in the last chapter of this book.

THE ESSENTIAL ACT

It follows from the above that the key professional activity is the *personal* relationship to the reader. A person in charge of a library system, however large or small, organises or should organise his library for this purpose, and where it is intensely felt, the professional service of all the members of a library is at the highest level. This seems so obvious that it is scarcely worth printing. Yet it is precisely at this point that so many library services fail, because the final act of dealing with a particular reader's needs can only be successful if it is based on a highly developed service, with all that this implies in the quantity and quality of stock, staff and organisation. If this were not so, the librarian would be nothing more than what the less well informed members of the body politic have always imagined him to be—a stamper out of books.

To conclude this discursive discussion of role and personality, it is of interest that many apologists and critics have dealt with this problem by analogy, and such an exercise is not without profit. The custodians were described by the eighteenth century poet:

' Unlearned men of books assume the care,
  As eunuchs are the guardians of the fair.'

Other analogies have revealed an awareness of the more positive qualities which are now required for the role. One writer referred to the librarian as a ' kind of celestial Pandarus ' guiding the reader to chambers of Truth and Beauty. (If any prospective librarian should feel dismay at this comparison, he should be reminded that the pander is a member of an ancient and necessary calling, who still plays an important role in international hospitality.) As Shakespeare's Troilus says, ' But Pandarus—O gods how you do plague me. I cannot come to Cressida but by Pandar '. The frequent comparison with midwifery is also relevant, and there is a significant implication that the librarian is interested only in those who are suffering from intellectual birth pangs, however short. Finally, the analogue of the librarian as a *catalyst* is perhaps particularly appropriate. The *Concise Oxford dictionary* says that catalysis is an ' effect produced by a substance that without undergoing change itself aids a chemical change in other bodies '. In other words, the librarian does not instigate the change but he facilitates it, and the significance of the analogy is that this facilitation often takes the form of *speeding up the process or the reaction.*

It happens, of course, that in despondent moments librarians wonder whether their job is ' worthwhile ' enough, or whether their merits are properly appreciated or their efforts recognised. Such misgivings sometimes underly the professional apologia at official conferences: the speakers protest too much. What they are *really* worried about is the human condition—what the Victorian books for children refer to as ' our lot '. If anyone doubts this, I would remind him that the members of other professions suffer the same pangs. The lawyer in his crooked world, the teacher on his treadmill, the doctor conscious of his quackery, the priest whom God forsakes—each has to face the moments of doubt. This should be a consolation to us all.

CONCLUSION

This survey can be summed up by noting that it is insufficient to assume that professionalism is necessarily something altogether to be wished for, and that in any case it represents a collection of ideas which continually change. Insofar as we may wish to propose that librarianship is a profession, then the claim can be upheld subject to the reservations noted above. Beyond this the discussion is sterile.

Reference has been made to the dangers inherent in professionalism as it often exists. In *Science and the modern world,* Whitehead refers to the unprogressive characteristics of professional organisations. It was suggested above that, as far as librarians are concerned, this alleged deficiency often takes the form of a failure to relate the world of our own to the world outside. At the same time it must be admitted that associations of any kind can be a protection against the so called mass society and the growth of a vast bureaucracy. Carr Saunders and Wilson state that the function of the professional is to bring knowledge to the service of power, and this definition is particularly appropriate for librarians.

13

the nature and purpose of librarianship

Librarianship, like most words, has several meanings. It refers to a profession, or to a body of knowledge which can be studied, or, finally, to the application of this knowledge to practical activity. In this chapter I am concerned solely with the last meaning: what do librarians do? If we are dealing with an activity we are discussing *function*. The *Concise Oxford dictionary* defines function as 'an activity proper to anything; a mode of action by which it fulfils its purpose'. We begin here then, by defining function (as in other chapters of this book there is an attempt to examine objectives, aims, goals or purposes).

The available definitions of librarianship all include four main areas of activity. They indicate that librarians are responsible for:

1 The collection of material appropriate for libraries.

2 The preservation of the material.

3 The organisation of the collections.

4 The dissemination of the material or the information which it contains. This may include interpretation.

Preservation and organisation (2 and 3) are often treated as one, so that the function has been expressed simply as acquisition, management and use of appropriate material. This is convenient, but the word 'use' is not accurate, and what is required is something to indicate 'making available'. Shera, in more general terms, has referred to 'the management of human knowledge'. Most fully developed modern library services include all four elements.

Some libraries carry out the first three functions only, and in unfavourable circumstances the first two may be all that is possible, and it is these which historically were so important. The history of libraries indicates how each culture maintained itself by the preservation of records, and how libraries were an indispensable agency in bridging the gaps in time between different civilisations. The library is thus an *active* medium of communication, because without the libraries the books would not have survived. This is what Professor Irwin has called ' the golden chain ', and this is how the intellectual content of the cultures of ancient Greece and Rome was preserved. Without this survival, even if evidence of early civilisations is to be found in rocks and ruins, we should be unable to interpret it, and our mental landscape would still be haunted by giants and trolls. Eventually even the legends themselves can survive only in the library.

We should be grateful therefore for the chains which tethered books in the old cathedral libraries, and for the frightful maledictions which the medieval monks called down to frighten delinquents in their libraries. References to the monks may serve also to remind us that this preservation process can be regarded as such only in retrospect. The modern librarian is conscious of his responsibilities to posterity, but it seems likely that this is only a recent attitude, and that the librarians of the past were innocent of any such intentions. If we now think of a golden chain it was not always thought of in this way in the past, and the concept obscures the fact that the chain must necessarily be incomplete and that some of the links are missing.

Librarianship has now built on to the traditional foundations a structure called ' the organisation of knowledge ', and a superstructure which enables that organised knowledge to be transmitted. (Elsewhere I have referred to these areas of librarianship as three levels of service divided according to the degree of service to the individual user.)

THE SPECIALISED FIELDS

Like other activities in industrialised countries, librarianship has become increasingly specialised. Various groups devise slogans for banners of their own and, unless restrained, begin to march away in all directions. All I can do is mention those types of librarianship where an accurate description may be defeated by areas of obscurity— and to stress aspects which are peculiar to one type of work.

People become specialists because they respond to a new social challenge. In librarianship the challenge is threefold. First, there is the response to types of material; second, there is the response to the needs of groups of readers; third, there is the response to areas of subject knowledge and their differences in breadth and depth. It is the modern developments in these three areas which have resulted in the growth of different types of librarianship.

THE SPECIALISED FIELDS: NATIONAL LIBRARIES

The primary function of the national library is clear enough. National libraries are set up to preserve the literature produced in a particular country, and this function is carried out by means of legal deposit laws, which ensure that every item published is collected and preserved in one or more national collections. This concept is often extended to include material in all languages *about* a country.

Beyond this activity there are other possible functions which national libraries may carry out, and many other libraries which may be called national because they are, for various reasons, of national importance. The word is, in consequence, used in this wider sense to cover many different types of organisation, and really has no exact meaning. There is the further difficulty that often libraries which are national in the wider, or even in the legal deposit sense, are also university or special libraries, for example, the university legal deposit libraries in Britain and in Scandinavia. I could best describe the situation simply by saying that there are different types of national library, but that the one essential and common function is that of legal deposit.

Because of this variation, much difficulty has been encountered in attempting to define the true nature of a national library. As Pierre Bourgeois, the Director of the Unesco symposium on ' National libraries: their problems and prospects ' in 1958, stated (page 2): ' We still do not know what a national library really is, nor can we name with certainty the functions it must fulfil in order to be called " national " '. He then asked whether it is urgent for us to know this and answers in the affirmative. Before offering our own answer (which was implied in the Unesco discussions), we should note some of the possible variations.

The secondary responsibilities include that of collecting or selecting current foreign literature, the setting up of national bibliographical and information services, and a leadership role in the planning of

224

library services generally—a role which may include library training and education. They are merely three of the most important of possible functions, and of these, the collection of world literature is of special significance. It increasingly happens that this type of provision is carried out by special libraries in particular fields; these come to be regarded as national libraries, and some of them also benefit by legal deposit. The outstanding example is the National Library of Medicine in America. There may also be national libraries for special readers, such as the blind.

Behind this development there lies the fact that the traditional all-embracing, general national library no longer relates to modern needs, partly because there is a clash between the several functions and purposes for which it was originally set up. Some degree of decentralisation has become necessary for national library provision in developed countries, even if it involves nothing more than subject divisions within the national library. This decentralisation or division of responsibility may also be necessary for functional reasons, notably with regard to the two conflicting functions of lending and reference. In Britain, for example, there is a separate lending system, with the National Central Library at its centre, and this is clearly a national library in the wider sense noted above. This distinction between lending and reference is necessary for practical purposes, but it is fundamentally an arbitrary one, since the reading material itself cannot logically be classified in this way. This complication is mentioned because, however well organised library services may be, there are likely to be gaps, for example, when people want to borrow material mainly for reference purposes, or to refer to material which is commonly lent—and not immediately available. This is usually possible for the staff in academic libraries to arrange, but outside the universities not so. This is why in Britain the London Library (the one remaining important private general subscription library) was set up and why it continues to be necessary.

Another increasingly important factor in modern library service is that the needs and methods of research workers in the sciences are different from those of scholars in the humanities, and it may be necessary to set up separate national libraries for the two areas.

To conclude, we should return to Pierre Bourgeois's statement quoted above, and ask why we do not know what a national library really is. Once we go beyond the legal deposit definition, the answer surely must be, first, that the pattern must be different in each country, and second, that it is impossible to define these wider functions without reference to a national library system as a whole. This conclusion, implied in the Unesco discussions, if correct, is most important, because plans and policies for national libraries are often worked out in isolation, and a national library is, or should be, merely one part of a national structure. (This is particularly relevant in underdeveloped countries, since in their case a wholly different pattern may be necessary.) That is why the term ' national librarianship ' is meaningless, and why the problem as stated is pseudo, and why a wider definition of functions for one particular library is not possible.

THE SPECIALISED FIELDS: UNIVERSITY LIBRARIES

On one level the functions of the university library are clear enough: they are naturally to serve the aims of the university, which are to transmit knowledge and to expand or increase knowledge by research. At the present time there is controversy concerning the social or national role of universities with reference to the needs of the state, but this does not concern us, since the library's function necessarily follows university aims whatever these may be. As noted above there is a conflict of functions with regard to preservation and current use; there is also a conflict from the library point of view between the needs of teaching and research. Apart from these obvious divergences, which are resolved by policy decisions on priorities, there is another factor which is peculiar to academic librarianship. In most library work the professional task is a two-way relationship between the reader and the librarian. In university and college and school libraries there is a third person involved, the teacher. This gives the work of the academic librarian an extra dimension, even greater complexity, since he is in a sense one of the bridges between the student and the teacher. Just as the special librarian requires subject knowledge, so the university librarian needs to be a scholar, and this implies that he has to help the student to help himself in the use of books for scholarly purposes. The function of the library is therefore educational, not only in the sense that a university is an educational institution, but also because the library itself has an educational function within the university. All libraries have this responsibility to some degree, but in academic libraries it is, or should be, of paramount importance.

THE SPECIALISED FIELDS: PUBLIC LIBRARIANSHIP

That mythical non-specialist ' the man in the street ' would naturally think of a public library as any library which is open to the public, and indeed the term is so used in countries where the public library tradition, as understood in Britain and the United States, has not developed. Since this book is a product of this tradition, we can safely describe a wider concept: this includes four main elements, *ie* first, that public libraries are available for the loan of material and for reference purposes to *all* citizens; second, that public libraries are *mainly* supported from public funds, either on a local or on a national basis. These are the two essential criteria. The third element is that their services as far as the individual is concerned should be *free*. This characteristic is built into the public library concept for historical reasons—so much so that public libraries in Britain in the nineteenth century were called ' free libraries '.

As we shall see, the social consequences were not wholly fortunate, but the free aspect is important because the movement developed as part of modern liberal democracy, which is based on the idea that there should be equal opportunities for all. It is implied that all citizens are *not* free to use the library if a charge is made. It will be apparent that in the affluent society this emphasis carries less weight, but at the present time it is still there. The fourth foundation is that all material should be made available as an integral part of the Rights of Man.

Little proof is required to show that these requirements are rarely met in full. The attempt to meet them constitutes the history of the public library movement, which is inevitably a story of struggle, like all democratic developments. If we return to our three challenges as described above, we find that public libraries came into existence to provide *every* kind of material (at least in theory) to *all* the people on *all* subjects. One has only to make this statement for it to become apparent that this is impossible and this is the historical dilemma of the public library.

THE SPECIALISED FIELDS: SPECIAL LIBRARIANSHIP
The cultural changes caused by the growth of technology have resulted in an extensive increase in the number and scope of special libraries. They are *primarily* concerned with the fourth of the activities defined above (dissemination of information), and they have been able to develop the required techniques intensively because they operate in a restricted subject area. It is necessary to examine the concept of special librarianship carefully, because there are differences of emphasis which are often hidden causes of controversy.

If we look at the three elements we can establish that the word 'special' originally applied to the subject area, which is restricted, and this is still the *main* distinction. The material is not *necessarily* different from that in other types of library, but it usually includes a large proportion of items on very specific topics or segments of information. Finally, the readers are usually members of a particular organisation. Most definitions stop here, but special librarianship in its developed form implies that these members have a *common purpose*. If we lay stress on this aspect it follows that some libraries in special subject fields are not special libraries in the full sense, and this would apply also to some college libraries. It remains to note that several definitions have been offered which concentrate neither on the subject nor on the special groups of readers, but on the special *activity* which special librarians undertake. Thus Heinkle claims that 'whenever the librarian does some of the readers' work he is giving " special service " '. When a primary part of his job is *doing research for readers,* he is a special librarian, regardless of the subject matter of the search or the type of library in which it is made. The emphasis is then shifted from *what* is done to *how* it is done. The difficulty about this definition considered by itself is that it would allow *any* librarian to claim that he is a special librarian at least some of the time, since this is one of the activities in the definition we started with. However, it is important to include this concept along with the others, because it is precisely on this element of the *type of work done* that the documentalists base their claim to be a different profession.

THE SPECIALISED FIELDS: DOCUMENTATION

In many countries there are people working in libraries who call themselves documentalists and not librarians. There are separate international associations, one for documentation and one for librarianship. It is important, therefore, that we should note the relationships between the two fields and historical background. There is a considerable literature on this matter, and the best modern exposition is Shera's *Documentation and the organisation of knowledge.* The present section is little more than a summary of his analysis, together with that of Foskett in the introduction to the English edition of the work.

There is small profit in examining the available definitions because we should find *in every case* that the definition would include some or all of the four activities mentioned above as characteristic of librarianship. The most succinct of these descriptions has been quoted from the *Schweizer lexicon*: ' The handling and organisation of scholarly materials '. This serves our purpose very well, since these seven words include the word ' scholarly '. Similarly, the definition offered by S C Bradford includes the words ' creative specialist '. We need go no further than this to arrive at the conclusion that, while librarianship is concerned with all types of material for all types of user, documentation on the other hand is primarily concerned with the world of specialised information, scholarship and research. In other words, documentation is simply this information aspect or function of librarianship carried out in depth.[1] For this reason it is confined to certain types of material and certain types of reader. It is ' an essential part of our modern system of graphic communication within the world of scholarship, an instrumental device to expedite the flow of recorded information *within* a group of specialists or between various groups of specialists '.

This, then, is the real distinction insofar as there is one, and according to the approach used here the nature of the activity is the same. There is a difference of degree, that is all.

The divergence between the two fields is not unconnected with the two cultures problem, and it was only natural that workers in special libraries should feel that the techniques in general librarianship which had developed in the later part of the nineteenth century were not relevant to their modern needs. At that time and for a long while afterwards, public librarians, for example, were preoccupied with concerns which did not include the provision of information by subject analysis. Those of their users who required such service went elsewhere, and it is only fair to add that in the UK a penny rate limitation usually meant that, even if the staff had been capable of dealing with specialised enquiries (which they were not), the financial resources for such activities were not there.

Before the emergence of the modern mass media of communication, the public library was necessarily more involved with mass enlightenment than it is now. Because of this, on a theoretical level it was difficult to integrate the new specialised requirements into the existing professional structure of ideas, which were undeveloped in any case. So the documentalists went another way, and in most European countries they had no choice, since ' general ' librarianship was so rooted in the humanities that it could not help. To quote Shera again, ' Thus an important part of the bibliographic mechanism for providing access to a large body of contemporary literature passed out of the hands of the library profession and insofar as the material was concerned the library was reduced to its older function of physical custodianship'. He is referring here to periodical literature and presumably to conditions in the United States. In the UK, although the tendency to set up a separate profession, with all that this implies, is present, it has been possible to a considerable extent to preserve professional unity. The sheep are obviously of different colours and breeds, but they are recognisably sheep and should stay within the fold.

THE SPECIALISED FIELDS: ARCHIVES

The preservation of records is one of the oldest librarianship activities. If we apply our threefold analysis, we find that archive work is specialised, because the type of material is distinct, the users are (more or less) a group and the 'subject' is historical. This type of material involves special techniques, such as 'calendaring', and special knowledge, such as palaeography or institutional history. It may be useful to add that collections of archives are rather like a library of unprinted books without indexes, and since their subject is really the history of institutions, such as a government department, the normal rules of subject classification do not apply. The archives concept for obvious reasons also involves the notion that the records are *complete*. The scope of these activities is unequivocal.

PROFESSIONAL AND OTHER QUALIFICATIONS

Special librarianship and documentation involve not only specialised techniques which come firmly within the sphere of librarianship, but also qualifications in subject areas, or subject knowledge as it is usually called. For some library posts it may be in dispute whether a qualified scientist (who must then learn library techniques) should be appointed, or alternatively a qualified librarian who must then learn the subject field. Ideally, both qualifications should be required, but librarians with scientific qualifications are in short supply. Much sterile argument has proceeded on this point, and clearly there may be fields so highly specialised that most individuals without subject qualifications could not undertake the work. It naturally depends on the abilities of individuals, and on the degree and intensity of specialisation required for particular posts. The same problem arises where language qualifications are essential, both in special and in academic and national libraries.

In the last resort this issue is not really relevant, because the documentalists' case that they are a separate profession must rest on the claim that their *techniques* are so highly developed that they have gone beyond the more limited realm of librarianship. It is this claim which cannot be substantiated, except (and this is a most important proviso) in countries where librarianship in the modern sense does not exist. Quite apart from the documentation issue, it remains true that the subject focus in special librarianship represents a serious problem in library education. In the case of archives there are disciplines and techniques which are not required by ' normal ' librarians, and to this extent archivists are a separate group who require different education and training. But this applies to other specialist librarians. Somebody has said that documentation is librarianship conducted by amateurs. One might equally say that the archivist is an antiquarian librarian, except that the modern archivist is also concerned with the present and the future.

IS LIBRARIANSHIP A SCIENCE?
This pseudo problem is still sometimes raised, and the short answer is that librarianship is both a science and an art. In each of the four areas listed in my initial definition, scientific techniques are required. The theoretical foundations, moreover, are largely sociological. But many of the typical professional activities (for example, book provision) remain an art in the traditional sense. Even management can be regarded both as an art and a science. There is no fundamental difference in approach on this matter between the Americans and the British, except in the use of language. There is however a different *emphasis*, and Europeans have been less eager to adopt scientific methods, and to prefer to avoid the term ' library science '. Some British librarians are fond of referring to their ' craft '—but this medieval term throws more light on the British professional past than on the nature of librarianship.

This description of the nature of librarianship is familiar enough, but it by no means follows that a statement based on this fourfold definition reflects the library situation everywhere. Many countries, as Lester Asheim has stressed, are still engaged in foundation activities. Librarianship in this sense is only possible or necessary in fully industrialised countries.

The preceding section considered the functions of librarianship. The next step is to examine for what purposes these functions are exercised. We are here dealing with aims, goals, or objectives. If these often contradictory ends can be integrated at all, then an adequate theory might become possible.

ONE: THE PRESERVATION OF MATERIAL (THE LIBRARY AS REPOSITORY)
I have already noted the importance and significance of the custodial function. At first sight this process seems to be an end in itself and not a purpose at all, and indeed many libraries have obsessively hoarded material without quite knowing why. On one level this is a symptom of 'underdevelopment', where even out of date books have a rarity value and there is insufficient money to replace them. It does happen thus that the means (preservation) becomes an end in itself.

Closer examination reveals that in developed library systems the principle that ' books are for use ' must still apply, and that the library which concentrates on the museum function for any part of its stock is, as a matter of policy, giving priority to the users of the future. Unlike the users of the present and the past, these people are not yet individualised and we have to refer to them under the collective term ' posterity '. The trouble with posterity is that it does not know what it wants, and we cannot send it a questionnaire. This may sound gratuitous but it serves to indicate the dilemma of the national library. This is why some national libraries, such as the British Museum, are required to preserve everything except items like books with blank pages, whose non-communication value is total. Another problem for national and university libraries is that they have other functions and purposes which conflict with the repository role. The readers of the present are inevitably more vocal in their demands. There are, of course, possible solutions, which are outside the scope of this section.

In this context we inevitably think of national and academic libraries first, but it is clear that all libraries are likely to have some material which should be rescued from its current enemies or friends. Public librarians have ' local collections ', which are important for archival reasons, and valuable private collections find their way into unexpected sanctuaries. The primary purpose of university libraries is to provide research material, but, in the humanities at least, the research process depends on the survival of the literary and other records of past time.

This type of material is often used at infrequent intervals and can therefore be stored in a different manner, and often in another place from the rest of the library. In this way the possibility of *collective* storage arises, and the libraries which exist for this purpose, such as the Center for Research Libraries in the United States, are organised solely for repository purposes, although current access is available. Public libraries in the United Kingdom which are organised within the regional co-operative bureaux have agreed to specialise in the provision of books and periodicals in allotted subject fields. Some of them have taken up, perhaps too light heartedly, a custodial role with regard to their special subjects. From the national point of view, the responsibility is to consider not only *what* should be kept for the future, but what degree of duplication is required in how many centres.

The role of the librarian considered as custodian is simple. He is by no means ' the little friend of all the world ', and must devote all his energies to overcoming the enemies of books. Historical and natural calamities are beyond his control, but he can be vigilant against the minor destructive forces which are chemical, human, animal, insectival, atmospheric, fungoid, etc. Bernard Shaw, in *Caesar and Cleopatra,* with reference to the alleged destruction of the library in Alexandria makes Caesar say in response to Theodotus' cry that the memory of mankind is burning ' a shameful memory. Let it burn '. For the librarian as custodian such thoughts are unthinkable, and all his attention must be concentrated on the new types of enemy which have to be identified. For example, on November 3 1967, *Time* magazine reported that 'At Baltimore Selective Service Office a Roman Catholic priest and two laymen poured two pints of blood over sixteen file drawers of records . . . All four were arrested and charged with mutilating public records '. It was of course easier to blot out the records than to stop the war in Vietnam. Libraries can be destroyed by a gesture.

TWO : RESEARCH
Since we are concerned here mainly with areas of uncertainty, the research purposes of libraries need not detain us for they are sufficiently clear. National and university libraries provide material for research as their main purpose. As we have seen, material is preserved in repository libraries for the research workers of the future. The pattern of research and the needs of research workers are changing in a manner which is a constant challenge to all research libraries. The

8*

methods of research also vary according to the subject fields. There is often a conflict with the research purpose and other purposes, for example, the provision of material for undergraduates. There is also the conflict which we have already noted between the needs of current and future research workers. As one American authority has indicated, ' The enormous diversity and unpredictable character of university research have forced university libraries into something of a dual function: first, they build and maintain a " working " library, oriented around the reasonably clear needs of students and faculty members and the materials most likely to be used in support of current research and teaching; and secondly the library acquires, keeps and services a collection of " permanent record " in which future needs are anticipated as far as good judgment and available resources permit, and in which the relatively inactive acquisitions of the past are retained for possible future use. These future uses, it is recognised are often entirely different from the original purpose of the publications.' The same writer points out that it is this growth of the American university library in the twentieth century (Harvard University 560,000 books and pamphlets in 1900, eight million in 1967).

It is clear that any library which possesses any kind of research material has a research purpose: it provides material *for* the research worker. The question (as in education) then arises: To what extent does the library itself take part in the research process? This brings us back to our previous discussions in relation to documentation. The immediate answer is that the librarian is concerned mainly or solely with *bibliographical* research—to assist the users of the library. Since bibliographical work, such as abstracting or indexing or, particularly, literature searching, involves an investigation of subject content, it happens that librarians may disagree about the extent to which they should ' do the work of the researcher for him '. Where should the process end? What we need note is that many libraries do in fact take an active part in the research activity, which is in any case usually partly bibliographical. Librarians provide research material and they assist with its use.

THREE: THE INFORMATION ROLE

In a preceding section it was claimed that documentation, which is concerned with the dissemination of information, should be regarded as an essential part of librarianship, and that if it is not, librarians may be reduced to their primitive condition of custodian, while the documentalists will have run off with their clothes. If it is not so considered, there seems little point in insisting that libraries should be taken into account when communication processes are studied. The concept of reference service implies that a fully organised modern library of any kind is capable of playing an active information role, at least to some degree or in certain subject areas. When this is done, it is clear that all information services are an essential element in the communication processes, which are so important in developed societies. The communication agencies, including television, the radio and the press, provide information, but in the first instance they must obtain many types of prior information from suitably organised library services, including their own. The library of the British Broadcasting Corporation is a very important one, and major newspapers need highly organised libraries in order to function at all.

Similarly, public relations officers in government departments, or in large industrial firms, or in public services, depend for their efficiency on library activities. Citizens advice bureaux inevitably have to use the techniques of librarianship, and apart from this they often work most efficiently by co-operation with public libraries. Fundamental to this information purpose is the concept of the library as a *clearinghouse*, in the sense that every information centre is inevitably part of a national system, even if there is no organised or recognised structure. In other words, the provision of information is essentially a co-operative activity based on library services, even if particular information officers or librarians operate with nothing more than themselves and a telephone. The basic professional activity resides in a full understanding of sources of information, whether they are in the first instance libraries or not. (For example, a particular item of information may be obtained from a periodical, or from a specialised organisation, but somewhere along the line librarianship techniques are involved. In every case the key to the process is provided by the actions of one or several individuals who either organise indexes to it or otherwise lead toward it, wherever it, may be.)

The modern emphasis on the importance of information has transformed librarianship as a practical activity and as a theoretical discipline. The most obvious evidence is the growth of the special library movement, particularly in the scientific and technical field. This has led to the creation of ' documentation ' services, which involve specialist subject knowledge and the interpretation of literature by information officers. As already noted, special librarianship in Britain has, on the whole, remained an increasingly important part of the library movement in general. It is true that Aslib was set up because special librarians considered they needed a separate organisation of their own, but Aslib has always stopped short of adopting a breakaway education or examination structure of its own. The last ten years have witnessed the creation of the Institute of Information Scientists, the members of which would probably claim it to be a unique entity, though it is important to remember that this body is in no sense a rival to Aslib or the Library Association, because the institute and its qualifications are open to a relatively small number of highly qualified scientific specialists.

The emphasis on scientific information has also resulted in the setting up of the National Lending Library for Science and Technology, the special services of the Ministry of Technology, and the new embryonic National Scientific Reference Library, based on the Patent Office and the British Museum. Because of the importance of information retrieval—a new electronic world of information activity has come into being, and the potentialities for the future are very considerable. This world of information retrieval is really an extension of the traditional procedures of library cataloguing and classification, when applied to ' bits ' of information. The same trend lies behind the classification developments represented by Ranganathan. Faceted classification schemes will be required in many fields where general schemes are no longer adequate. All this obliges the recognition that a new structure of librarianship theory is being created, although much remains to be done.

FOUR: EDUCATION

The degree to which libraries are ' educational ' depends on how one defines education. The only useful starting point is to analyse the various uses of the word.

Education as a lifelong process: Libraries are collections of books and other materials. It is clear that any book may have an educational value for a particular person, irrespective of its subject or its intellectual level. It is equally clear that in the widest sense anything that happens to anyone can be regarded as ' educational,' even falling down the stairs, or drinking too much, or driving on the wrong side of the road. Education in these terms is simply the accumulation of experience.

The private library: In a slightly more exact sense, those who extol the value of reading as an essential element in the development of the individual are thinking of the education-as-lifelong-process theme. All education which is real is self education, etc. In such a context the reader is stimulated, by his life situation, or by what happens to him, or by what he has read in the past, to continue his reading adventures. Since one book leads to another (the organic basic bibliography of the common reader), a library collection of some kind is essential, and this is the function of the private library. An individual collection inevitably possesses a value out of all proportion to its size, and innumerable lives have been sustained by the constant re-reading of a few works basic to a particular culture. At the present time there is much evidence to suggest that reading of this kind is in decline. An inherent weakness or limitation of the American type culture, which is becoming universal, rests on the misapplication of science to produce digests and ' potted ' versions. Abstracts are invaluable for summarising *information*: beyond this limited sphere they are a snare and a delusion.

Public libraries: It is this type of educational ' culture ' reading which public libraries traditionally exist to provide. They are still educational in this sense. McColvin used the phrase ' self development in an atmosphere of freedom '. This is a question-begging statement, but it serves to indicate the difference between this concept of education and the formal education process, which implies a course and a curriculum and prescribed readings. At the present time in Britain the public library does not have to be a *substitute* for formal education (which includes library provision), but a complement to it. This is the difference between the children's library as part of public library provision, and the school library.

The role of the public library in education can only be appreciated in relation to the education system as a whole. In Britain in the past, many people who did not have higher education opportunities ' educated ' themselves in the public library. At the present time their modern counterparts receive a university education, and the educational function of the public library has to this extent changed. (The role of adult education agencies like the Workers Education Association has been modified in a similar fashion.)

In view of this, it is appropriate that Unesco in its library programmes for underdeveloped countries should regard the public library as only one agency among others for the promotion of mass education and for the elimination of illiteracy, and it is considered natural for public library provision to be one of the responsibilities of the ministry of education. All this is straightforward, partly because ' new ' countries are still mainly rural, and there is not yet (indeed, there may never be) a large industrial proletariat such as existed in nineteenth century Britain.

A complex origin: If we examine the educational role of the British public library movement in the nineteenth century, we encounter a variety of social forces, most of which were related in some way to the class conflicts which the industrial revolution had produced. The full story is related by Altick in *The English common reader*. Various groups desired that the working classes should be ' educated ' for purposes which they considered paramount and self evident. It is useful to isolate the several influences which Altick discusses in detail.

The utilitarians, who were influenced by classical economies and Benthamite doctrines of social efficiency, recognised the need for technical or ' useful ' knowledge to be disseminated amongst the members of the new class of skilled workers or artisans. The philanthropists of the evangelical movement wished to provide an education based on what they regarded as Christian principles and knowledge. Both these movements, with their different approaches, combined to restrict the type of literature they considered suitable, and both were active in the struggle against doctrines which might endanger the social structure. Their influence was decisive, because they operated within a climate of opinion which could not tolerate government ' interference ' in economic or social processes. Education was one of these, and in retrospect it seems extraordinary that there was no system of state universal education until 1870, and even more remarkable that, even so, by mid-century at least half the people were more or less literate. In such an atmosphere the mechanics institute libraries, and later the public libraries, were crippled by social pressures which distorted their true educational value. Right from the beginning libraries were caught up in the conflict over the provision of imaginative literature.

For example, in the case of the Leeds Mechanics Institute, the middle class sponsors stated that ' it was desirable to confine the attention of the artisans to the study of science, which could not be done if a more interesting kind of literature were placed within their reach . . . such books would dissipate their attention '. Other institutes were closed down after disputes about such dangerous writers as Shelley. In addition to these pressures from the *advocates* of adult education, there were the numerous and often influential voices of those who opposed any extension of education to the lower orders at all. Because of them, the first public libraries Acts were limited and permissive, so that time after time special meetings of local voters (called in accordance with the provisions of the Act) turned down proposals to set up public libraries in the towns. From the vantage point of modern society liberated from the ' spectre ' of revolution which then haunted Europe, most of the arguments seem irrelevant. As Altick says, ' The issue of public subsidisation of reading was entangled in the far broader issues of social reform and *laissez faire*; and the whole subsequent history of the public library movement offers an instructive cross-section of English public opinion on such matters as taxation for the general benefit, the problem of drink, poverty and crime, and the relations of the inferior classes to the ruling one '. Such was the legacy of the public library movement. A hundred years later the alcoholic and the criminal are still with us, but they are not sent to the public library to be cured—and we can accept the educational role of the public library in a more limited sense.

The confusion has been reflected in official statements which have appeared in government and other reports: statements which are often eloquent, but largely meaningless. Pronouncements made since 1960 have, however, been more realistic. For example, the Report of the Working Party on Standards of Public Library Service states that the public library ' can . . . in large measure fill in the gaps in the knowledge and awareness of those people whose education and training has necessarily been of a specialised nature '.

Similarly, the Parliamentary Secretary to the Ministry of Education said in the House of Commons on February 5, 1964, ' We therefore see the public library as complementary to all branches of the education service . . .'. There is no need to go beyond this simple statement.

Formal education: The educational role of other types of library is more straightforward and need not detain us. In universities and colleges the library is geared to the educational needs of the institutions concerned: in secondary schools it is, or should be, an integral part of the curriculum. There is an increasing awareness that in academic libraries the library should take a more active part in the education process. The existence of tutor-librarians is an indication of this.

In the special library field many libraries provide textbooks and other material which is educational in the narrow sense for the members of their organisations who are studying for examinations. These organisations may be professional or ' learned ' societies, or government departments, or industrial firms.

Propaganda: Finally, we should take note of the large number of institutions whose aim is to promulgate particular opinions, or enlighten the public on specific issues. This is the realm of propaganda, and libraries are an essential part of it. We are back with the problem of 'education for what?', which is dealt with in the last chapter of this book.

FIVE: THE CULTURAL ROLE

In the section concerned with the educational purpose I mentioned 'culture reading', and noted that it could be regarded as educational in one sense, but not in any formal meaning. In many types of library, and especially in public libraries, this purpose is so important that it needs to be discussed separately.

I am using the term 'culture' as defined earlier in this book, and the distinction there made between material and ideal culture is relevant. It should be apparent that libraries are concerned with both aspects, and not, as is often assumed, with 'high culture' only.

Public libraries: In considering public libraries, we must first note that whether the function is regarded as 'educational' or not, this is or *was* the main purpose of public libraries, at least in developed countries. This has always been recognised, but controversy has arisen because these cultural responsibilities have been interpreted in different ways. Two main areas of dispute can be identified: 'high' versus 'low', and books versus other cultural activities.

As defined throughout this work, the word 'culture' includes all forms of recreational activity, including reading. For this reason we are discussing recreational reading under the cultural heading and not separately. This is the only way to avoid becoming bogged down in a sterile controversy about the nature of recreation. In many quarters there has been a tendency to regard what is called 'light' reading as recreational, and to elevate other types of reading into a separate category called 'serious', and therefore non-recreational. This is an untenable distinction, and as has been suggested elsewhere, derives from the puritanic tradition which regarded any pleasant activity as automatically wrong. It was this tradition which produced the extraordinary bias against imaginative literature of any kind, and eventually left the library world with the ridiculous dichotomy of novels versus the rest: fiction and 'non-fiction'. There could be no more damaging comment on public librarianship than to note that it has never succeeded in eliminating this absurd terminology. The answer should be not to invent another term, but simply to stop talking about non-fiction. The term ' subject-books ' is equally objectionable since it seems to suggest that novels have no subject. The distinction is a pseudo problem, and has distracted librarians so much that there has been an immense and repetitive professional literature about the provision of ' light fiction '. This is not to deny that there may be a problem concerning the provision of ' light ' literature generally, but this is not confined to the novel. The problem, it is hardly necessary to add, revolves round the value distinction we started with. If we apply strictly educational or academic, or aesthetic, or moral standards, certain types of literature are rightly regarded as rubbish, and the public library with financial resources which are inevitably limited may exclude some or all of this literature because it is rubbish. But *which* types of literature should be excluded can only be decided according to the needs of a particular community, and in relation to other recreational opportunities. The other sources for the supply of ' lower ' cultural recreation include the possibility of provision from ' commercial ' or subscription libraries (now much less prevalent than formerly), or the availability of cheap literature in paperback form, or the alternative entertainment provided by television and the mass media generally.

This reference to alternative types of provision does not, however, exhaust the problem, since ' light ' literature may serve a cultural purpose in adding to the sum of human satisfactions—happiness may be too strong a word. One other consideration is however worth noting. It is dangerous and fallacious to think of readers as types, since, quite apart from professional or vocational needs, any individual at different times will require different kinds of literature. With regard to the higher cultural role of the public library, there is clearly discernible a shift of emphasis away from the earlier missionary message. For example, P H Ennis, discussing the cultural-educational improvement programme of the early twentieth century in the United States, refers to the library faith of the time as ' a peculiar cultural imperialism that was part of the progressive era; everyone should read good books, everyone should develop his capacities to the fullest, everyone should be educated, freer and above all more refined '. He goes on to suggest that the affluent society no longer generates these attitudes, and that this type of cultural purpose should receive a lower priority. There can be little doubt that as far as readers are concerned, this kind of ' uplift ' motivation is less common, and this has probably affected the attitudes of younger librarians.

Turning to the debate about books versus other cultural activities, many librarians, and other 'friends of public libraries', like to think of the public library as the cultural centre of the community in the widest sense. Rightly, they regard literature as but one element in the full, or the good life, and therefore advocate the provision of lectures, concerts, exhibitions, dramatic productions, public readings and other activities which are cultural in the broad sense. They also employ secondary types of material such as gramophone recordings, reproductions of pictures and audio-visual media of every kind. These activities are undertaken for their own sake, and not necessarily to encourage the reading habit. These services in a public agency can be justified, when one considers that citizens who are cultivated in a 'literary' sense are very much in a minority. The programmes are usually described by the unfortunate term 'extension services'. They seem to be most appropriate where there is an absence of other agencies for this purpose.

If, as is here maintained, the public libraries' purpose should be regarded as cultural in this wide sense, it follows that some older traditions could with advantage be abandoned. For example, the public reference department, particularly in small libraries, could emphasise its information role as a cultural centre for the provision of every kind of *practical* information. This has nothing to do with research or quiet study, or even with reading. The concept presupposes a centre where people can talk, smoke and eat or drink. I am not suggesting that the other purposes of the public library mentioned here should be neglected. The problem of priorities remains.

Academic libraries: The cultural purpose of university, college and school libraries is, as we have seen, education and/or research. I have discussed formal education in terms of the curriculum. The cultural purpose of the academic library does, however, include education 'beyond the curriculum'. This is the peculiar responsibility of the librarian in his book selection activities. He is concerned with the 'gaps' between the subjects studied, and with the relations between them. Technical colleges have long sought to 'liberalise' their education. This can be done by including 'arts' subjects in the curriculum and in the library, and tutor librarians often play a valuable role in these activities. But the true liberalisation of education consists of teaching 'subjects' in such a manner that they are related to the rest of life. *Any* subject can be liberalised in this way, and this can be reflected in the book selection policies of the library. The academic librarian can help to overcome cultural division of whatever kind.

Special libraries: Many special libraries may attempt to provide culture reading beyond the immediate practical needs of the organisation which they serve, but the true cultural role of the special library is inevitably to be found in carrying out the purposes of the parent organisation.

NOTE

1 Thus Shera, in *Of librarianship, documentation and information science* (*op cit*) states unequivocally: ' Documentation, therefore . . . is nothing more than a form, or aspect of librarianship; it is . . . librarianship in a high key '.

He notes also that, at least in the USA, the meaning of documentation is becoming academic, as the term is becoming obsolete, and the American Documentation Institute is considering changing its name to the American Society of Information Scientists. Shera maintains that there will be a new consensus of opinion embracing librarians and information scientists. Librarians will then become a new kind of scholar librarian. In the light of this alleged trend it is interesting that an information scientist in the Soviet Union has coined the term ' Informatics '.

14

philosophies of librarianship

WHY PHILOSOPHY? In the introduction to this book I stated that I considered that certain subjects are proper studies for librarians. This claim rests on what used to be called a philosophy of librarianship. There is no generally accepted 'philosophy' of this kind, and most librarians would accept that the term is not particularly helpful. However, it continues to be used and we should try to discover what is meant.

The word 'philosophy' inevitably has many uses, and if we use it in the sense which implies a total systematic philosophic structure or system, existing as a thing in itself, then it is apparent that there can be no philosophy of librarianship. In education the position is the same, since philosophies of education derive from some other foundation or system of beliefs. If, however, we use the term in a different and more limited sense, which involves the pursuit of truth, or the setting up of principles as a guide to action, or the creation of theories which explain reality, then philosophy is necessary and inevitable, even if the word is not used.

Everybody displays attitudes of some kind, even if these are not fully conscious, and these are the rudiments of theory, or an embryonic philosophy. The search for an adequate theoretical structure has in recent years become more important in the UK because of developments in library education. Modern courses in librarianship, particularly when they are conducted at university level, require a theoretical foundation, firstly to provide a coherent pattern of study in each subject area, and secondly to link the various studies together. Within

244

the individual subjects considerable advances have been made: there is an adequate theory of classification, for example, and the principles of industrial management and administration can be applied to library organisation. This development has been generally welcome, but few have seen the need to establish an inclusive pattern in which these various studies can be placed.

THE RELEVANCE OF THEORY

We have already referred to the pragmatic British attitude to theory, although this pragmatism is really an embryonic theory in itself. There exists an assumption that many ideas may be perfectly sound, but that practice is something else. Proposals are 'all right in theory, but not in practice'. There is a philistine belief that theories are a frivolous luxury which practical men cannot afford. It seems not to occur to those who hold this view that in many areas if the theory cannot correspond with practice, then the theory is wrong, inadequate, incomplete or incorrect. Behind this lies the feeling, perhaps inevitable in what is still to some extent a Christian culture, that there is bound to be a gap between the ideal and the real. This is indeed so, and if we pursue the matter we come up against a conflict between moral principles and scientific theories. This confusion is inherent in the social sciences because they deal with human institutions, human nature and human values. The theory and practice of librarianship are part of the social sciences, and library science is concerned with social processes, but these involve ethical principles and value judgments. It follows that some, probably an increasing proportion, of its practices are amenable to the application of true scientific principles (for example, information retrieval), whereas others are not (for example, book selection). I have stressed this problem because it is one more manifestation of the so-called two culture split, which must concern us all. In the sphere of religion and ethics we recognise that there is a gap between our aspirations and what we achieve. It is within this gap that the various kinds of hypocrisy flourish, and it is this area which the novelist primarily explores. But in the scientific realm, if a theory does not correspond to the facts it is false, and should be abandoned. (The word 'wrong' indicates the nature of the problem, since it can be used either in an ethical or a scientific sense.) The communist world is caught up in this dilemma, because the communists claim that Marxism is a science, so that when they commit crimes they have to be designated as 'errors'. The real error is, of course,

245

to suggest that social life is wholly amenable to scientific or pseudo-scientific laws.

All I am suggesting is that theories have continually to be brought up to date to take account of new cultural and social situations. If they are not so revised, they will remain inadequate and incorrect.

RANGANATHAN

The pioneer work has been done by Ranganathan, and his ' five laws ' can be applied to all library studies. Because his approach is deductive and his laws seem simple to the point of absurdity, their value has been regularly underestimated or misunderstood in Anglo-Saxon countries where deductive theories are not usual. It is a fact that almost every aspect of modern librarianship can usefully be studied as part of one or other of these laws, and most deficiencies in library services can be shown to relate to a failure in observing them. From the teaching point of view, provided that the laws are satisfactorily applied to concrete situations (and this is a large proviso), the result can be an immense improvement on the vast jumble of disconnected facts which formerly passed as librarianship.

In spite of this achievement, there remain certain limitations and difficulties which should be noted. In the first place, as Ranganathan has himself admitted, these are not scientific but *moral* laws—even ideals. A moment's thought will make it apparent that in fact ' books are not for all ', that many libraries are not ' growing organisms ', that the appropriate reader is not found for every book, and so on. In other words, these are professional principles of conduct, or service ideals and the word ' science ' is misleading. This inevitably limits the scope and range of the theory. It is also limited by the lack of a social context, although there are obvious sociological implications: for example, ' books are for all ' assumes the desirability of total literacy, political democracy, and the emancipation of women. Those who consider, as I have considered in these chapters, that sociological factors represent a fundamental part of the theory of librarianship, must therefore go beyond the five laws in order to identify or discuss these factors. Nevertheless, their validity remains as a method of expressing professional principles which, inevitably, are not always put into practice.

THE TRADITIONAL VIEW: One unsatisfactory element in librarianship has always been that it seems to be inevitably an adjunct of something else. If this is always so, then the limitations of its scope must be recognised. Professor Irwin, if I understand him correctly, has taken this view. For example, he states ' The librarian as such is neither a maker of history nor a maker of literature. He is an intermediary, whose only memorial lies in the books he preserves and the scholars who read them; his fate is to serve as the anonymous channel of recorded tradition. It is noteworthy that the librarians of former ages, if they are remembered at all, are always remembered for something other than librarianship . . . If indeed there is one lesson that the history of libraries teaches us, it is that something over and above technical knowledge is needed to make the great librarian: a library cannot live on librarianship alone.' Here, at least at one point, Professor Irwin is stating that librarianship as such consists of ' technical knowledge ' and that is all. If this view is correct, then there is little more to be said; that is the end of the matter—with the traditional custodial function of the librarian. I have tried to suggest in earlier chapters of this work that, while it is true that the librarian is an intermediary, he may also be in the modern world something more—and that as soon as he starts to interpret the literature he is no longer merely a custodian. If this is the lesson that the history of libraries teaches us, then perhaps we should look at history again.

THE SECULAR MISSIONARIES: Many public librarians used in the past to regard themselves as agents in the struggle for popular education and enlightenment. This is the tradition implicit in the writings of L R McColvin, and in several official reports on public libraries in the UK, and explicit in Broadfield's book, *Philosophy of librarianship*. It reveals the application, or the attempted application, of nineteenth century liberal and ' progressive ' ideals. The positive side of this approach was the missionary wish to spread enlightenment and high culture, so that these should no longer remain the privilege of the few. This often took the form of a generous desire to share a personal response to literature. Such an enthusiasm can be found in the writings of Lawrence Clark Powell, the American librarian and library educator.

Admirable though these professional ideals were, they are inadequate today because they do not easily relate to the characteristic of a so-called mass culture. It is noteworthy that modern statements are sometimes positively hostile to this outlook, and younger librarians now often feel that other people's tastes in literature should be left alone—who is to say that a personal response should have a general value? For example, P H Ennis in a passage quoted in chapter 13 (p 241) concerning the cultural educational programme of the early twentieth century refers to a ' peculiar cultural imperialism '. He goes on to claim that this ' imperative ' is no longer important, at least in the USA, because of the changed cultural situation. (It may be of some significance that Ennis is a sociologist and not a librarian.) The challenge facing modern cultural workers is not at all to increase the number of people who can appreciate traditional high culture, but rather to work out an appropriate role in a cultural context of an entirely different order. If the positive side of this progressive tradition produced librarians as cultural missionaries, the negative side was the twentieth century struggle for liberal values under attack from the enemies of freedom.

It is my view that this concept should be preserved as an essential part of any modern view of librarianship, although a concentration on the fight against censorship and tyranny is not enough by itself, at least in societies which are relatively ' open '. Some would regard this liberal tradition as a religious hangover, or, more appropriately perhaps, as a Christian heresy, since it isolates one element in Christianity (the unique value of the individual) and ignores others. Arnold Toynbee has described Marxism also as a Christian heresy, which in our context isolates the missionary spreading of the Word according to infallible secular authorities. This is, of course, why the socialist countries have well developed library services. But we cannot adopt their library ' philosophy ', because we have taken the view that in closed societies librarianship in our sense cannot exist except as a travesty.

If there still remains a professional requirement to stress the importance of intellectual freedom, then this imperative should be restated in modern terms. For example, even within the realm of the information scientist it can be claimed that efficiency and progress are impossible if information services are not free, and if political or religious dogma obstruct the flow of communication. In the free world the secrecy is not due to direct political control, but arises from strategic considerations, or from the nature of competitive industry. Many have considered that advanced industrial states must eventually permit intellectual freedom in every field and on every level, partly because they cannot otherwise advance, and partly because universal education produces a large number of specialists and professional people who will not in the long run tolerate ideological control. The argument is that modern societies cannot exist without an intelligentsia—and that the information freedoms which become necessary will destroy dictatorships. This analysis is commonly applied to the Soviet Union, but there is not sufficient evidence for any safe predictions to be made. The key question is perhaps not whether, but *when,* authoritarian controls will break down, since in many fields scientists can continue to operate independently of political processes, and information can flow freely for a long time within restricted and isolated areas, without necessarily affecting society as a whole.

THE INFORMATION PROCESS

Both the practice and the theory of librarianship have become substantially modified by the development of special libraries, and the consequent emphasis on the information role and the techniques of information retrieval. As a result of this imposing new structure, with all its electronic devices, some have considered that it is in this world that the basic elements of a new theory of librarianship must be sought. This approach concentrates on the information process itself, without reference to the wider social and cultural issues which I have considered essential. D J Foskett's paper ' The creed of a librarian—no politics, no religion, no morals ' can be taken as an excellent example of this attitude. Having stressed the need for a philosophy (by which Foskett means an appropriate professional set of ideals), he then goes on to say that in providing reference service for readers, the librarian can only do so effectively if he possesses the quality of imaginative sympathy which will enable him ' to put himself in the reader's shoes ', and to ignore his own prejudices, attitudes, opinions and beliefs—hence the title of the paper. This ability is undoubtedly a central professional requirement and it is one which is necessary in other callings, for instance teaching or the priesthood. The individual separates himself as a librarian from himself as a man, and there need be no conflict. Foskett points out that the core of professional purpose depends for its success on library organisation, on systems of classification and indexing and so forth. All this is indeed true and important, but there is a deliberate limitation in the scope of the enquiry, and the key questions remain unanswered.

I am suggesting that the real problem begins where this enquiry stops, and that we should explore the social implications of this particular ideal (which is really a creed for the individual considered as a professional worker, and not as a person who inevitably has social even professional commitments) beyond the boundaries of the information process. The librarian, as librarian, provides information, but there may well be times when his convictions as a man will oblige him to ask 'What is the information for?'; (information is never an end in itself). And if the answer is that it is to be used for what the librarian as a man regards as totally evil purposes, then this indicates the real professional dilemma. Information has been defined as 'knowledge put to use', but if the librarian is indifferent to the nature of the use, he is not a man but a thing. There is a parallel with the moral responsibilities of the scientist whose research may result, for example, in improved methods of biological warfare. This was the dilemma of German liberal librarians during the Nazi period, and those who co-operated with the regime, for whatever reason, used this same argument that what they did or did not do as librarians had to be separated from their beliefs as men. The implication seems to be that a specialist can and should isolate his functions from other general human considerations. This is why the specialist provokes alarm and distrust, and the librarian should be the last person to submit to this form of intellectual betrayal. As I noted in the chapter on professional ideals, the librarian, particularly in special libraries, is not a free agent, and the point I am making here is that a conflict may arise between the aims of an organisation and professional ideals in the sense which includes a commitment to a wider system of values.

Ronald Staveley has made his own characteristic contribution to this discussion. In his paper 'Personal viewpoints', he notes that library philosophies rest on some foundation of general beliefs, and then goes on to discuss briefly the implications of certain well known systems of belief, such as humanism, existentialism, Platonism, pragmatism, logical positivism and Marxism. He notes that a library 'philosophy' might derive inspiration from any of these, but it cannot be said that any general conclusions emerge from his survey, and the impression is left that perhaps we might hop about and collect something valuable from any or all of them. If most of us who reject any closed system of traditional beliefs were honest enough to admit it, it may be that this is what we habitually do do, in the hope that the consequent hotch-potch will eventually add up to something coherent.

Insofar as a 'philosophy' does emerge from Staveley's survey, it is precisely this same concentration on the personal relationship of the librarian and the ' client ' and the message in the end is roughly similar to that of Foskett noted above. I return to this point at the end of this chapter.

THE COMMUNICATORS

Some librarians and some library school programmes have attempted to place theories and problems of communication at the centre of a theory of librarianship. In the considerable literature dealing with this subject, that part of it which concentrates on the communication process, as I have remarked in chapter 3, is limited in the same way as is the theory of information retrieval. It has also become a specialism in itself, with its own jargon, so that nothing is communicated except to other communicators—and the conclusions reached, if any, have little relevance to librarianship as a whole.

Apart from this literature, however, there does exist a substantial body of work which deals with social communication problems in general, and with the need for social control of the communication media. Raymond Williams has repeatedly called for a ' Communication centre ', and for an ' Institute of Communication research '. He has also insisted that communication should not be regarded as a secondary process, but as part of a primary struggle to learn, to educate and to understand. It is possible that the problem of communication does have this special importance, and if this is so, we should ask ourselves whether libraries and librarianship should be regarded as falling within this context.

Those who write books about communication problems rarely mention libraries, and it is not difficult to discover why. Libraries are largely dependent on other cultural agencies: they do not originate communications, but transmit them.

Williams refers to the people who generate communication processes as the contributors. He then distinguishes four man kinds of contributor, ie the creative artist, the performer, the reporter, the commentator or critic. At first sight the librarian appears to be none of these. He has been referred to as a middleman, but if we examine the communications world we shall find that modern communications are full of middlemen who all have a part to play. The communication systems are networks which depend on the co-operation of a number of people. This is true of radio, the film, the press and television; they are all collective enterprises, and the four types of activity mentioned above are inextricably mixed together. Communication depends on large scale organisation, and libraries are indeed one of those organisations. Modern life is so complex, and the quantity of literature so appalling, that it requires a high degree of library and bibliographical organisation before literature can be effectively used. This has to be done not just in isolated places but on a national scale, and librarians, to use the late Barbara Kyle's words, have a duty ' to preserve knowledge so that none is lost, organise knowledge so that none is wasted, and make knowledge available so that no one need be deprived '. This task is formidable indeed, and it seems no longer appropriate to refer to agencies which successfully perform it as ' anonymous channels '.

The librarian does not write the literature in his library, but it must be organised before it can be read, and the information his library contains cannot be reached if he fails to produce it when required. In so doing he may have to evaluate it and interpret the available sources. To this extent libraries are part of the national communication process, and library studies must include an examination of communication problems in society. In other words, librarianship must adopt those elements in communication studies which are relevant and adapt them for its own use.

THE SOCIOLOGY OF KNOWLEDGE

I noted above that the alleged theoretical failures in Britain may arise because full time education for librarianship on an extensive scale is relatively recent. Yet if we turn to the United States where library education is half a century old we find a similar situation. Many years ago Pierce Butler lamented the poverty of theory in American librarianship: more recently Jesse Shera, in the essays collected in *Libraries and the organisation of knowledge,* linked this weakness with the pragmatic tradition and the American predilection for useful knowledge, and a ' democratic ' hostility to philosophy. Shera has attempted to provide a theoretical foundation by insisting that the core of professional studies must be sought in the sphere of epistemology or, as he called it (in his earlier work with Margaret Egan *Bibliographic organisation*), social epistemology. This is a substantial contribution and the current preoccupation with the ' fluid ' state of the structure of knowledge has increased its importance. For example, Kenneth Boulding in *The image* (1956) claims that the problem of ' knowledge ', or what he calls our ' image ' of the world, is of fundamental importance because ' we are in the midst, or perhaps only at the beginning, of a profound reorganisation of the departmental structure of knowledge and of academic life . . . There is something abroad which might be called interdisciplinary movement '. Because, *inter alia*, of the *growth* of knowledge he draws the comforting conclusion that we must examine the process of education from the point of view of what is the *minimum* knowledge which must be transmitted. The student has usually operated on the principle of knowing as little as he can get away with. It is time, perhaps for this principle to be made respectable.

Shera states that the two fundamental questions for librarians are: 1) what is knowledge?; 2) how is it put to work? In my own case I was influenced by similar considerations in *Bibliography and the provision of books,* but the work suffers because it is limited to the second question above, *ie* I was concerned with social processes and the barriers to the free flow of information, without reference to the structure of knowledge itself. It may well be that this limitation came about because the approach was in the first instance bibliographical, whereas Shera has always rightly insisted that *classification* studies should provide the basis for bibliographic organisation. This is most important, particularly when one considers the still prevalent tendency to study reference material without an adequate link with the classification techniques which are inherent in information retrieval. At first sight knowledge about knowledge may seem ' academic ' in the old fashioned and useless sense, but this theoretical construct should provide a foundation for improved techniques of information retrieval. The practical application is possible, but the results remain within the realm of *method* or technique. The wider social context is missing, and it is this which is essential if we are thinking (as we are here) of aims, purposes or goals. Information retrieval is a means, not an end. The theoretical framework (quite properly) is constructed of concepts, not precepts; ideas not ideals. (In the case of the secular missionaries these missing components *are* present.) It may well be that a true sociology of knowledge should provide this context, but my impression is that as an academic discipline this study has developed very little.

To return to Shera's formula, it seems to me that the subject of our enquiry is not only ' what is knowledge?' and ' how is it put to work?' but also ' *for what purpose?*'. Without this third element our ' philosophy ' cannot be a guide to action, and in vocational education this is what is required. (Ranganathan would affirm that his ' five laws ' provide the answer to the third question, and that in studying the first and the second question we are learning how to obey the laws. He often writes as if they were eternal entities who become distressed when they are not obeyed!) It is perhaps Shera's deliberate exclusion of social values which gives his writing an almost sinister lucidity. For instance, in emphasising the importance of the search for order as a basic psychological need he refers to 'pattern seeking' in the sciences and 'pattern making' in the arts as if these were identical activities: the wider cultural implications are not considered.

With regard to education for librarianship, the study of the structure of knowledge can certainly be regarded as part of an essential core. But as Shera himself admits, 'Librarianship is a composite of many disciplines'. It all depends on what one means by a 'core', and whether a 'composite core' is a nonsense thing.

One is obliged to conclude that the theoretical foundations of librarianship are weak, not because of the limitations of library education or because of the Anglo/American anti-metaphysical tradition, but because there are certain unresolved and possibly inherent contradictions. Shera says 'one cannot remember Chaos', but one may have to live with it most of the time. Or, to be more precise, we can often construct orderly patterns only by the evasion of too many realities. The contradictions probably *can* be resolved, but on a level which librarianship cannot reach.

CONCLUSION

It appears from what I have said above that what is required is a new integration incorporating the various elements we have attempted to isolate—a combination of traditional custodial principles, the missionary approach and the rationale of a personal reference service. All this would need to be seen against the background of modern communication problems.

The attitudes expressed in the foregoing chapters of this book can be seen as explorations towards this integration process. In the nature of things they can only be explorations, and I have also stressed throughout my own personal preoccupations. Certain themes are constant, and one of them is the importance of background social and cultural studies for librarianship. I have implied that our professional attitudes inevitably rest on personal interpretations of the nature of modern culture. A key question I have asked is whether the librarian should regard himself mainly as the custodian of traditional high culture, and I have answered it in the negative. To some extent, therefore, this book may be regarded as an apologia for pop culture. The inference is that the librarian should be wholly responsive to the modern predicament, and in this role he cannot afford to become a ' square '. (Since the spectacle of middle aged souls trying to keep up with the young is often pathetic and always partial, one can only conclude that all librarians should retire at 40, a proposal which might encounter some opposition!)

Another assumption which has been present here is that the librarian should seek to be an intellectual, in the sense that the word is commonly understood in Britain. It might be thought that this is self evident and unworthy of discussion, but many of our colleagues go out of their way to repudiate such a suggestion as though it might contain some attack on their integrity as public and responsible persons. As stated here, this is not simply the traditional plea that the librarian should be a ' bookman ', or a scholar, but that he has certain cultural responsibilities. (It is ironic that, according to some reports, American librarians in their drive for status wish to be regarded as ' intellectuals ', while their British counterparts would rather be seen as a typical rotarian or ELK.)

Also present throughout the foregoing discussions is an uneasy awareness of the differences between science and the arts, and their implications for librarianship. In chapter one I asserted that the techniques and professional processes involved in all forms of librarianship are the same. In this last chapter, I can repeat that assertion only with a number of provisos. The emphasis of Foskett and Staveley mentioned above (and indeed many others) is surely the right one *as far as it goes*. If, therefore, we regard personal reference service as the key professional activity, the main problem is whether the growth of automation and specialisation in science will result in retrieval processes which are different in kind from those employed in the humanities. It is perhaps too early to answer this question with total confidence, but there are new trends developing which may be more significant than is generally appreciated. It has been claimed that in both fields, because the growth points in modern knowledge develop *between* traditional disciplines, the librarian will become increasingly important as an integrating agent. This implies that in science his role will remain decisive, whatever the machines may do in the retrieval of *facts*. It implies also that in the humanities new types of reference service must be evolved. Already valuable work has been reported

255

in some organisations and institutions. However, this work is certainly not yet typical, and it is significant that it is being done in colleges which are directly educational. The common element, therefore, in both science and the arts, is that the librarian's role is not simply to supply *information* in response to particular requests, or to make available material for those who require it, or to fill in gaps, but to *provide the connections*.

If those who prefer a more precise statement would ask ' *what* connections?', the answer can only be that if we knew what connections are required there would be no need to make them. ' Insights ' in the humanities cannot be planned or plotted, and the research scientist does not usually know what he is looking for. It is this which makes the library activity at its highest level worthwhile. Needless to say, there are other types of library work, and these are what they have always been except insofar as the machines are taking over.

Having agreed with those who stress personal reference service, I would also wish to add that this element by itself is clearly not enough, if we are thinking in terms of a satisfactory set of ideals. It is surely significant that those librarians who make a positive contribution in the field of reference service are motivated by something more than the wish to do a job well. It is here that we return to the missionary role, which involves the wider considerations that I have constantly stressed. Why in fact should anyone bother with the higher librarianship? Possibly the answer must be individual, and for some their religious beliefs would be relevant. My own personal bias probably derives from attitudes which might be called ' existentialist ' in a non philosophical sense. Among these attitudes which are relevant to librarianship is a belief in the importance of total ' awareness ', both with regard to the self and the world. Relevant also is a distrust of ' objective ' abstractions and an insistence on an appreciation of unique circumstances. Such an understanding recognises that theoretical formulations about life or the ' problem ' of living are irrelevant if they ignore subjective or inner realities. This attitude is valuable with regard to the reference role of the librarian, since he must deal with a series of unique information problems, and the subjective realities partly reside in the personality of the reader who requires assistance, and of the librarian who supplies it. The key factor is the personal relationship.

Beyond all this, the viewpoint reflected in these chapters is humanistic in the broad sense, which means nothing very precise except that it implies some kind of faith that in the long run the growth of human knowledge *may* help to modify the human condition for better rather than for worse. Like all worthwhile beliefs, this must be held without reference to the evidence, and if it is not held it is difficult to see why anyone should want to be a librarian at all (undertakers are equally well paid).

At the same time, even if we reject the view that the librarian, as well as his library network, is merely a kind of pipeline, it is as well that our professional claims should recognise the appropriate limits. Librarianship is not a way of life, and those who attempt to make it so become half, or non, persons. It has often been remarked (notably by the American Public Library Inquiry) that official professional statements about library ideals are too far removed from what actually happens in libraries. In the same way the ' idealism ' of library schools leaves students unprepared for what they eventually face in work situations.

There has always been a tendency, from which I myself have not always been immune, to inflate the content of our studies into a farrago of false pretensions. This happens because our studies have often been solemn rather than serious, and insufficiently rooted in social realities. It is these realities I have attempted to present.

further reading

The reading lists are not necessarily references to sources used but suggestions for further reading.

Chapter 1
Adorno, Theodor W: *Prisms,* Spearman, 1967.
Anderson, Perry: 'Components of the national culture', *Student power, ed* Cockburn, A and Blackburn, R, Penguin, 1969.
Annan, Noel: *The disintegration of an old culture* (Romanes lecture), OUP, 1966.
Arnold, Matthew: *Culture and anarchy,* CUP paperback, 1960.
Bergonzi, Bernard: *Innovations,* Macmillan, 1968.
Brown, J A C: *Freud and the post Freudians,* Penguin, 1964.
Brown, N O: *Life against death,* Routledge, 1959.
Eliot, T S: *Notes towards the definition of culture,* Faber, 1948.
Frye, Northrop and others: *The morality of scholarship, ed* Max Black, Cornell University, 1967.
Fyvel, T R: *Intellectuals today,* Chatto, 1968.
Getzels, J W and Jackson, P W: *Creativity and intelligence,* Wiley, 1962.
Hoggart, Richard: *Contemporary cultural studies* (pamphlet), Centre for Contemporary Cultural Studies, University of Birmingham, 1969.
Huxley, Aldous: *Literature and science,* Chatto, 1963.
Kluckhohn, Clyde: *Mirror for man,* Harrap, 1950.
Laing, R D: *The divided self,* Penguin, 1965.
Laing, R D: *The politics of experience,* Penguin, 1967.
Leach, E: *A runaway world* (Reith lectures), BBC, 1967.
Leavis, F R: *Two cultures; the significance of C P Snow,* Chatto, 1962.

Marcuse, H: *Eros and civilization*, Sphere Books, 1969.

Merton, Robert K: *Social theory and social structure*, Free Press, 1968.

Meyersohn, Rolf: *Sociology and cultural studies* (pamphlet), University of Birmingham, 1969.

Mills C W: *Power, politics and people, ed* Horowitz, I L, OUP, 1967

Moore, Tom: *Claude Levi-Strauss and the cultural sciences* (pamphlet), Centre for Contemporary Cultural Studies, University of Birmingham, 1968.

Mumford, Lewis: *Technics and civilization*, Routledge, 1946.

Mumford, Lewis: *The condition of man*, Mercury Books, 1963.

Nisbet, Robert A: *The sociological tradition*, Heinemann, 1967.

Ottaway, A K C: *Education and society*, Routledge, second edition 1962.

Peckham, Morse: *Man's rage for chaos: biology, behaviour and the arts*, Schocken, 1966.

Richmond, W K: *Culture and general education*, Methuen, 1963.

Ross, A S C ed: *Arts v Science*, Methuen, 1967.

Sampson, Anthony: *Anatomy of Britain today*, Hodder, 1965.

Shapiro, H L ed: *Man, culture and society*, OUP, 1956.

Snow, Sir Charles: *The two cultures and a second look*, CUP, 1964.

Sontag, Susan: *Against interpretation and other essays*, Eyre and Spottiswoode, 1967.

Spender, Stephen: *The struggle of the modern*, Methuen, 1965.

Steiner, C: *Language and silence*, Faber, 1967.

Stenhouse, L: *Culture and education*, Nelson, 1967.

Sweeney, F ed: *The knowledge explosion*, Farrar, Strauss and Giroux, 1966.

Tomkins, Calvin: *The bride and the bachelors*, Weidenfeld and Nicholson, 1965.

Trilling, Lionel: *Beyond culture*, Penguin, 1967.

Williams, Raymond: *Culture and society*, Chatto, 1958.

Williams, Raymond: *The long revolution*, Chatto, 1960.

Ziman, John: *Public knowledge: the social dimension of science*, CUP, 1968.

Chapter 2

Achebe, Chinuah: *Things fall apart*, Heinemann, 1965.

Achebe, Chinuah: *No longer at ease*, Heinemann, 1963.

Ashby, Eric: *African universities and western tradition*, OUP, 1964.
Benedict, Ruth: *Patterns of culture*, Routledge, 1935.
Chase, Stuart: *The proper study of mankind*, Pheonix, second edition 1965.
De Rougemont, Denis: *Passion and society*, Faber, 1940.
Fanon, Frantz: *The wretched of the earth*, Penguin, 1967.
Field, M J: *Search for security*, Faber, 1960.
Gluckman, Max: *Custom and conflict in Africa*, Blackwell, 1955.
Herskovitz, W R and M J *eds*: *Continuity and change in African cultures*, University of Chicago Press, 1959.
Hunter, Guy: *The new societies of tropical Africa*, OUP, 1962.
Johnson, J J: *Continuity and change in Latin America*, Stanford University Press, 1964.
Kimble, G H T: *Tropical Africa* (abridged), Anchor Books, 1962.
Lamming, George: *The pleasure of exile*, Michael Joseph, 1960.
Lewis, Oscar: *La Vida*, Pantheon, 1968.
Lloyd, P C: *Africa in social change*, Penguin, 1967.
Mead, Margaret: *Cultural patterns and technical change*, Mentor Books, 1955.
Mead, Margaret: *Growing up in New Guinea*, Pelican, 1942.
Mead, Margaret: *Coming of age in Samoa*, Pelican, 1943.
Moorehead, Alan: *The fatal impact*, Hamilton, 1966.
Ottenberg, Simon and Phoebe *eds*: *Cultures and Societies of Africa*, Random House, 1960.
Ward, Barbara: *The rich nations and the poor nations*, Hamish Hamilton, 1962.
Worsley, Peter: *The trumpet shall sound*, MacGibbon and Kee, 1958.
Worsley, Peter: *The third world*, Weidenfeld and Nicholson, 1958.

Chapter 3
Aranguren, J L: *Human communication*, Weidenfeld and Nicolson, 1967.
Berelson, Bernard and Janowitz, Morris *eds*: *Reader in public opinion and communication*, Macmillan, 1966.
Chase, Stuart: *The power of words*, Phoenix, 1955.
Ginzberg, Eli *ed*: *Technology and social change*, Columbia University Press, 1964.
Harrington, M: *The accidental century*, Penguin, 1967.
Kapp, R O: *The presentation of technical information*, Constable, 1948.

Mares, C: *Communication,* EUP, 1966.

Meredith, Patrick: 'Information, documentation and communication' *Library Association record* 63(6) June 1961.

Meredith, Patrick: 'Thoughts on communication' *Journal of documentation* September 1956.

Meredith, Patrick: *Instruments of communication,* Pergamon, 1966.

Ogden, C K and Richards, I A: *The meaning of meaning,* Routledge, tenth edition 1949.

Potter, Simeon: *Language in the modern world,* Penguin, 1966.

Schramm, W: *Communication satellites for education, science and culture,* Unesco, 1968.

Shera, Jesse H: *Documentation and the organization of knowledge,* Crosby Lockwood, 1966.

Whorf, B L: *Language, thought and reality,* Chapman and Hall, 1956.

Wootton, B: 'Some problems of communication' *Focus on information and communication, ed* Kyle, B, Aslib, 1965.

Chapter 4

Baker, Samm Sinclair, *The permissible lie,* Owen, 1969.

Barzun, Jacques: *The house of intellect,* Secker, 1959.

Boorstin, D J: *The image,* Penguin, 1963.

Brown, J A C: *Techniques of persuasion,* Penguin, 1963.

Dean, E Barbara: 'Television in the service of the library' *Library Association record* February 1969.

Gasset, J Ortega Y: *The revolt of the masses,* Allen and Unwin, 1961.

Great Britain: *Report of the Committee on Broadcasting,* Cmnd 1753, HMSO, 1962.

Groombridge, Brian: *Popular culture and personal responsibility: a study outline,* NUT, 1961.

Hall, Stuart and Whannel, Paddy: *The popular arts,* Hutchinson, 1964.

Halloran, James D: *Control or consent,* Sheed and Ward, 1963.

Halloran, James D: *The effects of mass communication,* Leicester University Press, 1964.

Hancock, A: *The small screen,* Heinemann, 1965.

Himmelweit, H T and Oppenheim, A N: *Television and the child,* OUP, 1958.

Hoggart, Richard: 'Mass communication in Britain' *The modern age, ed* Ford, B, Penguin, 1961.

9*

Hoggart, Richard: *The uses of literacy,* Penguin, 1958.

Huggett, F: *The newspapers,* Heinemann, 1968.

Huizinga, J: *Homo Ludens,* Beacon Press, 1950.

Innis, H A: *The bias of communication,* Canadian University Paperbacks, 1964.

Jacobs, Norman *ed: Culture for the millions,* Van Nostrand, 1961.

Leavis, F R and Thompson, D: *Culture and environment,* Chatto, 1933.

Lowenthal, L: *Literature—popular culture and society,* Prentice Hall, 1961.

Maclean, R: *Television in education,* Methuen, 1968.

McLuhan, M: *The medium is the massage,* Penguin, 1968.

McLuhan, M: *The Gutenberg galaxy,* Routledge, 1962.

McLuhan, M: *Understanding media,* Penguin, 1968.

Peterson, T, Jensen, J W, Rivers, W L: *The mass media and modern society,* Holt, Rinehart and Winston, 1965.

Riesman, David: *The lonely crowd,* Yale University Press, 1961.

Rosenberg, B and White, David: *Mass culture: the popular arts in America,* Free Press of Glencoe, 1952.

Schramm, Wilbar and others: *The new media: memo to educational planners,* Unesco, 1967.

Stearn, C E *ed: McLuhan hot and cool,* Penguin, 1968.

Steinberg, C S *ed: Mass media and communication,* Hasting House, 1966.

Stephenson, W: *The play theory of mass communication,* University of Chicago Press, 1967.

Thompson, Denys *ed: Discrimination and popular culture,* Penguin 1964.

Wertheim, Frederick: *Seduction of the innocent,* Museum Press, 1956.

Whitehouse, Mary: *Cleaning up TV,* Blandford Press, 1967.

Williams, Francis: *Dangerous estate,* Longmans, 1957.

Williams, Raymond: *Communications,* Penguin, 1962.

Worsley, Peter: ' Libraries and mass culture ' *Library Association record* 69(8) August 1967.

Chapter 5

American Library Association: *The first freedom,* ALA, 1960.

Astbury, Raymond *ed: Libraries and the book trade,* Bingley, 1968.

Bryant, E T: ' Book selection and censorship ' *Librarian* April 1955.

Craig, Alec: *The banned books of England*, Allen & Unwin, 1962.

Ernst, M L and Seagle, W: *To the pure: a study of obscenity and the censor*, Cape, 1928.

Fryer, Peter: *Private case, public scandal*, Secker, 1966.

Johnson, Pamela Hansford: *On Iniquity*, Macmillan, 1967.

Kronhausen, E and P: *Pornography and the law*, Ballantine, 1959.

Lawrence, D H: 'Pornography and obscenity' *in A propos of Lady Chatterley's lover*, Penguin, 1961.

Marcus, Steven: *The other Victorians*, Corgi, 1969.

Rembar, G: *The end of obscenity*, Deutsch, 1968.

Rolph, C H: *Books in the dock*, Deutsch, 1969.

Chapter 6

Anderson, Nels: *Work and leisure*, Routledge, 1961.

Asheim, L: 'Research on the reading of adults' *Library Trends* 1953.

Cipolla, Carlo M: *Literacy and development in the West*, Penguin, 1969.

Cruse, Amy: *The Victorians and their books*, Allen and Unwin, 1935.

Dalzeil, M: *Popular fiction 100 years ago*, Cohen and West, 1957.

Ennis, P H: 'The library consumer: patterns and trends' *Library Quarterly* April 1964.

Goody, Jack ed: 'Introduction' *Literacy in traditional societies*, CUP, 1968.

Goody, Jack and Watt, Ian: 'The consequences of literacy' *Literacy in traditional societies*, ed Goody, J, CUP, 1968.

Gray, William S ed: *Reading in an age of mass communication*, Appleton, 1949.

Groombridge, B: *The Londoner and his library*, Research Institute for Consumer affairs, 1964.

Hackett, Alice Payne: *70 years of best sellers, 1895-1956*, Bowker, 1967.

Hart, James D: *The popular book*, OUP, 1950.

Hatt, Frank: 'Public libraries in the 70's' *Library Association conference papers*, 1963.

Kaufman, Paul: 'English book clubs and their role in social history' *Libri* 14(1) 1964.

Leavis, Q: *Fiction and the reading public*, Chatto, 1932.

Orwell, George: *Critical essays*, Secker, 1951.

Tauber, M F and Stephens, I eds: *Library surveys*, Columbia University Press, 1967.

Turner, E S: *Boys will be boys*, Michael Joseph, 1957.

Unesco: *Basic facts and figures: international statistics relating to education, culture and mass education*, Unesco, 1960.

Unesco: *World illiteracy at mid century*, Unesco, 1957.

Webb, R K: *The British working class reader 1796-1848*, Allen and Unwin, 1955.

Chapter 7

'The American reading public' (special issue of *Daedalus* on publishing and bookselling, Winter 1963).

Arts Council of Great Britain: *The Arts Council and the public lending right*, Arts Council, 1968.

Barker, R E and Davies, G R eds: *Books are different: an account of the Net Book Agreement before the Restrictive Practices Court in 1962*, Macmillan, 1966.

Barker, R E: *Books for all*, Unesco, 1957.

Bingley, Clive: *Book publishing practice*, Crosby Lockwood, 1966.

Bingley, Clive: 'A world of books?' *Progress in library science 1966*, Butterworth, 1966.

Bingley, Clive: 'Why do book prices go on rising?' *Library Association record* 71(3) March 1969.

Calder, John: ' Some aspects of book publishing' *Library Association record* 69(10) October 1967.

Davies, G R: 'Libraries and bookselling' *Library Association record* 71(1) January 1969.

Library Association: 'Statement on proposals for a Public Lending Right' *Library Association record* 70(12) December 1968.

Mann, Peter and Burgoyne, Jacqueline: *Books and reading*, Deutsch, 1968.

Saunders, J W: *The profession of English letters*, Routledge, 1964.

Seymour Smith, F: 'Librarianship and the book trade' *Progress in library science 1966*, Butterworth, 1966.

Chapter 8

Adams, W: ' The place of professional education in the universities' *Applied social studies* January 1969.

Bantock, G H: *Education in an industrial society*, Faber, 1963.

Batty, C D: 'Librarianship by degrees' *Library world* 68 (798) December 1966.

Benge, R C: 'Some principles of library education: a discussion' *Ghana library journal* Vol 2 (2) 1968.

Bramley, Gerald: *A history of library education*, Bingley 1969.

Callander, Thomas: 'Presidential address: Library Association, 1968' *Library Association record* 70 (6) June 1968.

Carnovsky, Leon: 'The evaluation and accreditation of library schools' *Library quarterly* 37 (4) October 1967.

Cockburn, A and Blackburn, R: *Student power*, Penguin, 1969.

Daiches, David ed: *The idea of a new university: an experiment in Sussex*, Deutsch, 1964.

Fuller, R Buckminster: *Education automation*, Southern Illinois University Press, 1962.

Great Britain: Committee on Higher Education: *Higher education (Robbins report)*, Cmnd 2154, HMSO, 1963.

Great Britain: Department of Education and Science: Library Advisory Councils (England and Wales): *A report on the supply and training of librarians*, HMSO, 1968.

Great Britain: University Grants Committee: *Report of the Committee on University Teaching Methods (Hale Report)*, HMSO, 1964.

Guy, Leonard C: 'Teaching the management of libraries' *Library Association record* 70 (4) April 1968.

Hepworth, J B: 'Problems of orientation in professional education' *Library Association record* 71 (2) February 1969.

Holmes, Brian: *Problems in education: a comparative approach*, Routledge, 1965.

Hudson, Liam: *Contrary imaginations*, Penguin, 1967.

Keppel, Francis: *The necessary revolution in American education*, Harper, 1966.

Leavis, F R: *Education and the university*, Chatto, 1943.

Lowell, M H: *The management of libraries and information centres*, Scarecrow Press, 1968.

Martin, David, ed: *Anarchy and culture: the problem of the contemporary university*, Routledge, 1969.

New, P G: 'Educational escalation' *Library Association record* 71 (7) July 1969.

Ottaway, A K C: *Education and society*, Routledge, second edition, 1962.

Peters, R S ed: *The concept of education*, Routledge, 1967.

Peterson, A D C: *The future of education*, Cresset Press, 1968.

Pickering, G: *The challenge to education*, Watts, 1967.

' Recruitment and training' (articles by Edward Dudley, Miss L V Paulin, R S G Cook) *Library Association record* 71 (6) June 1969.

Revill, D H: 'Education for librarianship' *Library Association record* 71 (4) April 1969.

Richmond, Kenneth: *Culture and general education*, Methuen, 1963.

Robinson, Eric: *The new polytechnics*, Penguin, 1968.

Shera, Jesse H: *Libraries and the organization of knowledge* (part three), Crosby Lockwood, 1965.

Staveley, R: 'Professional education' *Five years work in librarianship 1961-1965*, Library Association, 1968.

Teece, A H: 'Recruitment in librarianship', *Library Association record* 71 (4) April 1969.

Whitehead, A N: *The aims of education*, Benn, 1962.

Young, M: *Rise of meritocracy*, Thames and Hudson, 1958.

Chapter 9
GEOGRAPHY AND SOCIAL FACTORS

Baguley, F W S: 'Library provision in a new town and on a new estate' *Library Association conference proceedings*, 1958.

Bendix, Dorothy ed: *Library service for the undereducated*, Drexel Institute of Technology, 1966.

Berry, John N: 'Getting into the Ghetto' *Library journal* 91 (August 1966).

Campbell, H C: *Metropolitan public library planning throughout the world*, Pergamon Press, 1967.

Carnovsky, Leon ed: *The public library in the urban setting*, University of Chicago Press, 1968.

Conant, Ralph: 'Black power in urban America' *Library journal* 93 (May 1968).

Conant, Ralph W ed: *The public library and the city*, MIT Press, 1965.

Dickinson, Robert E: *City and region*, Routledge, 1964.

Drennan, Henry T ed: 'War on poverty: the unifying theme' *Library journal* 89 (September 1964).

Freeman, T W: *The conurbations of Great Britain*, Manchester University Press, second edition, 1966.

Harrison, K C: 'Problems and opportunities in the merging of libraries' *Unesco bulletin for libraries* 22 (3) May-June 1968.

Hatt, P K and others: *Cities and society*, Free Press, 1957.

Jackson, Brian, *Working class community*, Routledge, 1968.

' Library service for a nation covering a large geographical area ', (Canada by W K Lamb; Soviet Union by J P Koudakov; United States by S A McCarthy) *Libri* 17 (3) 1967.

Moon, Eric: ' High John ' *Library journal* (January 1968).

Scientific American: *Cities,* Penguin, 1967.

POLITICS AND RELIGION

Altick, R D: *The English common reader*, University of Chicago Press, 1957.

Irwin, Raymond: *The English library*, Allen and Unwin, 1966.

Kelly, Thomas: *Public libraries in Great Britain before 1850* (pamphlet), Library Association, 1966.

GOVERNMENT RESPONSIBILITY

Benge, R C: ' Life without father ', *Library Association record*, February 1957.

Corbett, E V: ' Library service in the London boroughs ' *Library world* 68 (796) October 1966.

Nyren, Karl: ' The national dimension ' *Library journal* 92 (1) January 1967.

Ollé, James G: 'Andrew Carnegie: the unloved benefactor ' *Library world* 70 (826) April 1969.

Price, P P ' Recent national aid programmes for libraries in the United States ' *Unesco bulletin for libraries* 22 (3) May-June 1968.

Richnell, D T: ' The national library problem ' *Library association record* 70 (6) June 1968.

Robertson, William: *Welfare in trust* (chapter 3), Carnegie UK Trust, 1964.

Saunders, W L ed: *Librarianship in Britain today*, Library Association, 1967.

Vollans, Robert F ed: *Libraries for the people*, Library Association, 1968.

SPECIAL SERVICES

'American library services for the disadvantaged ', (editorial) *Assistant librarian* 62 (6) June 1969.

Lewis, M J: ' Library service to handicapped readers ', *Library Association record* 70 (5) May 1968.

Matthews, David: 'Library services for the blind' *Progress in library science 1967*, ed Collison, Butterworth, 1967.

Stoffle, Carla J: 'Public library service to the disadvantaged: a comprehensive annotated bibliography 1964-1968' *Library journal* 94 (2) (January 1969).

EDUCATION AND LIBRARIES

Beloff, Michael: *The plate-glass universities*, Secker and Warburg, 1968.

Beswick, Norman: 'The library-college—the true university' *Library Association record* 69 (6) June 1967.

Beswick, Norman W: 'Librarians and tutor-librarians' *Library-college journal* 2 (2) Spring 1969.

Great Britain: University Grants Committee: *Report of the Committee on Libraries*, HMSO, 1967.

Hatt, Frank: 'My kind of library tutoring' *Library Association record* 70 (10) October 1968.

Havighurst, Robert J: 'Educational changes: their implication for the library' *ALA bulletin* 61 (5) May 1967.

Lewis, David T: 'Polytechnic library development: a comparative view' *Library world* 70 (825) March 1969.

'Libraries in the new polytechnics' *Library Association record* 70 (9) September 1968.

Linden, R O: 'Tutor librarianship: a personal view' *Library Association record* 69 (10) October 1967.

Parry, Thomas: 'University libraries and the future' *Library Association record* 70 (9) September 1968.

Robinson, Eric E: 'Developments in higher education and their implications for libraries' *Library Association record* 71 (5) May 1969.

Roe, E C: *Teacher, librarian and children*, Crosby Lockwood, 1965.

INTERNATIONAL LIBRARIANSHIP

Coblans, Herbert: 'The contribution of Unesco to libraries and documentation' *Five years work in librarianship, 1961-1965*, Library Association, 1968.

Gummer, E N 'Books and libraries overseas: the world of the British Council' *Library Association record* 68 (9) September 1966.

Scoff, E: 'IFLA and FID: history and progress' *Library quarterly* 1962.

'Unesco's role in library development in the developing countries' *Libri* 1964 (3).

'Unesco's twentieth anniversary' (six articles) *Unesco bulletin* 20 (5) September-October 1966.

COMPARATIVE STUDIES

Conant, Ralph W: 'Sociological and institutional changes in American life: their implications for the library' *ALA bulletin* 61 (5) May 1967.

Foskett, D J: 'Comparative librarianship' *Progress in library science* 1965, Butterworth, 1965.

Hassendorfer, J: 'Comparative studies and the development of public libraries' *Unesco bulletin for libraries* 22 (1) January-February 1968.

McColvin, Lionel: *The chance to read*, Phoenix House, 1956.

Pahl, Ray: 'Friendly library: the library and the community' *Assistant librarian* 62 (6) June 1969.

Simsova, Silva: *A handbook of comparative librarianship*, Bingley, 1970.

Chapter 10

Bagrit, Leon: *The age of automation* (Reith lectures 1964), Penguin, 1966.

Brookes, B C: 'Scientific information and the computer' *Library Association record* 69 (6) June 1967.

Council on Library Resources Inc: *Automation and the Library of Congress*, Library of Congress, 1963.

Cox, N S M and others: *The computer and the library*, University of Newcastle, 1966.

Foskett, A C: 'Computers in libraries' *Five years work in librarianship 1961-1965*, Library Association, 1968.

Foskett, D J: 'The library in the age of leisure' *Library Association record* 69 (1) January 1967.

Ginzberg, E ed: *Technology and social change*, Columbia University Press, 1964.

Great Britain: Ministry of Technology: *Technical services for industry*, Ministry of Technology, 1968.

Grose, M W: 'The place of the librarian in the computer age' *Library Association record* 70 (8) August 1968.

Kent, A ed: *Library planning for automation*, Macmillan, 1965.

Licklider, J C R: *Libraries of the future*, MIT Press, 1965.

Stein, T: 'Automation and library systems' *Library journal* 1964, 2723-2734.

Vickery, B C: 'The future of libraries in the machine age' *Library Association record* 68 (7) July 1966.

Wasserman, Paul: *The librarian and the machine*, Gale Research Company, 1965.

Chapter 11

Almond, G A and Coleman, J S: *The politics of developing areas*, Princeton University Press, 1960.

Asheim, L: *Librarianship in the developing countries*, University of Illinois Press, 1966.

Benge, R C: 'The role of the librarian in Ghana' *Ghana library journal* 1 (3) October 1964.

Breese, Gerald: *Urbanization in newly developing countries*, Prentice Hall, 1966.

Carnovsky, L ed: *International aspects of librarianship*, University of Chicago Press, 1954.

Curle, Adam: *Educational strategy for developing societies*, Tavistock Publications, 1963.

Edwards, James: 'Libraries and the culture of Africa' *Library Association record* 66 (9) September 1964.

Gelfand, M A: *University libraries in developing countries*, Unesco, 1968.

Chapter 12

Carr-Saunders, A M and Wilson, P A: *The professions*, Cass, 1964.

'Code of ethics for librarians' (reprint of the ALA code 1938) *Library journal* 91 (19) November 1966.

Ennis, P H and Winger, H W: *Seven questions about the profession of librarianship*, University of Chicago Press, 1962.

'The future of the Library Association', (The membership of the Association by H D Barry; Education and research by D J Foskett; Policy and structure by P W Plumb; Means and ends by G Hare) *Library Association record* 70 (6) June 1968.

Marshall, J D, Shirley, W and Shores, L eds: *Books - libraries - librarians*, Shoe String Press, 1955.

Marshall, J D *ed*: *Of, by and for librarians,* Shoe String Press, 1960.
Millerson, Geoffrey: *The qualifying associations,* Routledge, 1964.

Chapter 13
Astall, Roland: *Special libraries and information bureaux,* Bingley, 1966.
Burkett, Jack *ed*: *Trends in special librarianship,* Bingley, 1968.
Davinson, Donald: *Academic and legal deposit libraries,* Bingley, 1965.
Foskett, D J: 'The intellectual and social challenge of the library service' *Library Association record* 71 (2) February 1969.
Garceau, Oliver: *The public library in the political process,* Columbia University Press, 1949.
Humphreys, K W: 'National library functions' *Unesco bulletin for libraries,* July-August 1966.
Jolley, L: 'Function of the university library' *Journal of documentation* 1962, 133-142.
Landheer, B: *Social functions of libraries,* Scarecrow Press, 1957.
Leigh, Robert D: *The public library in the United States,* Columbia University Press, 1950.
Line, M B: 'The functions of the university library' *University and research library studies, ed* W L Saunders, Pergamon Press, 1968.
Ollé, James: 'Free books in an affluent society' *Library world* December 1962.
Shera, Jesse H: 'Of librarianship, documentation and information science' *Unesco bulletin* 22 (2) March-April 1968.
Shores, L and others: *The library-college,* Drexel Press, 1966.
Snow, C P: 'Presidential address' *Library Association record* 64 (11) November 1962.
Taylor, Robert S: 'The interface between librarianship and information science and engineering' *Special libraries* 58 (January 1967).
Unesco: *National libraries: their problems and prospects,* Unesco, 1958.

Chapter 14
Benge, R C: *Bibliography and the provision of books,* AAL, 1963.
Boulding, Kenneth: *The image,* University of Michigan Press, 1956.
Broderick, D: 'The librarian in today's society' *Library journal* 92 (7) April 1967.

Butler, Pierce: *An introduction to library science,* University of Chicago Press, 1961.

Caldwell, W: ' Libraries and the social structure ' *Assistant librarian* October 1968.

Foskett, D J: *The creed of a librarian,* Library Association, Reference, Special and Information Section, North Western Group, 1962.

Foskett, D J: *Science, humanism and libraries,* Crosby Lockwood, 1964.

Gardner, F M: ' Presidential address ', *Library Association record* 66 (8) August 1964.

Hatt, Frank: ' The right to read and the long revolution ' *Library Association record* 65 (1) January 1963.

Mukherjee, A K: *Librarianship its philosophy and history,* Asia Publishing House, 1966.

Ranganathan, S R *Five laws of library science,* Asia, second edition reprinted 1964.

Shera, Jesse H: *Libraries and the organisation of knowledge* (part one), Crosby Lockwood, 1965.

Staveley, Ronald: *Personal viewpoints,* University College London School of Librarianship and Archives, 1964.

subject index

275

name index